THE 100 MOST INFLUENTIAL
WORLD LEADERS
OF ALL TIME

The Britannica Guide to the World's Most Influential People

The 100 Most Influential

WORLD LEADERS
of All Time

Edited by Amy McKenna, Senior Editor, Geography and History

Britannica®
Educational Publishing

IN ASSOCIATION WITH

ROSEN
EDUCATIONAL SERVICES

Published in 2010 by Britannica Educational Publishing
(a trademark of Encyclopædia Britannica, Inc.)
in association with Rosen Educational Services, LLC
29 East 21st Street, New York, NY 10010.

Distributed exclusively by Rosen Educational Services.
For a listing of additional Britannica Educational Publishing titles, call toll free (800) 237-9932.

First Edition

Britannica Educational Publishing
Michael I. Levy: Executive Editor
Marilyn L. Barton: Senior Coordinator, Production Control
Steven Bosco: Director, Editorial Technologies
Lisa S. Braucher: Senior Producer and Data Editor
Yvette Charboneau: Senior Copy Editor
Kathy Nakamura: Manager, Media Acquisition
Amy McKenna: Senior Editor, Geography and History

Rosen Educational Services
Hope Lourie Killcoyne: Senior Editor and Project Manager
Nelson Sá: Art Director
Matthew Cauli: Designer
Introduction by Michael I. Levy

Library of Congress Cataloging-in-Publication Data

The 100 most influential world leaders of all time / edited by Amy McKenna, senior editor.
    p. cm.—(The Britannica guide to the world's most influential people)
"In association with Britannica Educational Publishing, Rosen Educational Services."
Includes index.
ISBN 978-1-61530-015-0 (library binding)
1. World history. 2. Biography. 3. Heads of state—Biography. 4. Statesmen—Biography.
5. Politicians—Biography. 6. Social reformers—Biography. 7. Political activists—Biography.
8. Religious leaders—Biography. 9. Leadership—Case studies. 10. Influence (Psychology)—
Case studies. I. Title: One hundred most influential world leaders of all time.
D21.3.A13 2010
321.0092'2—dc22

2009030358

Manufactured in the United States of America

On the cover: *Marking his 100th day as the 44th president of the United States, Barack Obama,
the first African American to hold the office, speaks during a town hall meeting at Fox Senior High
School in Arnold, Mo., April 29, 2009.* Saul Loeb/AFP/Getty Images

CONTENTS

155

241

INTRODUCTION

What does it mean to be a leader? Does it require that a person hold political office and rule masses? Does it include only those who made a positive impact on society or also those who wreaked devastation and destruction? Do humanitarians or activists who never held office but who had the ability to stir thousands and millions with a vision of a different, better world merit inclusion?

Many very different types of leaders are profiled in this book, which is arranged chronologically by date of birth. It ends with Osama bin Laden and Barack Obama. One is a mastermind of terrorist acts that have killed thousands and another a politician who overcame the weight of hundreds of years of slavery and discrimination against blacks to become the first African American elected president of the most powerful country in the world. They are opposites in almost every imaginable way. Bin Laden leads a global jihad against Western values, and Obama, the symbolic leader of the West, was the recipient of the 2009 Nobel Peace Prize. They are linked, however, in their ability to inspire loyal followers—in bin Laden's case to commit destruction and in Obama's to believe that ordinary citizens, acting together, can change a sometimes seemingly bleak world for the better—and in their lasting impact on the world in which they and future generations will live.

The world today has some 6.7 billion people, most of whom adhere to one religion or another. In the 13th century BCE, Moses delivered his people from Egyptian slavery and received the Ten Commandments, establishing Judaism as the world's first great monotheistic religion. Although Jews make up but a small fraction of the world's population today, monotheism flourishes, with Christians and Muslims together accounting for more than half the world's population.

Jesus' Christian followers were once persecuted by the Romans until Constantine I the Great became the first Roman emperor to convert to Christianity; now, more than two billion people call themselves Christians. In the 7th century Muhammad founded Islam, and he is considered by Muslims to be the last of the Great Prophets; his name is now invoked several billion times a day by nearly 1.5 billion Muslims around the world. Others, such as Confucius in 6th–5th-century-BCE China and Buddha in the area around Nepal and India about the same time, have inspired hundreds of millions of people, and their teachings remain central to the daily lives of vast numbers today. And, though these figures still have relevance thousands of years after their deaths, the world continues to produce religious leaders—Martin Luther and his Reformation in Europe, Ruhollah Khomeini and his Islamic Revolution in Iran, John Paul II and his more than 25-year leadership as head of the Roman Catholic Church, and the Dalai Lama—who have represented challenges to existing religious views or have spread the reach of their religious doctrine.

While some have founded religions, others have founded countries. George Washington is almost universally revered in the United States as the "Father of His Country," securing independence on the battlefield and then turning down an offer to become king. The American Revolution began the process of independence in the so-called New World, which had been subject to colonial domination by European powers. Less than 40 years after the American Revolution had been won, another American revolution of sorts, led by Simón Bolívar in Latin America, helped throw off Spanish rule there. Bolívar's name is still a symbol to revolutionary leaders in Latin America. Indeed, Hugo Chávez leads his own "Bolivarian Revolution" in Venezuela today.

In Europe, too, new countries were formed in what are generally thought of as ancient lands—Giuseppe Garibaldi helped create a unified Kingdom of Italy in 1861, while Otto von Bismarck helped forge a German empire in 1871. Old empires fell away and were replaced with modern states in the 20th century. Vladimir Lenin established in Russia the world's first communist regime, one that, though it collapsed nearly 75 years later, continues to have a lasting influence on our world. Out of the ashes of the Ottoman Empire, Kemal Atatürk helped found modern Turkey. Eamon de Valera won Irish independence from Great Britain. Ibn Sa'ūd created a country, Saudi Arabia, that bears his family's name. And, Mao Zedong led a 30-year struggle in China, creating a communist state in 1949 that 60 years later continues to rule over the world's largest population. Sometimes individuals have led peaceful resistance movements that have freed their people—as Mohandas Gandhi did in India. After World War II, as peoples yearned to become free, David Ben-Gurion in Israel, Kwame Nkrumah in Ghana, Julius Nyerere in Tanzania, and Ho Chi Minh in Vietnam fought for and achieved their country's independence in different ways. Nelson Mandela in South Africa is yet another story of resistance—sometimes armed and sometimes peaceful. He was jailed from 1964 to 1990 by his apartheid government, which legally discriminated against the overwhelmingly black population in favour of minority whites, before being released, helping end apartheid, ushering in a peaceful transition to democracy, and becoming the first black president of the new, multiracial South Africa.

Some of the world's greatest leaders have earned their place here from victories—and defeats—on the battlefield. Alexander the Great won a vast 4th-century-BCE empire that eventually stretched from Europe to India.

Attila commanded the Huns, leading them in invasions against the Balkans, Greece, and Italy. His empire, however, died shortly after he did in 453 CE. Charlemagne had himself crowned Holy Roman emperor in 800, following military conquests that expanded his kingdom outward from what is modern-day Germany. A millennium later, Napoleon led French forces in Europe to stunning victories, but his defeats in Russia and, later, at Waterloo proved his downfall. Outside of Europe, Chinggis Khan was one of the greatest warriors the world has ever seen, leading his Mongols in amassing an empire that stretched from Mongolia to the Adriatic Sea in the 12th–13th century. At about the same time, Saladin, founder of the Ayyūbid dynasty, fought in the Middle East against Christian Crusaders, capturing Jerusalem to end nearly nine decades of occupation by Christians.

The 20th century brought advances in technology—making war even more devastating than it was during Napoleon's time. It is estimated that some 35 to 60 million people died during World War II, and for this reason the leaders of the major combatants usually top any list of influential leaders. Italy's Il Duce, Benito Mussolini, the world's first fascist dictator, joined an alliance in Europe with Germany's Adolf Hitler under whose dictatorial rule most of Europe fell and some six million Jews died in the Holocaust. Together, Hitler and Mussolini formed the Axis with Japan in the Pacific. Hirohito, emperor of Japan, though playing a limited political role, was the symbolic leader of his country. His national radio address in 1945, the first time many Japanese had heard his voice, announced the country's surrender, and the next year he renounced his quasi-divine status, helping to engineer Japanese democracy after the war. Franklin D. Roosevelt, though afflicted with debilitating polio, managed to win re-election to four terms as president of the United States and led the Allies. He was joined by Winston Churchill, whose steely nerves helped calm Britain during relentless bombing by the German Luftwaffe, while Charles de Gaulle led the Free French against German occupation. A fourth ally was Joseph Stalin, whose rule in the Soviet Union resulted in purges, famine, and the deaths of some 20 million; initially signing a pact with Hitler, he joined the Allies following Hitler's invasion of the Soviet Union.

From the ashes of World War II came dreams to build a Europe that would be free from the traditional English-French-German rivalry that had plunged the continent into two world wars. Jean Monnet and Robert Schuman may never have led a government, but they helped found the European Coal and Steel Community, the forerunner of today's European Union. The EU now encompasses 27 countries—from Portugal in the west, Malta in the south, Finland in the north, and Romania in the east—helping to integrate the continent both politically and economically and ward off war.

Upholding the European ideal was but one way in which statesmen and activists have influenced the arc of history without ever possessing formal power. Frederick Douglass, one of the greatest human rights leaders of the 19th century, helped lead the American abolition movement. Though slavery had been abolished in the United States in 1865, African Americans still suffered from discrimination, so in the next century Martin Luther King, Jr., used nonviolent protest and civil disobedience, modeled on Gandhi's movement in India, to achieve political equality before he was struck down by an assassin's bullet in 1968. Eleanor Roosevelt, wife of Franklin, was a tireless campaigner for human rights, playing a major role in drafting and gaining adoption of the Universal Declaration of

Human Rights—considered humanity's Magna Carta (Great Charter) to many.

Eleanor Roosevelt was but one woman whose imprint has been made on a society traditionally dominated by men. One of her predecessors as first lady, Abigail Adams, wrote in 1776 in a letter to her husband, John Adams, the great revolutionary and the second president of the United States, "I desire you would remember the ladies and be more generous and favorable to them than your ancestors." (Neither Adams nor her husband made the list of 100.) Too often, however, women have not been remembered in history. Still, their contributions have been enormous. Cleopatra, who ruled as queen of Egypt for decades, eventually committed suicide, and history was rewritten to portray her as predatory and immoral rather than as the woman she was: strong and smart, a philosopher and a scientist. Women were also discriminated against in the hereditary monarchies of Europe, which favoured males in deciding who would rule. Though her father, Henry VIII, had divorced or had killed several wives to find one who would produce a male heir, Elizabeth I eventually became queen of England, ruling for 45 years and giving her name to an age. Catherine II the Great of Russia was empress for more than three decades, and during her time she brought Russia into full participation in the political and cultural life of Europe. While Elizabeth and Catherine ruled from palaces, Joan of Arc earned her mark on the battlefield. She died at age 19, burned at the stake, but before then she led the French to win improbable battles, mostly due to the confidence that her men had in her, despite her youth, gender, and lack of military know-how. Margaret Thatcher, the "Iron Lady," became Britain's first woman prime minister in 1979 and helped win the Cold War. Other strong women have reached the pinnacle of power only to be murdered. Indira Gandhi of India served four terms as prime minister of the world's largest democracy but then was assassinated by extremists, while Benazir Bhutto, in neighbouring Pakistan, was the first woman in modern history elected to lead a predominantly Muslim country, and while campaigning in 2007 for what would most likely have been another term as prime minister was killed by an assassin. Today, Aung San Suu Kyi, winner of the 1991 Nobel Peace Prize, continues the fight for freedom, the face of hope in an authoritarian Myanmar (Burma) whose leadership has mostly kept her under house arrest.

Selecting the most influential anything is inherently fraught with difficulties, and choosing those individuals who have left a lasting impression on the world—both during their times and long after they perished—was nearly impossible. The stories that follow represent both the best—and worst—of humanity and provide a journey across time and across the globe—a trek that will provide keen insight into the art of leadership and the countless followers who were drawn into a cause, an upheaval, or a new dawn.

MOSES

(flourished 14th–13th century BCE)

Moses, a Hebrew prophet, teacher, and leader, delivered his people from Egyptian slavery and founded the religious community known as Israel, based on a covenant relationship with God. As the vehicle and interpreter of the Covenant, including the Ten Commandments, he exerted a lasting influence on the religious life, moral concerns, and social ethics of Western civilization.

According to the biblical account in Exodus and Numbers, Moses—whose Hebrew name is Moshe—was a Hebrew foundling adopted and reared in the Egyptian court. Raised there, according to the biblical account, by his biological mother, who was hired to be his nanny, Moses came to know of his Hebrew lineage. As an adult, while on an inspection tour, Moses killed an Egyptian taskmaster who was beating a Hebrew slave. Fearing the wrath of the pharaoh, Moses fled to Midian (mostly in northwest Arabia), where he became a shepherd and eventually the son-in-law of a Midianite priest, Jethro. While tending his flocks, he saw a burning bush that remained unconsumed by the flames and heard a call from the God—thereafter called Yahweh—of Abraham, Isaac, and Jacob to free his people, the Hebrews, from their bondage in Egypt. Because Moses was a stammerer, his brother Aaron was to be his spokesman, but Moses would be Yahweh's representative.

Ramses II, who reigned 1279–13 BCE, was probably the pharaoh of Egypt at the time. He rejected the demand of this unknown God and responded by increasing the oppression of the Hebrews. The biblical text states that Moses used plagues sent by Yahweh to bend Ramses' will. Whether the Hebrews were finally permitted to leave Egypt or simply fled is not clear. According to the biblical account, the pharaoh's forces pursued them eastward to the Sea of

Moses Showing the Tables of the Law to the People, *oil painting by Rembrandt, 1659.* Courtesy of Staatliche Museen Preussischer Kulturbesitz Gemaldegalerie, Berlin

Reeds, a papyrus lake (not the Red Sea), which the Hebrews crossed safely but in which the Egyptians were engulfed. Moses then led the people to Mount Sinai (Horeb), which lies at the southern tip of the Sinai Peninsula. Yahweh appeared to Moses there in a terrific storm, out of which came the Covenant between Yahweh and the people of Israel, which included the Ten Commandments. Moses began issuing ordinances for specific situations and instituted a system of judges and hearings of civil cases.

After leaving Mount Sinai and continuing the journey toward Canaan, Moses faced increasing resistance and frustration from the Hebrew people and once got so angry at them that, according to tradition, Yahweh accounted it as a lack of faith and denied him entrance into Canaan. As his last official act, Moses renewed the Sinai Covenant with the survivors of the wanderings and then climbed Mount Pisgah to look over the land that he could not enter. The Hebrews never saw him again, and the circumstances of his death and burial remain shrouded in mystery.

Tradition states that Moses wrote the whole Pentateuch, but this is untenable. Moses did formulate the Decalogue, mediate the Covenant, and begin the process of rendering and codifying interpretations of the Covenant's stipulations. In a general sense, therefore, the first five books of the Hebrew Bible can be described as Mosaic. Without him there would have been no Israel and no collection known as the Torah.

BUDDHA GOTAMA

(fl. *c.* 6th–4th century BCE, Lumbini, near Kapilavastu, Śākya republic, Kosala kingdom [India]—d. Kusinārā, Malla republic, Magdha kingdom [India])

Buddha Gotama (also called Siddhārtha) was the founder of Buddhism. The term *buddha*, literally meaning "awakened one" or "enlightened one," is not a proper name but rather a title, and Buddhists traditionally believe that there will be innumerable buddhas in the future as there have been in the past and that there are other buddhas in other presently existing cosmos as well. The Buddha who belongs to the present era of the cosmos in which we are living is often referred to as Gotama. When the term the Buddha is used, it is generally assumed that it refers to the Buddha Gotama.

According to virtually all Buddhist traditions, the Buddha lived many lives before his birth as Gotama; these previous lives are described in Jātakas (birth stories), which play an important role in Buddhist art and education. Most Buddhists also affirm that the Buddha's life was continued in his teachings and his relics. The Pāli Tipitaka, which is recognized by scholars as the earliest extant record of the Buddha's discourses, and the later Pāli commentaries are the basis of the following account in which history and legend are inextricably intertwined.

The Buddha was born in the 6th or 5th century BCE in the kingdom of the Śākyas, on the borders of present-day Nepal and India. Gotama is said to have been born of the king and queen of the Śākyas, Suddhodna and Mahāmāyā. The Buddha's legend, however, begins with an account of a dream that his mother, Mahāmāyā, had one night before he was born. A beautiful elephant, white as silver, entered her womb through her side. Brahmins (Vedic priests) were asked to interpret the dream, and they foretold the birth of a son who would become either a universal monarch or a buddha. The purported site of his birth, now called Rummindei, lies within the territory of Nepal. (A pillar placed there in commemoration of the event by Aśoka, a 3rd-century BCE Buddhist emperor of India, still stands.) The child was given the name Siddhattha (Siddhārtha in Sanskrit), which means "one whose aim is accomplished."

Gotama is said to have led a sheltered life of great luxury, which was interrupted when, on three excursions outside of the palace, he encountered an old man, an ill man, and a corpse. Each time he asked a servant to explain the phenomenon and was told that all men are subject to such conditions. Gotama then met up with a wandering ascetic and decided that he must discover the reason for the man's display of serenity in the midst of such misery. Renouncing his princely life, Gotama went in search of teachers who could instruct him in the way of truth. He took up the practice of various austerities and extreme self-mortifications, including severe fasting. These experiences eventually led Gotama to the conviction that such mortifications could not lead him to what he sought.

Buddhist mythology states that the Buddha went to meditate beneath a pipal tree (*Ficus religiosa*), now known as the bodhi tree. There he was tempted by Mara (the Buddhist Lord of the Senses), but Gotama remained unmoved. Later that night the Buddha realized the Four Noble Truths, achieving enlightenment during the night of the full moon day of the month of May (Vesakha) at a place now called Bodh Gayā.

After this enlightenment, the story continues that the Buddha sought out five companions and delivered to them his first sermon, the *Dhammacakkappavattana Sutta* ("Sermon on Setting in Motion the Wheel of Truth"), at Sarnath. An ancient stupa marks the spot where this event is said to have occurred. The Buddha taught that those in search of enlightenment should not follow the two extremes of self-indulgence and self-mortification. Avoiding these two extremes, the Thatāgata ("He Who Has Thus Attained") discovers the middle path leading to vision, knowledge, calmness, awakening, and nirvana.

This middle path is known as the Noble Eightfold Path and consists of right view, right thought, right speech, right action, right living, right endeavor, right mindfulness, and right concentration. The First Noble Truth is that sentient existence is *dukkha*, always tainted with conflict, dissatisfaction, sorrow, and suffering. The Second Noble Truth is that all this is caused by selfish desire—craving or *tanha*, "thirst." The Third Noble Truth is that there is nirvana—emancipation, liberation, and freedom for human beings from all this. The Fourth Noble Truth, the Noble Eightfold Path, is the way to this liberation.

After this sermon the five companions became the Buddha's first disciples, were admitted by him as monks (bhikkhus), and became the first members of the *sangha* ("community," or "order"). After the Buddha had trained followers, his mission was fulfilled. At Kusinara (now called Kasia) on the full moon day of the month of Vesakha (May), the Buddha Gotama entered *parinirvāṇa*—an end to the cycle of being reborn. His body was cremated by the Mallas in Kusinara, but a dispute over the relics of the Buddha arose between the Mallas and the delegates of rulers of several kingdoms. It was settled by a venerable Brahmin on the basis that they should not quarrel over the relics of one who preached peace. Stupas were then built over these relics.

CONFUCIUS

(b. 551 BCE, Qufu, state of Lu [now in Shandong Province, China]—d. 479 BCE, Lu)

Confucius (originally named Kong Qiu) is China's most famous teacher, philosopher, and political theorist, and his ideas have influenced the civilization of East Asia and some other parts of the surrounding area.

Confucius's life, in contrast to his tremendous importance, seems starkly undramatic, or, as a Chinese expression states, it seems "plain and real." Confucius's humanity was not revealed truth but an expression of self-cultivation and the ability of human effort to shape its own destiny. The faith in the possibility of ordinary human beings to become awe-inspiring sages and worthies is deeply rooted in the Confucian heritage, and the insistence that human beings are teachable, improvable, and perfectible through personal and communal endeavour is typically Confucian.

Although the facts about Confucius's life are scanty, they do establish a precise time frame and historical context. Confucius was born in the 22nd year of the reign of Duke Xiang of Lu (551 BCE). The traditional claim that he was born on the 27th day of the eighth lunar month has been questioned by historians, but September 28 is still widely observed in East Asia as Confucius's birthday. It is an official holiday in Taiwan, referred to as "Teacher's Day."

Confucius was born in Qufu in the small feudal state of Lu in what is now Shandong Province, which was noted for its preservation of the traditions of ritual and music of the Zhou civilization. His family name was Kong and his personal name was Qiu, but he is referred to as either Kongzi or Kongfuzi (Master Kong) throughout Chinese history. The adjective "Confucian," derived from the Latinized *Confucius*, is not a meaningful term in Chinese — nor is the term *Confucianism*, which was coined in Europe as recently as the 18th century.

Confucius's ancestors were probably members of the aristocracy who had become virtual poverty-stricken commoners by the time of his birth. His father died when

Confucius was only three years old. Instructed by his mother early in life, Confucius then distinguished himself as an indefatigable learner in his teens. He recalled toward the end of his life that at age 15 his heart was set upon learning. A historical account notes that, even though he was already known as an informed young scholar, he felt it appropriate to inquire about everything while visiting the Grand Temple.

Confucius had served in minor government posts, managing stables and keeping books for granaries before he married a woman of similar background when he was 19. It is not known who Confucius's teachers were, but he made a conscientious effort to find the right masters to teach him, among other things, ritual and music. His mastery of the six arts—ritual, music, archery, charioteering, calligraphy, and arithmetic—and his familiarity with the classical traditions, notably poetry and history, allowed him to become a teacher himself in his 30s.

Confucius is known as the first teacher in China who wanted to make education broadly available and who was instrumental in establishing the art of teaching as a vocation and as a way of life. Before Confucius, aristocratic families had hired tutors to educate their sons in specific arts, and government officials had instructed their subordinates in the skills needed to perform their jobs. But Confucius was the first person to devote his whole life to learning and teaching for the purpose of transforming and improving society. He believed that all human beings could benefit from self-cultivation. He inaugurated a humanities program for potential leaders, opened the doors of education to all, and defined learning not merely as the acquisition of knowledge but also as character building.

For Confucius the primary function of education was to provide the proper way of training exemplary persons (*junzi*), a process that involved constant self-improvement and continuous social interaction. Although he emphatically noted that learning was "for the sake of the self," he found public service integral to true education. Confucius confronted those who challenged his desire to serve the world. He resisted the temptation to live apart from the human community, opting instead to try to transform the world from within. For decades Confucius tried to be actively involved in politics, wishing to put his humanist ideas into practice through government channels.

In his late 40s and early 50s, Confucius served first as a magistrate, then as an assistant minister of public works, and eventually as minister of justice in the state of Lu. He likely accompanied King Lu as his chief minister on one of the diplomatic missions. Confucius's political career was, however, short-lived. His loyalty to the king alienated him from the power holders of the time — the large Ji families — and his moral rectitude did not sit well with the king's inner circle, who enraptured the king with sensuous delight. At 56, when he realized that his superiors were uninterested in his policies, Confucius left the country in an attempt to find another feudal state to which he could render his service. Despite his political frustration, he was accompanied by an expanding circle of students during this twelve-year exile. His reputation as a man of vision and mission spread. A guardian of a border post once described him as the "wooden tongue for a bell" of the age, sounding heaven's prophetic note to awaken the people (*Analects*, 3:24). Indeed, Confucius was perceived as the heroic conscience who knew realistically that he might not succeed but, fired by a righteous passion, continuously did the best he could. At the age of 67, he returned home to teach and to preserve his cherished classical traditions by writing and editing. He died in 479

BCE, at the age of 73. According to the *Records of the Historian*, 72 of his students mastered the "six arts," and those who claimed to be his followers numbered 3,000.

ALEXANDER THE GREAT

(b. 356 BCE, Pella, Macedonia—d. June 13, 323 BCE, Babylon)

Alexander the Great (also known as Alexander III) was the king of Macedonia (336–323 BCE) who overthrew the Persian Empire. Already in his lifetime the subject of fabulous stories, he later became the hero of a full-scale legend bearing only the slightest resemblance to his historical career.

LIFE

Alexander was born in 356 BCE at Pella in Macedonia to Philip II and Olympias. From the age of 13 to 16 he was taught by Aristotle, who inspired him with an interest in philosophy, medicine, and scientific investigation. He soon showed military brilliance, helping win the Battle of Chaeronea at the age of 18.

In 336, after his father's assassination, Alexander succeeded without opposition. He promptly exerted his power over other Greek states, taking Thessaly and Thrace before marching on to Thebes, which his army brutally razed. Some 6,000 Thebans were killed, and all survivors were sold into slavery. The other Greek states were cowed by this severity and surrendered to him.

BEGINNINGS OF THE PERSIAN EXPEDITION

In the spring of 334, Alexander crossed the Dardanelles Strait with his army, accompanied by surveyors, engineers, architects, scientists, court officials, and historians. From the outset Alexander seems to have envisaged an unlimited operation. He confronted his first Persian army at the Granicus (now called Kocabaş) River, near the Sea of Marmara. His victory there exposed western Asia Minor to the Macedonians, and most cities hastened to open their gates.

Asia Minor and the Battle of Issus

In the winter of 334–333, Alexander conquered western Asia Minor, and in the spring of 333, he advanced along the coastal road to Perga. At Gordium in Phrygia, legend records his cutting of the Gordian knot, which could only be untied by the man who was to rule Asia; but this story may be apocryphal or at least distorted. From Gordium he pushed on to Ancyra (now called Ankara) and south from there. Meanwhile, the Persian king Darius III and his army had advanced toward Alexander, meeting at Issus. In the battle that followed, Alexander won a decisive victory and Darius fled.

Conquest of the Mediterranean Coast and Egypt

From Issus Alexander marched south into Syria and Phoenicia. In reply to a letter from Darius offering peace, Alexander replied arrogantly, demanding unconditional surrender to himself as lord of Asia. After taking Byblos (modern Jubayl) and Sidon (Arabic Ṣaydā), he was refused entry into the island city of Tyre. He thereupon prepared to use all methods of siegecraft to take it, but the Tyrians resisted, holding out for seven months before Alexander finally stormed the city in July of 332. The storming of Tyre is considered to be his greatest military achievement. While the siege of Tyre was in progress, Darius sent a new offer. He would pay a huge ransom for his family (under

Alexander's domain since the Battle of Issus) and cede all his lands west of the Euphrates. Alexander declined. After Tyre, Alexander advanced south, reaching Egypt in November of 332, where the people welcomed him, and the Persian satrap Mazaces wisely surrendered. While in Egypt, Alexander visited the oracle of the god Amon, the basis of his later claim to divinity; he also founded the city of Alexandria, near the western arm of the Nile.

Alexander's conquest of Egypt had completed his control of the whole eastern Mediterranean coast, and in the spring of 331, he returned to Tyre and prepared to advance into Mesopotamia. During his advance, he won a decisive battle, on the plain of Gaugamela, with Darius on October 31. Alexander pursued the defeated Persian forces for 35 miles (56 kilometres), but Darius escaped. Alexander took Babylon, then pressed on over the Zagros range into Persia proper and entered Persepolis and Pasargadae. In the spring of 330 Alexander marched north into Media and occupied its capital Ecbatana. By this time, Alexander's views on the empire were changing, and he had come to envisage a joint ruling people consisting of Macedonians and Persians.

In midsummer of 330, Alexander headed east via Rhagae (modern Rayy, near Tehrān) and the Caspian Gates, where he learned that Bessus, the satrap (governor) of Bactria, had deposed Darius, had him stabbed, and left him to die. Alexander sent Darius's body for burial with due honours in the royal tombs at Persepolis. Bessus was later captured and killed for the murder of Darius.

Campaign Eastward, to Central Asia

Darius's death left no obstacle to Alexander's claim to be Great King. Crossing the Elburz Mountains to the Caspian Sea, Alexander seized Zadracarta in Hyrcania and received the submission of a group of satraps and

Persian notables, after which he continued eastward. Meanwhile, Alexander ruthlessly quashed real or imagined conspiracies among his men. His actions elicited widespread horror but strengthened his position among his critics.

Alexander pressed on during the winter of 330–329 up the valley of the Helmand River, through Arachosia, and over the mountains past the site of modern Kābul into the country of the Paropamisadae. There he founded Alexandria by the Caucasus. Crossing the Hindu Kush northward over the Khawak Pass, Alexander continued on to the Jaxartes (modern Syr Darya) River, the boundary of the Persian Empire. On the site of modern Khujand (Khojent) on the Jaxartes, he founded a city, Alexandria Eschate, or "the farthest." In 328 he attacked the Bactrian chief Oxyartes and the remaining barons who held out in the hills of Paraetacene (modern Tajikistan). Among the captives was Oxyartes' daughter, Roxana. In reconciliation Alexander married her, and the rest of his opponents were either won over or crushed.

Shortly afterward, Alexander embraced Eastern absolutism and adopted Persian royal dress and customs.

INVASION OF INDIA

In early summer 327, Alexander left Bactria and recrossed the Hindu Kush. His advance through Swāt and Gandhāra was marked by the storming of the almost impregnable pinnacle of Aornos (modern Pir-Sar), which lay a few miles west of the Indus and north of the Buner rivers. In spring of 326, crossing the Indus River near Attock, Alexander entered Taxila. In June, Alexander fought his last great battle on the left bank of the Hydaspes (modern Jhelum) River. He founded two cities there, Alexandria Nicaea (to celebrate his victory) and Bucephala (named after his horse Bucephalus, which died there).

Alexander had advanced to the Hyphasis (probably the modern Beas) River when his army mutinied. On finding the army adamant, he agreed to turn back. Alexander then proceeded down the Indus River, with half his forces on shipboard and half marching down the two banks, brutally pillaging as they went along.

CONSOLIDATION OF THE EMPIRE

In the spring of 324, Alexander was back in Susa. There Alexander held a feast to celebrate the seizure of the Persian Empire. Attempting to further his policy of fusing Macedonians and Persians into one master race, he and 80 of his officers took Persian wives. This policy of racial fusion brought increasing friction to Alexander's relations with his Macedonian people, who had no sympathy for his changed concept of the empire. His determination to incorporate Persians on equal terms in the army and the administration of the provinces was bitterly resented. The issue came to a head later that year at Opis, when Alexander's decision to send home Macedonian veterans was interpreted as a move toward transferring the seat of power to Asia. There was an open mutiny involving all but the royal bodyguard; but when Alexander dismissed his whole army and enrolled Persians instead, the opposition broke down. An emotional scene of reconciliation was followed by a vast banquet with 9,000 guests to celebrate the end of the misunderstanding and the partnership in government of Macedonians and Persians. Ten thousand veterans were sent back to Macedonia with gifts, and the crisis was surmounted.

Also in 324, Alexander demanded that he should be accorded divine honours. At this point, he seems to have become convinced of his own divinity and demanded its acceptance by others, a symptom of growing megalomania and emotional instability. The cities perforce complied, but often ironically: The Spartan decree read, "Since Alexander wishes to be a god, let him be a god."

The next year, Alexander suddenly fell ill in Babylon after a prolonged banquet and drinking bout; he died 10 days later. His body, diverted to Egypt, was eventually placed in a golden coffin in Alexandria. He received divine honours in Egypt and elsewhere.

ASSESSMENT

As a general, Alexander is among the greatest the world has known. He showed unusual versatility, both in the combination of different arms and in adapting his tactics to the challenge of enemies who used unique forms of warfare. His strategy was skillful and imaginative. His use of cavalry was so effective that he rarely had to fall back upon his infantry for the final defeat.

Alexander's short reign marks a decisive moment in the history of Europe and Asia. His expedition and his own personal interest in scientific investigation brought many advances in the study of geography and natural history. His career led to the moving of the great centres of civilization eastward and initiated the new age of the Greek territorial monarchies; it spread Hellenism in a vast colonizing wave throughout the Middle East.

SHIHUANGDI

(b. c. 259 BCE, Qin state, northwestern China — d. 210 BCE, Hebei)

Born in 259 BCE, Shihuangdi (also known as Zhao Zheng or Ying Zheng) was emperor (reigned 221–210 BCE) of the Qin dynasty (221–207 BCE) and creator of the first unified Chinese empire. His gigantic funerary compound—now known as the Qin tomb, located near the modern city of Xi'an—is a significant Chinese archaeological site.

Zhao Zheng was the son of Zhuangxiang, who later became king of the state of Qin in northwestern China. His mother was a former concubine of a rich merchant, Lü Buwei, who, guided by financial interests, managed to install Zhuangxiang on the throne, even though he had not originally been designated as successor. The legend, once widely accepted, that Zheng was actually Lü Buwei's natural son is probably a myth.

When Zheng, at age 13, formally ascended the throne in 246 BCE, Qin already was the most powerful state and was likely to unite the rest of China under its rule. The central states had considered Qin to be a barbarous country, but by that time its strong position on the mountainous western periphery enabled Qin to develop a strong bureaucratic government and military organization. This was the basis of the totalitarian state philosophy known as legalism.

Zheng was officially declared of age in 238. By 221, with the help of espionage, extensive bribery, and the ruthlessly effective leadership of gifted generals, Zheng had eliminated the remaining six rival states that made up China at that time and created a unified Chinese empire under the supreme rule of the Qin. To herald his achievement, Zheng assumed the sacred titles of legendary rulers and proclaimed himself Shihuangdi ("First Sovereign Emperor").

As emperor he initiated a series of reforms aimed at establishing a fully centralized administration, thus avoiding the rise of independent satrapies, or provinces. He abolished territorial feudal power in the empire, forced the wealthy aristocratic families to live in the capital, Xianyang, and divided the country into 36 military districts, each with its own military and civil administrator. He also issued orders for almost universal standardization—from weights, measures, and the axle lengths of carts to the written language and the laws. Construction began on a network of roads and canals, and fortresses erected for defense against barbarian invasions from the north were linked to form the Great Wall.

The last years of Shihuangdi's life were dominated by an ever-growing distrust of his entourage—at least three assassination attempts nearly succeeded—and his increasing isolation from the common people. Almost inaccessible in his huge palaces, the emperor led the life of a semi-divine being. Upon his death, he was buried with more than 6,000 life-sized terra-cotta soldier and horse figures—forming an "army" for the dead king—in a gigantic funerary compound hewn out of a mountain and shaped in conformity with the symbolic patterns of the cosmos. His death immediately led to the outbreak of fighting among supporters of the old feudal factions, which ended in the collapse of the Qin dynasty and the extermination of the entire imperial clan by 206.

Shihuangdi certainly had an imposing personality and showed an unbending will in pursuing his aim to unite and strengthen the empire. His despotic rule and the draconian punishments he meted out were dictated largely by his belief in legalist ideas. With few exceptions, the traditional historiography of imperial China has regarded him as the villain par excellence, inhuman, uncultivated, and superstitious. Modern historians, however, generally stress the endurance of the bureaucratic and administrative structure institutionalized by Shihuangdi, which, despite its official denial, remained the basis of all subsequent dynasties in China.

JULIUS CAESAR

(b. July 12/13, 100? BCE, Rome [Italy]—d. March 15, 44 BCE, Rome)

G aius Julius Caesar was a celebrated Roman general and statesman, the conqueror of Gaul (58–50 BCE), victor in the Civil War of 49–45, and dictator (46–44). He was launching a series of political and social reforms when he was assassinated by a group of nobles in the Senate House on the Ides of March.

LIFE

In 78 BCE Caesar started preparing for his political career by acting as a prosecuting advocate in Rome. He then

Julius Caesar, *marble bust; in the Capitoline Museums, Rome.* Alinari/Art Resource, New York

went to Rhodes to study oratory under a famous professor Molon. En route he was captured by pirates (one of the symptoms of the anarchy into which the Roman nobility had allowed the Mediterranean world to fall). Caesar raised his ransom, raised a naval force, captured his captors, and had them crucified—all this as a private individual holding no public office.

In 69 or 68 Caesar began his political ascent when he was elected quaestor (the first rung on the Roman political ladder) of the province of Farther Spain (modern Andalusia and Portugal). He then was elected one of the curule aediles for 65, and pontifex maximus in 63 before being elected a praetor in 62. He obtained the governorship of Farther Spain for 61–60, but returned to Rome in 60 to stand for the consulship for 59, to which he was elected. The value of the consulship lay in the lucrative provincial governorship to which it would normally lead.

The First Triumvirate and the Conquest of Gaul

In 60, Caesar formed a political alliance, the so-called first triumvirate, with Pompey, a Roman general and statesman, and Marcus Licinius Crassus, also a Roman statesman. After a year as consul, Caesar was sent to govern the province of Cisalpine Gaul and Illyricum. When the governor-designate of Transalpine Gaul suddenly died, this province was also assigned to Caesar at Pompey's request.

Caesar set out to conquer the rest of Gaul, which he accomplished between 58 and 50. This campaign showcased his skills as a leader, an organizer, and a general. He fought alongside his soldiers as they conquered the tribes in Gaul. Caesar also made several raids into Britain and what is now Germany during this period.

The crisis of Caesar's Gallic war came in 52, when Vercingetorix, the chieftain of the Arverni tribe, led a general uprising of the Gauls against Caesar. After an initial defeat at Noviodunum Biturigum, Vercingetorix effectively used guerrilla warfare, but Caesar ultimately destroyed the rebellion. During 52–51, Caesar crushed a number of sporadic further revolts, completing his conquest in 50.

THE CIVIL WAR OF 49–45

During his conquest of Gaul, Caesar had been equally busy preserving and improving his position at home. Meanwhile the triumvirate was unraveling: Crassus was killed in battle in 53 and Pompey, who had grown wary of Caesar's increasing power, eventually sided with Caesar's enemies among the Roman nobility in the Senate.

War was brewing. The source of this tension was the issue of whether there should be an interval between the date at which Caesar was to resign his provincial governorships—and thus, command over his armies—and the date at which he would enter his proposed second consulship. If there were to be an interval, Caesar would be a private person during that time, vulnerable to attack by his enemies. If prosecuted and convicted, he would be ruined politically and possibly killed. Therefore, Caesar had to make sure that, until his entry on his second consulship, he should continue to hold at least one province with the military force to guarantee his security. The issue had been debated in the Senate several times before the body resolved that Caesar should be treated as a public enemy if he did not lay down his command. Meanwhile, Pompey had been offered—albeit without proper Senate authorization—command over all troops in Italy, which he accepted. When the Senate would not order Pompey to give up his command simultaneously, Caesar led his forces across the Rubicon River, the boundary between his province of Cisalpine Gaul and Italy proper, committing the first act of the Roman Civil War, which would last for four years.

In 49 Caesar drove his opponents out of Italy to the eastern side of the Straits of Otranto and later crushed Pompey's army in Spain. Caesar pursued Pompey, eventually into Egypt, where Pompey was murdered by an Egyptian officer. Caesar spent the winter besieged in Alexandria and dallying with Queen Cleopatra. In 47 he fought a brief local war in northeastern Anatolia with Pharnaces, king of the Cimmerian Bosporus; Caesar's famous words, *Veni, vidi, vici* ("I came, I saw, I conquered"), are his own account of this campaign.

Caesar then returned to Rome, but a few months later—now with the title of dictator—he left for Africa, where his opponents had rallied. In 46 he crushed their army at Thapsus and returned to Rome, only to leave in November for Farther Spain to deal with a fresh outbreak of resistance, which he crushed on March 17, 45, at Munda. He then returned again to Rome to start putting the Greco-Roman world in order. But before this could happen, he was assassinated the next year in the Senate House at Rome on March 15.

Caesar's death was partly due to his clemency and impatience, which, in combination, were dangerous for his personal security. Although capable of committing atrocities against those he deemed "barbarians," Caesar amnestied his political opponents wholesale and gave a number of them responsible positions in his new regime. Gaius Cassius Longinus, who was the moving spirit in the plot to murder him, and Marcus Junius Brutus, the symbolic embodiment of Roman republicanism, were both former enemies. "Et tu, Brute" ("You too, Brutus") was Caesar's expression of his particular anguish at being stabbed by a man whom he had forgiven, trusted, and loved.

ACCOMPLISHMENTS

Caesar changed the course of the history of the Greco-Roman world decisively and irreversibly, and even today many people are familiar with his name as a title signifying a ruler who is in some sense uniquely supreme or paramount—the meaning of *Kaiser* in German, *tsar* in the Slavonic languages, and *qaysar* in the languages of the Islamic world.

Caesar is recognized for reforming the Roman calendar, which was inaccurate and manipulated for political purposes; the Roman month Quintilis, in which he was born, was renamed July in his honour. Caesar's calendar, the Julian calendar, was established in the year 46 BCE and is used by some Eastern Orthodox Christian churches for their liturgical year. And the Gregorian calendar, now in widespread use throughout the world, is the Julian, slightly corrected by Pope Gregory XIII.

Caesar was a master public speaker and was well known for his writings, although most of his material has been lost. Only his accounts of the Gallic War and the Roman Civil War survive. All Caesar's speeches and writings apparently served political purposes. His accounts of his wars are subtly contrived to make the unsuspecting reader see Caesar's acts in the light that Caesar chooses. The accounts are written in the form of terse, dry, factual reports that look impersonal and objective; yet every recorded fact has been carefully selected and presented. The mark of Caesar's genius in his writings is that, although they were written for propaganda, they are nevertheless of outstanding literary merit.

CLEOPATRA

(b. 70/69 BCE — d. August of 30 BCE, Alexandria)

Cleopatra VII Thea Philopator was the last ruler of the Ptolemaic dynasty in Egypt. Her life has captivated historians and writers.

Cleopatra (Greek for "famous in her father") was the daughter of King Ptolemy XII Auletes. She was of Macedonian descent and had little, if any, Egyptian blood. When Ptolemy XII died in 51 BCE, the throne passed to his young son, Ptolemy XIII, and daughter, Cleopatra VII. It is likely, but not proven, that the two married soon after their father's death. The 18-year-old Cleopatra—older than her brother by about eight years—became the dominant ruler. Evidence shows that the first decree in which Ptolemy's name precedes Cleopatra's was in October of 50. Soon after, Cleopatra was forced to flee Egypt for Syria, where she raised an army, and in 48 BCE returned to face her brother. The arrival of Julius Caesar brought temporary peace.

Cleopatra realized that she needed Roman support, or, more specifically, Caesar's support, if she was to regain her throne. Caesar and Cleopatra became lovers and spent the winter besieged in Alexandria. Roman reinforcements arrived the following spring, and Ptolemy XIII fled and drowned in the Nile. Cleopatra, now married to her brother Ptolemy XIV, was restored to her throne. In June of 47, she gave birth to Ptolemy Caesar (known to the people of Alexandria as Caesarion, or "little Caesar"). Whether Caesar was the father of Caesarion, as his name implies, is not known. Cleopatra was in Rome when Caesar was murdered in 44, after which she returned to Alexandria. Shortly thereafter, her coruler, Ptolemy XIV, died, and Cleopatra now ruled with her infant son, Ptolemy XV Caesar.

Mark Antony eventually became the heir apparent of Caesar's authority—or so it seemed. Caesar's great-nephew and personal heir, Octavian, was a sickly boy who seemed easily controlled. Antony, now controller of Rome's eastern territories, summoned Cleopatra to Tarsus, in Asia Minor, to answer charges that she had aided his enemies in the aftermath of Caesar's assassination. She entered the city by sailing up the Cydnus River in a barge while dressed as the goddess Isis. Antony, who equated himself with the god Dionysus, was captivated. Forgetting his wife, Fulvia, Antony returned to Alexandria with Cleopatra, where they formed a society of "inimitable livers," whose members lived what some historians have interpreted as a life of debauchery and folly and others have interpreted as lives dedicated to the cult of the mystical god Dionysus.

In 40 Cleopatra gave birth to twins, whom she named Alexander Helios and Cleopatra Selene. Antony had already left Alexandria to return to Italy, where he was forced to conclude a temporary settlement with Octavian, who, during Antony's absence, had become more of a threat. As part of this settlement, he married Octavian's sister, Octavia (Fulvia having died). Three years later Antony was convinced that he and Octavian could never come to terms. His marriage to Octavia now an irrelevance, he returned to the east and reunited with Cleopatra. Antony needed Cleopatra's financial support for a military campaign in Parthia. In return, Cleopatra requested the recovery of much of Egypt's eastern empire, including large portions of Syria and Lebanon, and even the rich balsam groves of Jericho.

The Parthian campaign was a costly failure. Nevertheless, in 34, Antony celebrated a triumphant return to Alexandria, followed by a celebration known as "the Donations of Alexandria." Antony proclaimed Caesarion to be Caesar's son—thus relegating Octavian, who had been adopted by Caesar as his son and heir, to legal illegitimacy. Alexander Helios, Cleopatra Selene, and their infant brother Ptolemy were all awarded Roman territory to rule, and it was clear to Octavian, watching from Rome, that Antony intended his extended family to rule the civilized world. A propaganda war erupted when Octavian, claiming to have read Antony's will, told the Roman people that not only had Antony bestowed Roman possessions upon a foreign woman, but he also intended to be buried beside her in Egypt. The rumour quickly spread that Antony intended to transfer the capital from Rome to Alexandria.

Antony and Cleopatra spent the winter of 32–31 in Greece. The Roman Senate deprived Antony of his prospective consulate for the following year, and it then declared war against Cleopatra. The naval Battle of Actium, in which Octavian faced the combined forces of Antony and Cleopatra on September 2, 31, was a disaster for the Egyptians. Antony and Cleopatra fled to Egypt, and Cleopatra retired to her mausoleum as Antony went off to fight his last battle. Receiving the false news that Cleopatra had died, Antony stabbed himself with his sword. When he found out she was still alive, he had himself carried to her and died in her arms. After Cleopatra buried Antony, she, too, committed suicide. The means of her death is uncertain, though Classical writers came to believe that she had killed herself by means of an asp, a poisonous snake and symbol of divine royalty. After their deaths, Egypt fell under Roman domination.

The lives of most Egyptian queens have been forgotten over time, but the story of Cleopatra's life has endured through the ages. The official Roman version of a predatory, immoral Cleopatra passed into Western culture, where it was retold and reinterpreted as the years passed. Meanwhile, Muslim scholars, writing after the Arab conquest of Egypt about 640 CE, developed their own version of the queen. Their Cleopatra was first and foremost a scholar and a scientist, a gifted philosopher, and a chemist. In the late 20th century, Cleopatra's ethnic heritage became the subject of intense academic debate, with some African American scholars embracing Cleopatra as a black African heroine.

JESUS CHRIST
(b. *c.* 6 BCE, Judaea—d. *c.* 30 CE, Jerusalem)

To the faithful Christian, Jesus, the founder of the Christian faith, is the son of God and God incarnate whose sacrifice on the cross offers the promise of salvation and whose life and passion are the fulfillment of the Jewish Scriptures.

Although the earliest accounts of Jesus' life—the Synoptic Gospels of Matthew, Mark, and Luke and the more philosophical Gospel of John—are marked by inconsistencies and differing agendas and no independent account by contemporary authors exists, a picture of his life can be discerned from Scripture. According to Matthew, Jesus was born to the house of David, as foretold in Jewish scripture and messianic traditions. He was born to Mary, the wife of a carpenter named Joseph. According to Luke the birth occurred during the time of a census held by Augustus, and according to Matthew, during the reign of Herod the Great. Although the chronology of the Gospels is inconsistent, they do agree that Jesus was born in the town of Bethlehem—in support of Jewish messianic teachings—and raised in the Galilean town of Nazareth. Little is told of Jesus' early life except for the stories found in Luke concerning the presentation of Jesus at the Temple and the encounter of Jesus with the teachers in the Temple.

While his birth and youth, according to the evangelists, fulfilled scriptural prophecy, it was the adult ministry of Jesus that established the foundation of the faith. Once again the Gospels are not wholly consistent—differences in the length of the ministry and the number of visits to Jerusalem exist—but a coherent picture of the ministry does emerge. It begins with the baptism of Jesus by John the Baptist. Jesus recognized the importance of John's teachings and sought baptism from John. This episode may suggest that Jesus was a follower of John, and the affinities they had with the teachings of the Essenes and related Judaic teachings make this possible. However, John acknowledged that Jesus was the greater of the two and would go beyond John's own ministry. Jesus began to preach and recruited a number of disciples, including the twelve Apostles. Jesus' ministry was characterized by charismatic preaching. The moral authority of his sermons in some ways challenged existing law but also, as Jesus said, fulfilled the law. His preaching, which was often in the form of parables, spoke of the coming of the kingdom of God and demanded repentance of the people in preparation for the coming of the kingdom. Jesus was also a healer—curing a woman of an effusion of blood, healing the sick, and raising Lazarus from the dead—often in apparent violation of Sabbath prohibitions and Jewish laws of purity. The Gospels also record that Jesus was a miracle worker and that he calmed the seas, changed water into wine, and fed a great multitude with a few loaves and fishes.

The final chapter of Jesus' life involved his visit to Jerusalem. His entry at Passover, riding a donkey, was heavily symbolic and evoked the messianic traditions of Judaism. It was in this final, although possibly not first, visit to Jerusalem that Jesus probably came to the attention of the authorities. There was an incident at the Temple of Jerusalem in which he cast out the various merchants, declaring the Temple a house of prayer and not a den of thieves. He was questioned by Jewish leaders who, according to the Gospels, sought to put him in the wrong over his attitude toward the secular authority and matters concerning resurrection. While in Jerusalem Jesus responded to the questions of the Scribes saying that the highest commandment is to love God. He also prophesied the impending destruction of Jerusalem and the world.

The most important events of his time in Jerusalem involved his Last Supper and Passion, the events surrounding his trial and death. He established the new covenant by instituting the Eucharist and sharing the bread and wine—representing his body and blood—with the disciples, who were told to do this in his memory. He was betrayed by one of these disciples, Judas Iscariot, who revealed Jesus's whereabouts to the chief priests and elders for 30 pieces of silver. Jesus was condemned to death. For the Jewish authorities he was guilty of violating the law of Moses and blasphemy, and for the Romans he was guilty of inciting the overthrow of Roman authority. Indeed, the Romans reserved the horrible punishment of crucifixion for their most dangerous political criminals. Recognizing himself as the suffering servant, Jesus quietly accepted his fate, forbidding his followers to defend him in the garden of Gethsemane when he was arrested and enduring his punishment. While suffering on the cross, he sought forgiveness for those around him and commended his soul to God. The sacrifice on the cross was followed by the burial and by the resurrection of Jesus three days later. Having risen, he met Mary Magdalene and other women before revealing himself to his disciples and commanding them to make disciples of all nations and baptizing them in the name of the Father, and of the Son, and of the Holy Spirit (Matthew 28:20).

To understand the teachings of Jesus fully, it is necessary to place him in the context of the Judaism of his time. Jesus was in many ways an observant Jew—honoring the Passover, attending the Temple, and adhering to biblical teaching. During his lifetime there was a wide range of messianic teachings, from the violence of the Zealots to the otherworldly teachings of the Essenes, which foresaw the coming of a savior from the house of David. Notions of the "son of man" as an eschatological figure were current in Jewish circles as well. The Pharisees, moreover, taught a doctrine that included bodily resurrection, angel, and Satan, pertaining to the end of humankind.

Although Jesus was a part of contemporary Judaism, he made these traditions uniquely his own. Reluctant to identify himself as the messiah, he called himself the son of man and placed himself in the contemporary messianic context. His moral reform is outlined in the Sermon on the Mount, in which he taught that the kingdom of God awaits the peacemakers, the poor in spirit, and those who have suffered in Jesus' name. Drawn from Jewish tradition, the doctrine Jesus taught was one of repentance and moral reform, the love of God and service to his will—service that Jesus undertook with his Passion on the cross. The Passion, Christians believe, was rewarded with resurrection and thus offers the hope of salvation to all.

CONSTANTINE I

(b. Feb. 27, after 280? CE, Naissus, Moesia [now Niš, Serbia]—d. May 22, 337, Ancyrona, near Nicomedia, Bithynia [now İzmit, Turkey])

Constantine I (also known as Constantine the Great) was the first Roman emperor to profess Christianity. He not only initiated the evolution of the empire into a Christian state but also provided the impulse for a distinctively Christian culture that prepared the way for the growth of Byzantine and Western medieval culture.

Constantine was born probably in the later 280s CE. A typical product of the military governing class of the later 3rd century, he was the son of Flavius Valerius Constantius, an army officer, and his wife (or concubine) Helena. Constantine was brought up in the Eastern Roman Empire at the court of the senior emperor Diocletian at Nicomedia (modern İzmit, Turkey). He encountered Christianity in court circles as well as in the cities of the East. From 303, during the great persecution of the Christians, which began at the court of Diocletian at Nicomedia and which was enforced with particular intensity in the eastern parts of the empire, Christianity became a major issue of public policy.

In 305 the two emperors, Diocletian and Maximian (of the Western Roman Empire), abdicated. Passed over as successor to the throne, Constantine joined his father at Gesoriacum (modern Boulogne, France) and fought to make himself emperor. They crossed together to Britain and fought a campaign in the north before Constantius's death at Eboracum (modern York) in 306. Immediately declared emperor by the army, Constantine then threw himself into a complex series of civil wars. After his victory at the Milvian Bridge near Rome in 312, he became Western emperor; the East was to be shared by Licinius and his rival Maximinus. Licinius defeated Maximinus and became the sole Eastern emperor but lost territory in the Balkans to Constantine in 316. After a further period of tension, Constantine attacked Licinius in 324, defeating him at Adrianople and Chrysopolis (respectively, modern Edirne and Üsküdar, Turkey) and becoming sole emperor of East and West.

Constantine's adherence to Christianity was closely associated with his rise to power. He fought the Battle of the Milvian Bridge in the name of the Christian God, having received instructions in a dream to paint the Christian monogram on his troops' shields. It was at this time that he adopted Christianity, according to the account given by the Christian apologist Lactantius. A somewhat different version, offered by the historian Eusebius, tells of a vision seen by Constantine during the campaign against Maxentius, in which the Christian sign appeared in the sky with the words *in hoc signo vinces* ("In this sign, conquer").

Constantine had met Licinius at Mediolanum (modern Milan) in 313 to confirm a number of political and dynastic arrangements. A product of this meeting has become known as the Edict of Milan, which extended toleration to the Christians and restored any personal and corporate property that had been confiscated during the previous period of persecution. But Constantine went far beyond the joint policy agreed upon at Mediolanum, donating property for religious use. He also began issuing laws allowing the church and its clergy fiscal and legal privileges and immunities from civic burdens.

During his reign Constantine became involved in various ecclesiastical issues, including the Donatist schism in North Africa. The Donatists maintained that those priests and bishops who had once lapsed from the Christian faith could not be readmitted to the church, an opinion not held by the rest of the church. Despite Constantine's interventions into the matter from 313 to the early 320s, the schism did not end in his lifetime.

Constantine also became involved in the Arian heresy, another ecclesiastical issue. Arius, a priest of Alexandria, maintained that Christ was not the equal of the Father but was created by Him. Athanasius, leader of the bishops in the West, claimed that the Father and Son, though distinct, were equal, and of the same substance. The quarrel threatened to divide the Christian church. To settle the matter, Constantine called together a worldwide council of bishops at Nicaea in 325. However, the conclusions reached at the Council of Nicaea did not resolve the dispute.

Constantine was an earnest student of his religion. In later years he commissioned new copies of the Bible for the growing congregations at Constantinople. He composed a special prayer for his troops and went on campaigns with a mobile chapel in a tent. He issued numerous laws relating to Christian practice and susceptibilities. For instance, he abolished the penalty of crucifixion and the practice of branding certain criminals; enjoined the observance of Sunday and saints' days; and extended privileges to the clergy while suppressing at least some offensive pagan practices. Many churches throughout the empire owed their development, directly or indirectly, to Constantine's interest or sponsorship.

The greatest political crisis of Constantine's reign occurred while he was visiting Rome in 326. In his absence from the East, and for reasons that remain obscure, Constantine had his eldest son, the deputy emperor Crispus, and his own wife Fausta, Crispus's stepmother, slain. The visit to Rome was also not a success. Constantine's refusal to take part in a pagan procession offended the

Romans; and when he left after a short visit, it was never to return. These events set the course of the last phase of the reign of Constantine. After his defeat of Licinius, he had renamed Byzantium as Constantinople. Immediately upon his return from the West, he began to rebuild the city on a greatly enlarged pattern, as his permanent capital and the "second Rome." The dedication of Constantinople (in May of 330) confirmed the divorce, which had been in the making for more than a century, between the emperors and Rome.

Constantine fell ill at Helenopolis while preparing for a campaign against Persia. He attempted to return to Constantinople but was forced to stop near Nicomedia, where he died. He was buried at Constantinople in the Church of the Apostles, whose memorials, six on each side, flanked his tomb.

ATTILA

(d. 453)

Attila was king of the Huns from 434 to 453 (ruling jointly with his elder brother Bleda until 445). Known as Flagellum Dei (in Latin "Scourge of God"), he was one of the greatest of the barbarian rulers who assailed the Roman Empire, invading the southern Balkan provinces and Greece and then Gaul and Italy. In legend he appears under the name Etzel in the *Nibelungenlied* and under the name Atli in Icelandic sagas.

The empire that Attila and his elder brother Bleda inherited seems to have stretched from the Alps and the Baltic in the west to somewhere near the Caspian Sea in the east. Their first known action after becoming joint rulers was the negotiation of a peace treaty with the Eastern Roman Empire that required the Romans, in order to avoid being attacked by the Huns, to double the amount of tribute they had been paying to the Huns and in the future pay 700 pounds (300 kilograms) of gold each year.

The failure of the Romans to pay the promised tributes prompted Attila to launch assaults on the Danubian frontier of the Eastern Empire in 441. He captured and razed a number of important cities, including Singidunum (Belgrade). The Eastern Romans managed to arrange a truce for the year 442, but Attila resumed his attack in 443. He began by taking and destroying towns on the Danube and then drove into the interior of the empire toward Naissus (Niš) and Serdica (Sofia), both of which he destroyed. He next turned toward Constantinople, took Philippopolis, defeated the main Eastern Roman forces in a succession of battles, and reached the sea both north and south of Constantinople. It was hopeless for the Hun archers to attack the great walls of the capital; so Attila turned on the remnants of the empire's forces, which had withdrawn into the peninsula of Gallipoli, and destroyed them. In the peace treaty that followed, he obliged the Eastern Empire to pay the arrears of tribute, which he calculated at 6,000 pounds of gold, and he tripled the annual tribute, henceforth extorting 2,100 pounds of gold each year.

Attila murdered his brother Bleda in 445 and became the sole ruler of the Huns. He made his second great attack on the Eastern Roman Empire in 447, but little is known of the details of the campaign. He devastated the Balkan provinces and drove southward into Greece, where he was only stopped at Thermopylae. The three years following the invasion were filled with complicated negotiations between Attila and the diplomats of the Eastern Roman emperor Theodosius II. The treaty by which the war was terminated was harsher than that of 443; the Eastern Romans had to evacuate a wide belt of territory south of the Danube, and the tribute payable by them was continued, although the rate is not known.

Attila's next great campaign was the invasion of Gaul. He announced that his objective in the West was the kingdom of the Visigoths (a Germanic people who had conquered parts of the two Roman empires) centred on Tolosa (Toulouse). He also announced that he had no quarrel with the Western emperor, Valentinian III. But in the spring of 450, Honoria, the emperor's sister, asked Attila to rescue her from a marriage that had been arranged for her. Attila thereupon claimed Honoria as his wife and demanded half the Western Empire as her dowry. He then invaded Gaul in 451, but was defeated by an alliance between Aetius, a Roman general, and Theodoric, the Visigothic king. The decisive engagement was the Battle of the Catalaunian Plains, although some authorities would place it at Maurica (both places are unidentified). After fierce fighting, in which Theodoric was killed, Attila withdrew and shortly afterward retired from Gaul. This was his first and only defeat.

In 452 the Huns invaded Italy and sacked several cities, including Aquileia, Patavium (Padua), Verona, Brixia (Brescia), Bergomum (Bergamo), and Mediolanum (Milan). Aetius could do nothing to halt them. But the famine and pestilence raging in Italy in that year caused the Huns to leave anyway.

In 453 Attila intended to attack the Eastern Empire, after the new emperor Marcian had refused to pay the subsidies agreed upon by his predecessor, Theodosius II. But during the night following the last of his marriages, Attila died in his sleep. Those who buried him and his treasures were subsequently put to death by the Huns so that his grave might never be discovered. He was succeeded by his sons, who divided his empire among themselves.

MUHAMMAD

(b. c. 570, Mecca, Arabia [Saudi Arabia]—d. June 8, 632, Medina)

Muhammad—also known as the Messenger of God (Rasūl Allāh) or the Prophet (al-Nabī)—founded the religion of Islam and the Muslim community. Although biographical statements occur in the Qur'an, most of what is known about Muhammad's life comes from the Hadith, hagiographies (especially Ibn Ishāq's mid-8th-century *Sīra*), and Muslim histories (such as al-Tabarī's *Kitāb al-rusul wa'l-mulūk*, 9th–10th century). The life, teachings, and miracles of the Prophet have been the subjects of Muslim devotion and reflection for centuries.

Muhammad (in full, Abū al-Qāsim Muhammad ibn 'Abd Allāh ibn 'Abd al-Muttalib ibn Hāshim) was born after the death of his father, 'Abd Allāh, and was first placed in the care of his mother and his paternal grandfather, and, after their deaths, his uncle Abū Tālib. During his early life in Mecca, his merchant activities resulted in his marriage in about 595 to the wealthy widow Khadīja, who bore him at least two sons, who died young, and four daughters. The best known of these daughters was Fātimah, whom he gave in marriage to his cousin 'Alī to repay the kindness of Abū Tālib. Until Khadīja's death in 619, Muhammad took no other wife.

In about 610, while meditating in a cave in the mountains outside Mecca, Muhammad had a vision of a majestic being (later identified with the angel Gabriel) and heard a voice saying to him, "You are the Messenger of God." This marked the beginning of his career as prophet. From this time, at frequent intervals until his death, he received messages that he believed came directly from God or through Gabriel. Around 650 the messages were collected and written in the Qur'an. Muhammad's later experiences of receiving messages were mainly auditory, with no vision to accompany them. Muhammad rendered these with his voice into a "recitation" (*qur'ān*) of God's word.

Muhammad began preaching publicly in about 613. Although his preaching was basically religious, it contained an obvious critique of the beliefs, conduct, and attitudes of the rich merchants of Mecca. Attempts were made to get him to soften his criticism, and pressure was placed upon his supporters by the Quraysh rulers of the city. About 619, with the deaths of Khadīja and Abū Ṭālib, Muhammad lost the protection of his clan. This meant that he could be attacked and thus could no longer spread his religion in Mecca.

In looking for a safe place to practice their beliefs, Muhammad began negotiations in about 620 with clans in Yathrib (later called Medina, "The City of the Prophet"). He and some of his followers emigrated there, arriving on September 24, 622. This is the celebrated Hijra, which may be interpreted as "emigration," although the basic meaning is the severing of kinship ties. It is the traditional starting point of Islamic history. The Islamic Era (*ah* or Anno Hegirae) begins on the first day of the Arabic year in which the Hijra took place—July 16, 622, in the Western calendar.

In Medina, Muhammad set out to solidify his status. In a series of agreements, known collectively as the Constitution of Medina, he formalized his role as an arbitrator of disputes and as a prophet. It was during Muhammad's years at Medina that most of the Qur'an's rules concerning worship, family relations, and society were revealed.

Although Muhammad first sought to align himself and his followers with Jewish tribes of Medina and with their religion, relations between the two groups soon became strained. According to Muslim sources, Jews rejected Muhammad's claims to prophethood and seem to have joined with his opponents to defeat him.

A few emigrants from Mecca, with the approval of Muhammad, went on *razzias* (*ghazawāt*, or raids) in the hope of intercepting Meccan caravans passing near Medina on their way to Syria. In 624 the raids led to military conflict with Mecca. On March 15, 624, near a place called Badr, there was a battle in which at least 45 Meccans were killed, while only 14 Muslims died. To Muhammad this was a divine vindication of his prophethood, and the victory of Badr greatly strengthened him. In April of 627, a great confederacy of 10,000 men moved against Medina, but the army withdrew after a two-week siege. In 629 the Meccans formally surrendered and were promised a general amnesty. Although Muhammad did not insist on their becoming Muslims, many soon did so.

Ever since the Hijra, Muhammad had been forming alliances with nomadic tribes. When he was strong enough to offer protection, he made it a condition of the alliance that the tribe become Muslim. Muhammad was soon militarily the strongest man in Arabia. By this time in Medina he had also repelled all serious challenges to his control. Jews in settlements north of Medina surrendered to him and assumed what would later be called *dhimmī* (protected) status, as did Christians in other parts of Arabia.

In 632, after performing one last pilgrimage to Mecca, Muhammad fell ill in Medina and died in the arms of his wife 'Ā'isha, the daughter of his friend Abu Bakr. Since no arrangement had been made for his succession, the Prophet's death provoked a major crisis among his followers. The dispute over the leadership of the Muslim community eventually resulted in the most important schism in the history of Islam: the one between Sunni Muslims, led by the caliph (or official successor), and Shi'ite Muslims, led by the imam (or religious leader). Majoritarian religious doctrine precluded the appearance of another prophet.

After his death Muhammad's remains were interred in his mosque. It was not long before caliphs began to expand the site and add new, more permanent architectural features. The mosque-tomb in Medina was to become the second most sacred site for Muslims, and pilgrimage there, while not a duty like the hajj, is considered a highly laudatory undertaking.

Muhammad's prophetic calling is a belief that Muslims are required to acknowledge in the *shahāda* (creed), and it constitutes one of the principal subjects of theological discourse. He is considered an exemplary holy man whose words and deeds are remembered in the Hadith, which form the basis of the sunna, one of the roots of Islamic law (*fiqh*) and customary Muslim practice. Indeed, jurists regarded him as the foremost lawgiver, and philosophers saw in him the fulfillment of the ideal of Plato's philosopher-king. For Sufis, Muhammad was the ascetic and preeminent visionary and the ancestral founder of their myriad orders. More recently he has been seen by some as the first unifier of the Arab peoples and the model for armed resistance against Western imperialism.

'ALĪ

(b. *c.* 600, Mecca—d. January 661, Kūfa, Iraq)

The cousin and son-in-law of Muhammad, 'Alī was the fourth caliph (successor to Muhammad), reigning from 656 to 661. The question of his right to the caliphate resulted in the split in Islam into Sunni and Shi'ite branches. He is revered by the Shi'ites as the first imam, the true successor to the Prophet.

'Alī (in full, 'Alī ibn Abī Ṭālib) was the son of Abū Ṭālib, chief of a clan of the Quraysh. When his father became impoverished, 'Alī, who was five years old at the time, was taken under the care of his cousin Muhammad, then still a businessman in Mecca, who himself had been cared for by 'Alī's father as a child. When Muhammad began his career as a prophet, 'Alī, only 10 years old, became one of the first converts to Islam. Later, he married Muhammad's daughter Fāṭimah, who bore him two sons, Ḥasan and Ḥusayn.

'Alī is said to have been a courageous fighter in the expeditions Muhammad conducted to consolidate Islam. He was also one of Muhammad's scribes and led several important missions. When the inhabitants of Mecca finally accepted Islam without a battle, it was 'Alī who smashed their idols in the Ka'ba (holy shrine).

Muhammad died on June 8, 632. Some say he had nominated 'Alī as his successor while he was returning from his "farewell pilgrimage" to Mecca. Others maintain that Muhammad died without naming a successor. 'Alī, while attending the last rites of the Prophet, was confronted by the fact that Abū Bakr, Muhammad's closest friend and the father of 'Ā'isha, one of the Prophet's wives, had been chosen as caliph. 'Alī did not submit to Abū Bakr's authority for some time, but neither did he actively assert his own rights, possibly in order to prevent bloody tribal strife. He retired and led a quiet life in which religious works became his chief occupation. The first chronologically arranged version of the Qur'an is attributed to him, and his knowledge of Hadith aided the caliphs in various legal problems.

'Alī became caliph following the murder of 'Uthmān, the third caliph. His brief reign was difficult due mostly to the corrupt state of affairs he inherited. He based his rule on the Islamic ideals of social justice and equality, but his policy was a blow to the interests of the Quraysh aristocracy of Mecca, who had grown rich in the Muslim conquests. In order to embarrass 'Alī, they demanded that he bring the murderers of 'Uthmān to trial. When he refused, a rebellion against him was instigated, led by two prominent Meccans and 'Ā'isha. This rebellion, known as the Battle of the Camel (the camel ridden by 'Ā'isha), was crushed by 'Alī's forces. A second rebellion was on the point of defeat when its leader, Mu'āwiya, a kinsman of 'Uthmān and the governor of Syria, proposed arbitration. 'Alī was forced by his army to accept adjudication, greatly weakening his position. Soon he had to fight some of the very people who had earlier forced him to accept arbitration but now denounced it. Known as Khawārij (Seceders), they were defeated by 'Alī in the Battle of Nahrawān. Meanwhile, Mu'āwiya followed an aggressive policy, and by the end of 660 'Alī had lost control of Egypt and of the Hijaz. While he was praying in a mosque at Kūfa in Iraq, a Khārijite struck 'Alī with a poisoned sword. Two days later 'Alī died and was buried at Nujaf, near Kūfa. His mausoleum became one of the principal Shi'ite pilgrimage centers.

'Alī's political discourses, sermons, letters, and sayings, collected by ash-Sharīf ar-Radī in a book entitled *Nahj al-balāghah* ("The Road of Eloquence") with commentary by Ibn Abī al-Hadīd, are well known in Arabic literature. Muslims consider him to be an embodiment of the virtues of justice, learning, and mystical insight. In popular piety he is regarded as an intercessor with God, and certain quasi-gnostic groups maintain that he is the Perfect Man. Some, like the 'Alawī of Syria, even hold that he is a human incarnation of God.

CHARLEMAGNE

(b. April 747 — d. Jan. 28, 814, Aachen, Austria [now in Germany])

Charlemagne (also known as Charles I or Charles the Great) reigned as king of the Franks (768–814), king of the Lombards (774–814), and emperor (800–814). Although he was never crowned as such, he is considered to be the first Holy Roman Emperor.

LIFE AND REIGN

Charlemagne's father, Pippin III, became the unofficial ruler of the Franks in 747. Upon deposing Childeric III, the last king of the Merovingian dynasty, in 751, Pippin became king of the Franks—the first monarch of what would be known as the Carolingian dynasty. When Pippin died in 768, his realm was divided between Charlemagne and his brother, Carloman. Almost immediately the rivalry between the two brothers threatened the unity of the Frankish kingdom. The death of Carloman in 771 ended the mounting crisis, and Charlemagne, disregarding the rights of Carloman's heirs, took control of the entire Frankish realm.

The first three decades of Charlemagne's reign were dominated by military campaigns, which were prompted by a variety of factors: the need to defend his realm against external foes and internal separatists, a desire for conquest and wealth, a keen sense of opportunities offered by changing power relationships, and an urge to spread Christianity.

Charlemagne's most demanding military undertaking pitted him against the Saxons, longtime adversaries of the Franks whose conquest required more than 30 years of campaigning. This long struggle, which led to the annexation of a large block of territory between the Rhine and the Elbe rivers, was marked by pillaging, broken truces, hostage taking, mass killings, deportation of rebellious Saxons, draconian measures to compel acceptance of Christianity, and occasional Frankish defeats.

The Frisians — Saxon allies living along the North Sea east of the Rhine — were also forced to surrender.

While the conquest of Saxony was in progress, Charlemagne undertook other campaigns. He invaded the Lombard kingdom in 774, which ended with his assumption of the Lombard crown and the annexation of the kingdom's territory in northern Italy. Concerned with defending southern Gaul from Muslim attacks, Charlemagne invaded Spain in 778, which ended in the disastrous defeat of the Frankish army, immortalized three centuries later in the epic poem *The Song of Roland*. Despite this setback, Charlemagne persisted in his effort to make the frontier in Spain more secure. In 781 he created a sub-kingdom of Aquitaine with his son, Pippin, as king. From that base Frankish forces mounted a series of campaigns that eventually established Frankish control over the Spanish March, the territory lying between the Pyrenees and the Ebro River.

In 787 and 788, Charlemagne forcibly annexed Bavaria, whose leaders had long resisted Frankish domination. That victory was followed by successful Frankish campaigns in 791, 795, and 796 that hastened the disintegration of the Avar empire. Charlemagne captured a huge store of treasure, claimed a block of territory south of the Danube, and opened a missionary field that led to the conversion of the Avars and their former Slavic subjects to Christianity.

Charlemagne's military successes resulted in an ever-lengthening frontier, which needed to be defended. His vast holdings covered all of the present-day countries of France, Switzerland, Belgium, and The Netherlands; half of Italy and Germany; and parts of Austria and Spain. Through a combination of military force and diplomacy, he established relatively stable relations with a variety of potentially dangerous enemies.

Charlemagne was mindful of the obligation of a Frankish ruler to maintain the unity of his realm. This burden was complicated by the ethnic, linguistic, and legal divisions between the populations under Frankish domination. For assistance in asserting his power to command, Charlemagne relied on his *palatium*—a shifting assemblage of family members, trusted lay and ecclesiastical companions, and assorted hangers-on—which constituted an itinerant court following the king as he carried out his military campaigns.

To exercise his authority locally, Charlemagne continued to rely on royal officials known as counts, who represented royal authority in territorial entities called counties. Their functions included administering justice, raising troops, collecting taxes, and keeping peace. Bishops also continued to play an important role in local government. He integrated the central and the local administration by regularizing and expanding the use of *missi dominici*. These royal agents were charged with making regular circuits through specifically defined territories to announce the king's will, to gather information on the performance of local officials, and to correct abuses.

The record of Charlemagne's reign indicates his awareness of new developments affecting economic and social conditions. Evidence suggests that he was concerned with improving agricultural production, establishing a monetary system better attuned to actual exchange operations, standardizing weights and measures, expanding trading ventures into areas around the North Sea and Baltic Sea, and protecting merchants from excessive tolls and robbery. Royal legislation sought to protect the weak against exploitation and injustice. The king helped to clarify the incipient lord-vassal system and utilized that form of social contract to promote order and stability.

Charlemagne's program for meeting his royal religious responsibilities was formulated in a series of synods made up of both clerics and laymen. The suggested reforms focused on strengthening the church's hierarchical structure, clarifying the powers and responsibilities of the hierarchy, elevating the quality of the clergy, protecting and expanding resources, standardizing liturgical practices, intensifying understanding of the basic tenets of the faith and improvement of morals, and rooting out paganism. As the reform movement progressed, its scope broadened to vest the ruler with authority to discipline clerics, to assert control over ecclesiastical property, to propagate the faith, and to define orthodox doctrine.

Charlemagne's reign was also noted for a variety of activities that together produced a cultural *renovatio* (or restoration), later called the Carolingian Renaissance. The prime goal of Charlemagne's royal cultural policy was the extension and improvement of Latin literacy, which required the expansion of the educational system and the production of books containing the essentials of Christian Latin culture. A royal library was created, containing works that permitted a deeper exploration of Latin learning and the Christian faith. A royal scriptorium—a writing room in monastic communities used by scribes copying manuscripts—was established. This played an important role in propagating the Carolingian minuscule, a new writing system that made copying and reading easier. Charlemagne's court circle composed poetry, historiography, and religious writings—works that exemplified advanced levels of intellectual activity and linguistic expertise.

The antecedent to Charlemagne being named emperor of the Romans occurred in 799, when Pope Leo III was physically attacked by a faction of Romans who believed that he was guilty of tyranny and serious personal misconduct for supporting Charlemagne. Leo fled to Charlemagne, who provided an escort that restored Leo III to the papal office. In late 800, Charlemagne went to Rome to determine what further action would be taken. After a series of deliberations with Frankish and Roman clerical and lay notables, it was arranged that, in lieu of being judged, the pope would publicly swear an oath purging himself of the charges against him. Two days after Leo's act of purgation, as Charlemagne attended mass on Christmas Day in the basilica of St. Peter, the pope placed a crown on his head, while the Romans assembled for worship proclaimed him "emperor of the Romans." In 813 Charlemagne assured the perpetuation of the imperial title by bestowing the imperial crown on his son, Louis the Pious. In January 814 Charlemagne fell ill with a fever and died a week later.

ASSESSMENT

Although he received only an elementary level of formal education, Charlemagne possessed considerable native intelligence, intellectual curiosity, a willingness to learn from others, and religious sensibility—all attributes which allowed him to comprehend the forces that were reshaping the world around him.

His renewal of the Roman Empire in the West provided the ideological foundation for a politically unified Europe. His rule served as a standard to which many generations of European rulers looked for guidance in defining and discharging their royal functions. His religious reforms solidified the organizational structures and the liturgical practices that eventually enfolded most of Europe into a single "church." His cultural renaissance provided the basic tools—schools, curricula, textbooks, libraries, and teaching techniques—upon which later cultural revivals would be based. The impetus he gave to the lord-vassal relationship and to the system of agriculture known as manorialism—in which peasants held land from a lord in exchange for dues and service—played a vital role in establishing the seignorial system. The seignorial system, in which lords exercised political and economic power over a given territory and its population, in turn had the potential for imposing political and social order and for stimulating economic growth. Although his economic and social initiatives were motivated chiefly by his moral convictions, these measures gave modest support to movements that eventually ended the economic depression and social instability that had gripped western Europe since the dissolution of the Roman Empire in the 4th and 5th centuries.

WILLIAM I

(b. c. 1028, Falaise, Normandy [France]—d. Sept. 9, 1087, Rouen)

One of the greatest soldiers and rulers of the Middle Ages, William I (also known as William the Conqueror) reigned as duke of Normandy from 1035 and king of England from 1066 until his death in 1087. He made himself the mightiest noble in France and then changed the course of England's history with his conquest of that country.

William was an illegitimate son of Robert I, duke of Normandy, and his concubine Herleva. When Robert died in 1035, he was succeeded by William, who was only seven. He was accepted as duke by the Norman magnates and by his overlord, King Henry I of France. William and his supporters had to overcome enormous obstacles, including William's illegitimacy and the fact that he had

William I. Photos.com/Jupiterimages

acceded as a child. His weakness led to a breakdown of authority throughout the duchy: private castles were erected, public power was usurped by lesser nobles, and warfare broke out.

By 1042, when William was 15 and began to play a personal part in the affairs of his duchy, the worst was over. But his attempts to recover rights lost during the anarchy led to a series of baronial rebellions from 1046 until 1055, mostly led by his kinsmen.

In 1049 William negotiated with Baldwin V of Flanders for the hand of his daughter, Matilda. The wedding took place before the end of 1053, possibly in 1052. Four sons were born to the couple—Robert (the future duke of Normandy), Richard (who died young), William Rufus (his father's successor in England), and Henry (Rufus's successor). Among the daughters was Adela, who became the mother of Stephen, king of England from 1135 to 1154.

Between 1054 and 1060, William was threatened by the combined menace of internal revolt and the new alliance against him between King Henry and Geoffrey Martel, count of Anjou. After suppressing the rebels, William decisively defeated the invading forces of Henry and Geoffrey at the Battle of Mortemer in 1054. After a second victory, at Varaville in 1057, the duke was in firm control of Normandy. His position was secured even further when both Henry and Geoffrey died in 1060 and were succeeded by weaker rulers. William then became the most powerful ruler in northern France.

After negotiating with his cousin Edward the Confessor, the king of England, William had been named heir to the English throne in 1051. When Edward died childless on January 5, 1066, his brother-in-law, Harold, earl of Wessex, was accepted as king by the English magnates. William decided to fight for his crown. He proceeded carefully, first taking steps to secure his duchy and to obtain international support for his venture. He also appealed to volunteers to join his army of invasion and won numerous recruits from outside Normandy.

On September 27, William and his army set sail for the southeastern coast of England. The following morning he landed, took the unresisting towns of Pevensey and Hastings, and began to prepare for battle. William's forces were in a narrow coastal strip, hemmed in by the forest of Andred. On October 13, Harold emerged from the forest, but the hour was too late to push on to Hastings, and he took up a defensive position instead. Early the next day, before Harold had prepared his exhausted troops for battle, William attacked. Although the English phalanx initially held firm, ultimately William's forces gained the upper hand. Harold was killed in the battle, and the English surrendered. On Christmas Day, 1066, William was crowned king in Westminster Abbey.

William, although newly king of England, was already an experienced ruler. In Normandy he had replaced disloyal nobles and ducal servants with his friends, limited private warfare, and recovered usurped ducal rights, defining the duties of his vassals. The Norman church flourished under his reign, as he adapted its structures to English traditions. Like many contemporary rulers, he wanted the church in England to be free of corruption but also subordinate to him. During his reign, church synods were held much more frequently, and he also presided over several episcopal councils. He also promoted monastic reform by importing Norman monks and abbots, thus quickening the pace of monastic life in England and bringing it into line with continental developments.

William left England early in 1067 but had to return in December to deal with rebellions. To secure his hold on

An English axman in combat with a Norman knight at the Battle of Hastings, detail from the Bayeux Tapestry; in the Musée de la Tapisserie, Bayeux, France. Giraudon/Art Resource, New York

the country, he introduced the Norman practice of building castles, including the Tower of London. The rebellions, which were crushed by 1071, destroyed the English higher aristocracy and replaced it with an aristocracy of Norman lords, who introduced patterns of landholding and military service that had been developed in Normandy. To secure England's frontiers, William invaded Scotland in 1072 and Wales in 1081, creating special defensive "marcher" counties along the Scottish and Welsh borders.

In 1086 William ordered a complex census of all the people and lands of England, which is summarized in the two volumes of the Domesday Book, one of the greatest administrative accomplishments of the Middle Ages.

Despite his duties as king, William remained preoccupied with the frontiers of Normandy. There was also an issue with William's oldest son and heir, Robert Curthose (later Robert II), who, given no appanage (grant of land from the royal domain) and seemingly kept short of money, left Normandy in 1077 and plotted with his father's enemies. While fighting with King Philip I of France to enforce his last outstanding territorial claim, William suffered an injury from which he never recovered.

Before his death, he settled the matter of his inheritance. Although William was tempted to make the loyal Rufus his sole heir, in the end he compromised: Normandy and Maine went to Robert, and England went to Rufus. Henry was given great treasure with which to purchase an appanage.

URBAN II

(b. *c.* 1035, Châtillon-sur-Marne, or Lagery, or Lagny, Champagne, France — d. July 29, 1099, Rome [Italy])

Pope Urban II served as head of the Roman Catholic Church from 1088 to 1099. He developed ecclesiastical reforms begun by Pope Gregory VII, launched the Crusade movement, and strengthened the papacy as a political entity.

Originally named Odo of Châtillon-sur-Marne, or Odo of Lagery, or of Lagny, he was born of noble parents in the Champagne region of France. After studies in Soissons and Reims, he took the position of archdeacon in the diocese of Reims, probably holding that position from 1055 to 1067. Subsequently he became a monk and then prior superior at Cluny, the most important centre of reform monasticism

Pope Urban II. © Photos.com/Jupiterimages

in Europe in the 11th century. In 1079 he went to Rome on a mission for his abbot, Hugh of Cluny. While in Rome he was made cardinal and bishop of Ostia (the seaport for Rome) by Gregory VII. In 1084 Gregory VII sent him as papal legate to Germany. During the crisis of Gregory VII's struggle with Henry IV, the Holy Roman Emperor, over some cancelled agreements, Odo remained loyal to the legitimate papacy. After Gregory VII's death in 1085, he also served his successor, Victor III, who died in September 1087. After a long delay, Odo was elected pope on March 12, 1088, and was thereafter called Urban II.

As pope, Urban II found active support for his policies and reforms among several groups: the nobility, whose mentality and interests he knew; the monks; the canons regular, for whom he became patron and legislator; and also, increasingly, the bishops. He attempted, with moderation and tolerance, to reconcile the church-state traditions of his age with ecclesiastical notions of reform.

From 1095 Urban was at the height of his success. Several important church councils took place during this time, the first in 1095 at Piacenza, Italy, at which reform legislation was enacted. The second occurred in 1095 at Clermont, where Urban preached the First Crusade. In 1098 at Bari, Italy, he worked for a reunion between Greek Christians and Romans. In 1099 at Rome, reform legislation was again passed. Urban's idea for a crusade and his attempt to reconcile the Latin and Greek churches sprang from his idea of the unity of all Christendom and from his experiences with the struggles against the Muslims in Spain and Sicily. While the First Crusade led to military success with the conquest of Jerusalem in 1099, the project for union failed. Urban's pontificate not only led to a further centralization of the Roman Catholic Church but also to the expansion of papal administration. It contributed to the development of the Roman Curia, the administrative body of the papacy, and to the gradual formation of the College of Cardinals. The term *Curia Romana* first appeared in a bull written by Urban in 1089.

Urban died in Rome in 1099. Despite many problems that were still unsolved, the victory of medieval reform papacy was secured. Urban was beatified in 1881 by Pope Leo XIII.

SALADIN

(b. 1137/38, Tikrīt, Mesopotamia [now in Iraq]—d. March 4, 1193, Damascus [now in Syria])

Saladin, one of the most famous of Muslim heroes, was the Muslim sultan of Egypt, Syria, Yemen, and Palestine and founder of the Ayyūbid dynasty. In wars against the Christian Crusaders, he captured Jerusalem on October 2, 1187, ending its nearly nine decades of occupation by the Franks.

Saladin (Ṣalāḥ al-Dīn Yūsuf ibn Ayyūb) was born into a prominent Kurdish family in 1137 or 1138. Growing up in Aleppo, Ba'lbek, and Damascus, Saladin was apparently an undistinguished youth, with a greater taste for religious studies than military training. His formal career began when he joined the staff of his uncle Asad al-Dīn Shīrkūh, an important military commander under the emir Nūr al-Dīn. In 1169, after Shīrkūh's death, Saladin was appointed both commander of the Syrian troops in Egypt and vizier of the Fāṭimid caliph there.

Saladin's position was further enhanced when, in 1171, he abolished the weak and unpopular Shī'ite Fāṭimid caliphate, proclaiming a return to Sunni Islam in Egypt. Although he remained for a time theoretically a vassal of Nūr al-Dīn, that relationship ended with the emir's death in 1174. From that year until 1186, Saladin zealously pursued a goal of uniting, under his own standard, all the Muslim territories of Syria, northern Mesopotamia, Palestine, and Egypt. This he accomplished by skillful diplomacy backed when necessary by the swift and resolute use of military force. Gradually his reputation grew as a generous and virtuous but firm ruler, devoid of pretense, licentiousness, and cruelty. In contrast to the bitter dissension and intense rivalry that had up to then hampered the Muslims in their resistance to the Crusaders, Saladin's singleness of purpose induced them to rearm both physically and spiritually.

Saladin's every act was inspired by an intense and unwavering devotion to the idea of jihad, or holy war. It was an essential part of his policy to encourage the growth and spread of Muslim religious institutions. He courted their scholars and preachers, founded colleges and mosques for their use, and commissioned them to write edifying works, especially on the jihad itself.

Saladin also succeeded in turning the military balance of power in his favour—more by uniting and disciplining a great number of unruly forces than by employing new or improved military techniques. On July 4, 1187, aided by his own military good sense and by a phenomenal lack of it on the part of his enemy, Saladin trapped and destroyed an exhausted and thirst-crazed army of Crusaders at Ḥaṭṭīn, near Tiberias in northern Palestine. The losses in the ranks of the Crusaders in this one battle were so great that the Muslims were quickly able to overrun nearly the entire kingdom of Jerusalem. Acre, Toron, Beirut, Sidon, Nazareth, Caesarea, Nāblus, Jaffa (Yafo), and Ascalon (Ashqelon) fell within three months. But Saladin's crowning achievement and the most disastrous blow to the whole Crusading movement came on October 2, 1187, when the city of Jerusalem, holy to both Muslims and Christians alike, surrendered to Saladin's army after 88 years in the hands of the Franks. Saladin planned to avenge the slaughter of Muslims in Jerusalem in 1099 by killing all Christians in the city, but he agreed to let them purchase their freedom provided that the Christian defenders left the Muslim inhabitants unmolested.

His victory deeply shocked the West and led to the call for the Third Crusade (1189–92), which matched him against Richard I (the Lionheart), whom he was able to fight to a draw. When King Richard left the Middle East in October 1192, the battle was over. Their stalemate resulted in a peace that gave the Crusaders only a small strip of land from Tyre to Yafo (Jaffa). Saladin withdrew to his capital at Damascus, where he died the next year.

CHINGGIS KHAN

(b. 1162, near Lake Baikal, Mongolia—d. Aug. 18, 1227)

One of the most famous conquerors in history is the Mongolian warrior-ruler Chinggis Khan. He was also known as Genghis Khan, although his original name was Temüjin. He consolidated tribes into a unified Mongolia and then extended his empire across Asia to the Adriatic Sea.

The chronology of Temüjin's early life is uncertain. He may have been born in 1155, in 1162 (the date favoured today in Mongolia), or in 1167. According to legend, his birth was auspicious because he came into the world holding a clot of blood in his hand. He is also said to have been of divine origin, his first ancestor having been a gray wolf, "born with a destiny from heaven on high." Yet his early years were anything but promising. When he was nine, his father, Yesügei, a member of the royal Borjigin clan of the

Mongols, was poisoned by a band of Tatars, another nomadic people, in continuance of an old feud. With Yesügei dead, the remainder of the clan—led by the rival Taychiut family—abandoned Yesügei's widow, Höelün, and her children, seizing the opportunity to usurp power. Temüjin was later captured by the Taychiut, who, rather than killing him, kept him around their camps, wearing a wooden collar. One night, when they were feasting, Temüjin knocked down the sentry with a blow from his wooden collar and fled. Although the Taychiut searched all night for him, he was able to escape.

Temüjin rose to defeat several rival clans, including the Merkit, Jürkin, Kereit, and the formidable Tartars, ruthlessly crushing them and leaving him master of the steppes. In 1206 a great assembly was held by the River Onon, and Temüjin was proclaimed Chinggis Khan. The title probably meant Universal Ruler. He distributed thousands of families to the custody of his own relatives and companions, replacing the existing pattern of tribes and clans by something closer to a feudal structure.

The year 1206 was a turning point in the history of the Mongols and in world history, when the Mongols were first ready to move out beyond the steppe. Mongolia itself took on a new shape. The petty tribal quarrels and raids were a thing of the past. A unified Mongol nation came into existence as the personal creation of Chinggis Khan and has survived to the present day, despite many challenges. Chinggis Khan was ready to start on his world conquest, and the new nation was organized, above all, for war. His troops were divided up on the decimal system, were rigidly disciplined, and were well equipped and supplied. The generals were his own sons or men he had selected and were absolutely loyal to him.

The great conquests of the Mongols, which would transform them into a world power, were still to come. For now, China was the main goal. Chinggis Khan first secured his western flank by a tough campaign against the Tangut kingdom of Xixia, a northwestern border state of China. His forces then fell upon the Jin empire of northern China in 1211. In 1214 he allowed himself to be bought off, temporarily, with a huge amount of treasure, but in 1215 operations were resumed, and Beijing was taken. Subsequently, the more systematic defeat of northern China was in the hands of his general Muqali. Chinggis Khan himself carried out the conquest of the Muslim empire of Khwārezm, in the region of the Amu Darya (Oxus) and Syr Darya (Jaxartes). This war was provoked by the governor of the city of Otrar, who massacred a caravan of Muslim merchants who were under Chinggis Khan's protection. War with Khwārezm would doubtless have come sooner or later, but now it could not be avoided. During this war the Mongols earned their reputation for savagery and terror. City after city was stormed, the inhabitants massacred or forced to serve as advance troops for the Mongols against their own people. Fields, gardens, and irrigation works were destroyed as Chinggis Khan pursued his implacable vengeance against the royal house of Khwārezm. He finally withdrew in 1223 and did not lead his armies into war again until the final campaign against Xixia in 1226 and 1227.

Chinggis Khan's military genius could adapt itself to rapidly changing circumstances. Initially his troops were exclusively cavalry, riding the hardy, grass-fed Mongol pony that needed no fodder. With such an army, other nomads could be defeated, but cities could not be taken. But before long the Mongols were able to undertake the siege of large cities, using mangonels, catapults, ladders, burning oil, and even diverting rivers. It was only gradually, through contact with men from the more settled states, that Chinggis Khan came to realize that there were more sophisticated ways of enjoying power than simply raiding, destroying, and plundering. It was a minister of the khan of the Naiman—the last important Mongol tribe to resist Chinggis Khan—who taught him the uses of literacy and helped reduce the Mongol language to writing. It was only after the war against Khwārezm, probably in late 1222, that Chinggis Khan reportedly learned from Muslim advisers the "meaning and importance of towns." And it was another adviser, formerly in the service of the Jin emperor, who explained to him the uses of peasants and craftsmen as producers of taxable goods. He had intended to turn the cultivated fields of northern China into grazing land for his horses.

Chinggis Khan chose his successor, his son Ögödei, with great care, and passed an army and a state in full vigour on to him. At the time of his death in 1227, Chinggis Khan had conquered the landmass extending from Beijing to the Caspian Sea, and his generals had raided Persia and Russia. His successors would extend their power over the whole of China, Persia, and most of Russia.

HONGWU

(b. Oct. 21, 1328, Haozhou [now Fengyang, Anhui Province], China—d. June 24, 1398, Nanjing)

Hongwu is the reign name of the Chinese emperor who reigned from 1368 to 1398 and who founded the Ming dynasty, which ruled China for nearly 300 years. During his reign, the Hongwu emperor instituted military, administrative, and educational reforms that centred power in the emperor.

The future Hongwu emperor was born as Zhu Chongba, a poor peasant in 1328. Orphaned at 16, he became a monk to avoid starvation—a common practice for the sons of poor peasants. In 1352 he joined a rebel force and changed his name to Zhu Yuanzhang, rising from the ranks and eventually taking over leadership of the group. Zhu Yuanzhang attacked and captured towns and cities in eastern China and, on reaching the Yangtze River (Chang Jiang) delta, encountered educated men of the gentry class. Some decided to join his movement, and Zhu had the foresight to seek their guidance. From them he learned the rudiments of the Chinese language and studied Chinese history and the Confucian classics. More significant, he learned the principles of government and built up an effective administration in local areas alongside the military structure. Moreover, he was persuaded by his scholars to present himself as a national leader against the Mongols rather than as a popular rebel.

After defeating rival national leaders, Zhu proclaimed himself emperor of the Ming dynasty in 1368, establishing his capital at Nanjing. Hongwu ("Vastly Martial") was adopted as his reign title, and he is usually referred to as the Hongwu emperor, though Taizu (his temple name) is more strictly correct. He drove the last Yuan (Mongol) emperor from China that year and reunified the country by 1382.

The Hongwu emperor was cruel, suspicious, and irrational, especially as he grew older. Instead of eliminating Mongol influence, he made his court resemble the Mongol court and established himself as the autocratic ruler for the rest of the dynasty. He eliminated the posts of prime minister and central chancellor and had the next level of administration report directly to him. He restricted certain groups that were prone to intrigue in the past. He prohibited eunuchs from participating in government, forbade the empress to meddle with court politics, and appointed civilian officials to control military affairs. Of lowly peasant origins, he always was aware of the popular misery that administrative corruption could engender, and he savagely punished malpractices.

The Hongwu emperor felt that, after the Mongol expulsion, the scholars were the most dangerous group in country. Nevertheless, his interest in restoring traditional Chinese values involved rehabilitating the Confucian scholar class, and from experience he knew that effective government depended upon the scholars. He therefore encouraged education and purposely trained scholars for the bureaucracy. At the same time he used methods to deprive them of power and position and introduced the use of heavy bamboo as a punishment at court, often beating scholar-officials to death for the slightest offense. He felt that scholars should be mere servants of the state, working on behalf of the emperor. Because of the emperor's attitude, a great many members of the gentry were discouraged from embarking on official careers.

In foreign relations the Hongwu emperor extended the Ming Empire's prestige to outlying regions. Southern Manchuria was brought into the empire. Outlying states, such as Korea, the Liuqiu Islands, Annam, and other states, sent tribute missions to acknowledge the supreme rule of the Ming emperor. Not satisfied with the expulsion of the Mongols, he sent two military expeditions into Mongolia, reaching the Mongol capital of Karakorum itself. Ming forces even penetrated Central Asia, taking Hami (in the Gobi) and accepting the surrender of several states in the Chinese Turkistan region. When Ming emissaries traversed the mountains to Samarkand, however, they were met with a different reception. Timur (one of history's greatest conquerors) was building a new Mongol empire in that region, and the Chinese envoys were imprisoned. Eventually, they were released, and Timur and the Ming exchanged several embassies, which the Chinese regarded as tributary missions. The Hongwu emperor was less successful with Japan, whose buccaneers ravaged the Chinese coast. Three missions went to Japan, armed with inducements and threats, but all were unable to curb piracy—because the Japanese authorities were themselves helpless.

After the Hongwu emperor's death in June 1398, he was succeeded by his grandson, Yunwen. The Hongwu emperor's posthumous name is Gaodi.

JOAN OF ARC

(b. *c.* 1412, Domrémy, Bar, France—d. May 30, 1431, Rouen; canonized May 16, 1920; feast day May 30; French national holiday, second Sunday in May)

French national heroine Joan of Arc is remembered for leading the French army in a momentous victory at Orléans, which repulsed an English attempt to conquer France during the Hundred Years' War.

Joan was a peasant girl who from an early age believed she heard the voices of St. Michael, St. Catherine, and St. Margaret. When Joan was about 16, the voices began urging her to aid France's Dauphin (crown prince) and to save France from English conquest. The crown of France at the time was in dispute between the dauphin Charles (later Charles VII) and the Lancastrian English king Henry VI. Henry's armies were in alliance with those of Philip the Good, duke of Burgundy, and were occupying much of the northern part of the kingdom.

Dressed in men's clothing, Joan was granted an audience with the Dauphin. Upon meeting with his court, she immediately greeted the king, who was hidden among his couriers. She convinced him, his advisers, and the church authorities to support her. They mustered troops and on April 27 set out for Orléans, which had been besieged since October 12, 1428, and was almost totally surrounded by a ring of English strongholds. On the morning of May 6, Joan and her troops crossed to the south bank of the river and advanced toward a fort. The English immediately evacuated in order to defend a stronger position nearby, but Joan attacked the fort and took it by storm. Very early on May 7 the French advanced against the fort of Les Tourelles and attacked until the English capitulated, handing Joan and the troops an impressive victory.

The French and English armies again came face to face at Patay on June 18, 1429. Joan promised success to the French, and indeed the English army was defeated along with its reputation for invincibility. On July 16 Joan and the royal army reached Reims, which opened its gates. The next day, in Joan's presence, the Dauphin was crowned king as Charles VII.

In September 1429, Joan launched an unsuccessful attack on Paris. Wounded in the fighting, she continued to encourage the soldiers until they finally had to abandon the attack. The next day Joan sought to renew the assault, but they were ordered by Charles's council to retreat.

On May 23, 1430, Joan was captured by the Burgundians and later sold to the English. Joan was brought to trial before a church court. The theologists at the University of Paris, who acted as arbiter in matters concerning the faith—and in collaboration with the English—insisted that she be tried as a heretic and for witchcraft.

The trial began in February 1431 with the reading of 70 charges that had been drawn up against Joan. These were based mainly on the contention that her whole attitude and behaviour showed blasphemous presumption, including her claims to hear voices. Perhaps the most serious charge was of preferring what she believed to be the direct commands of God to those of the church. On May 23 Joan was informed that she was condemned to be burned to death unless she took back her claims. She hesitantly signed a statement indicating that she recanted, but many historians think she did not understand what was meant. After signing the statement, Joan's punishment was changed from death to life imprisonment. A few days later, she again asserted that she had been divinely inspired, which was taken to signify relapse. As a result, on May 29, the church court decreed that Joan was to be handed over to the civil authorities. They did so the next morning, and she was burned to death at the stake.

More than 20 years later, on the order of Pope Calixtus III following a petition from the d'Arc family, proceedings were instituted in 1455–56 that revoked and annulled the sentence of 1431. Joan was canonized by Pope Benedict XV on May 16, 1920.

MARTIN LUTHER

(b. Nov. 10, 1483, Eisleben, Saxony [Germany] — d. Feb. 18, 1546, Eisleben)

M artin Luther was the preacher, biblical scholar, and linguist whose Ninety-five Theses — an attack on various Roman Catholic ecclesiastical abuses — precipitated the Protestant Reformation.

Luther was the son of a prosperous copper miner. In 1502 he graduated from the University of Erfurt. He took his M.A. in 1505, afterwards entering the monastery of the eremitical order of St. Augustine. He was ordained priest in April 1507, and in 1508 he went to the University of Wittenberg, where he took his Doctorate of Theology in 1512 and received the chair of biblical theology.

After a long period of religious doubts and guilt at what he saw as his failure to obey God's law, Luther found relief through a sudden conviction that justification came through faith; that salvation is a divine gift of grace; that

Christ represents God's forgiving mercy; and that the soul, free from the burden of guilt, may serve God with a joyful obedience.

Luther was moved to public protest in 1517 by Johann Tetzel, a Dominican friar, who claimed that the faithful could purchase a letter of indulgence for the forgiveness of their sins. The ostensible purpose of this practice was to fund rebuilding of St. Peter's basilica in Rome.

In protest, Luther drew up the Ninety-five Theses and, according to legend, fastened them on the door of the Castle Church in Wittenberg, on October 31, 1517. These were tentative opinions, to some of which Luther himself was not committed. The closing section attacked those who refused to recognize that to be a Christian involved embracing the cross and entering heaven through tribulation. Luther sent copies of the theses to the archbishop of Mainz and to his bishop, but further copies were circulated. The archbishop forwarded the documents to Rome in December 1517, with the request that Luther be inhibited. The pope merely instructed the vicar general of the Augustinians to deal with Luther through the usual channels. In October the Cardinal Cajetan at Augsburg ordered him to recant.

In June 1520 the pope issued the papal bull *Exsurge Domine* ("Lord, Cast Out") against 41 articles of Luther's teaching, followed by the burning of Luther's writings in Rome. Luther replied in a series of treatises issued in 1520, the second of which, *De captivitate Babylonica ecclesiae praeludium* ("A Prelude Concerning the Babylonian Captivity of the Church"), reduced the seven sacraments of the church to three (baptism, the Lord's Supper, and penance). It also denied mass and attacked transubstantiation, made vehement charges against papal authority, and asserted the supremacy of Holy scripture and the rights of individual conscience. In January 1521 the pope issued the bull of formal excommunication (*Decet Romanum Pontificem*), although it was several months before the condemnation was received throughout Germany.

On April 17, 1521, Luther appeared before civic and religious authorities at the Diet of Worms. When required to recant his assertions, he stated that he would not go against his conscience unless convinced of his error either by Scripture or by evident reason. The emperor cut the proceedings short and Luther was allowed to depart. Luther's enemies, nonetheless, salvaged something when a rump Diet passed the Edict of Worms. It declared Luther to be an outlaw whose writings were denounced. The edict fettered his movements for the rest of his days. Luther departed to Wartburg, where he remained until March 1522. There he translated the New Testament into German. This volume was published in September 1522 and, like his later translation of the Hebrew Bible (1534), had deep and lasting influence on the language, life, and religion of the German people.

In 1523 he issued a treatise *Von weltlicher Obrigkeit* ("Of Earthly Government"), in which he distinguished between the two realms of spiritual and of temporal government, and stressed the sinfulness of rebellion against lawful authority. In May 1525, after the Peasants' War had broken out, Luther published the *Ermahnung zum Frieden* ("Exhortation for Freedom"), sympathizing with justified grievances, but repudiating the notion of a so-called Christian rebellion and claiming that the worldly kingdom cannot exist without inequality of persons.

In June 1525 Luther married Katherina von Bora, a former nun who had fled her convent. His home and family meant a great deal to him and was an emblem for him of Christian vocation. He included domestic life among the three hierarchies of Christian existence in this world, the other two being political and church life.

HENRY VIII

(b. June 28, 1491, Greenwich, near London, Eng.—d. Jan. 28, 1547, London)

As king of England from 1509 to 1547, Henry VIII presided over the beginnings of the English Renaissance and the English Reformation. He is remembered for taking six wives in his quest for a male heir.

Henry was the second son of Henry VII, first of the Tudor line, and Elizabeth, daughter of Edward IV, first king of the short-lived line of York. When his elder brother, Arthur, died in 1502, Henry became the heir to the throne. Soon after his accession in 1509, Henry married his brother's widow, Catherine of Aragon.

Henry was determined to engage in military adventure. Europe was consumed by rivalries between the French and Spanish kingdoms, mostly over Italian claims. Against the advice of his older councillors, in 1512 Henry joined his father-in-law, Ferdinand II of Aragon, against France and ostensibly in support of a threatened pope, to whom the devout king for a long time paid almost slavish respect. Henry himself displayed no military talent, but a real victory was won by the earl of Surrey at Flodden (1513) against a Scottish invasion. Despite the pointlessness of the fighting, the appearance of success was popular.

Henry's first chief minister, Thomas Cardinal Wolsey, exercised nearly complete control over policy in 1515–27. By 1515 Wolsey was archbishop of York, lord chancellor of England, and a cardinal of the church. More important, he was the king's good friend, to whom was gladly left the active conduct of affairs.

In 1527 Henry pursued a divorce from Catherine, who had not provided a male heir to the throne—after several stillbirths and early deaths, only their daughter Mary (born in 1516) survived. He wished to marry Anne Boleyn, a lady of the court, but Pope Clement VII denied him the necessary annulment.

In 1532 Henry's new minister, Thomas Cromwell, initiated a revolution when he decided that the English church should separate from Rome. This allowed Henry to marry Anne in January 1533. In May a new archbishop, Thomas Cranmer, presided over the formality of a trial that annulled Henry's first marriage, and in September, the princess Elizabeth was born. The pope retaliated with a sentence of excommunication.

Henry was declared the Supreme Head of the Church of England in 1534 by the Act of Supremacy. The monasteries throughout England were dissolved, and their vast lands and goods were turned over to the king, who in turn granted those estates to noblemen who would support his policies. Although Henry made changes to the government of the church, he refused to allow any changes to be made in its doctrines. Before his divorce he had opposed the teachings of Martin Luther in *Assertio septem sacramentorum adversus Martinum Lutherum* (1521), which had prompted the pope to give Henry the title Defender of the Faith. After the separation from Rome, Henry persecuted with equal severity the Catholics who adhered to the government of Rome and the Protestants who rejected its doctrines.

Cromwell's decade, the 1530s, was the only period of the reign during which a coherent body of policies was purposefully carried through. Cromwell's work greatly enlarged Henry's power, especially by transferring to the crown the wealth of the monasteries and from new clerical taxes. The union of England and Wales was completed in 1536, and Ireland was made a kingdom in 1541 with Henry as king of Ireland. Old friends such as Sir Thomas

More, refusing to accept the new order, were killed, and the king's earlier reputation as a champion of light and learning was permanently buried under his enduring fame as a man of blood.

The king now embarked on the series of matrimonial adventures that made him appear both a monster and a laughingstock. He soon tired of Anne, who failed to produce a male heir. In 1536 she was executed, with other members of the court, for alleged treasonable adultery. Henry immediately married Jane Seymour, who bore him his son Edward but died in childbirth (1537). The next three years were filled with attempts to replace her, and the bride chosen was Anne, sister of William, the duke of Cleves, a pawn in Cromwell's policy for a northern European alliance against dangers from France and the Emperor. But Henry hated her at first sight and at once demanded his freedom, an end achieved by a quick divorce.

The Cleves fiasco destroyed Cromwell, enabling his many enemies to turn the king against him. In July 1540 his head fell on the scaffold. Henry had by now become truly dangerous; always secretive and suspicious, now he was beginning to show paranoiac tendencies. Convinced that he controlled everyone, he was in fact readily manipulated by those who knew how to feed his suspicions and pander to his self-righteousness. His temperamental deficiencies were aggravated by what he regarded as his undeserved misfortunes and by ill health. Henry grew enormously fat. His mind did not weaken, but he grew restless, peevish, and totally unpredictable. Often melancholy and depressed, he was usually out of sorts and always out of patience. In 1540 he married the 20-year-old Catherine Howard, whose folly in continuing her promiscuity, even as queen, led to her execution in 1542. The next year, he married once more, to the calm and obedient Catherine Parr.

In 1542 hostilities ensued between the Holy Roman Emperor and the king of France. Henry joined the emperor; the Scots promptly joined the French. Henry personally managed both the war and the subsequent negotiations, and he displayed amazing energy, despite illness. But energy is not the same thing as competence, and the war proved ruinous. Yet, even after the emperor made peace with France (1544), Henry would not let go until two years later. As the year 1546 drew to a close, it was apparent to all observers that the king had not long to live, and he died early the next year.

ELIZABETH I

(b. Sept. 7, 1533, Greenwich, near London, Eng.—d. March 24, 1603, Richmond, Surrey)

Elizabeth I (also called the Virgin Queen or Good Queen Bess) reigned as queen of England during a period, often called the Elizabethan Age, when England asserted itself vigorously as a major European power in politics, commerce, and the arts.

Elizabeth was the daughter of Henry VIII and his second wife, Anne Boleyn. Before Elizabeth reached her third birthday, her father had her mother beheaded on charges of adultery and treason. When in 1537 Henry's third wife, Jane Seymour, gave birth to a son, Edward, Elizabeth receded into relative obscurity, but she was not neglected. She spent much of the time with her half brother Edward. She also profited, after the age of 10, from the loving attention of her stepmother, Catherine Parr—the king's sixth and last wife. Under a series of distinguished tutors, Elizabeth received the rigorous education normally reserved for male heirs.

With the death of Henry VIII in 1547, Elizabeth's frail 10-year-old brother, Edward, came to the throne. Upon his death in 1553, Elizabeth's life was in peril. Edward, who had been raised Protestant in his father's new church, was succeeded by Elizabeth's older half sister Mary, a religious zealot set on returning England, by force if necessary, to the Roman Catholic faith. This attempt, along with her unpopular marriage to the ardently Catholic king Philip II of Spain, aroused bitter Protestant opposition in England. In a charged atmosphere of treasonous rebellion and inquisitorial repression, Mary suspected Elizabeth of plotting with the Protestants to gain the throne and had her imprisoned for two months in the Tower of London. Elizabeth narrowly escaped death.

When Mary died on November 17, 1558, Elizabeth came to the throne amid bells, bonfires, patriotic demonstrations, and other signs of public jubilation. The queen began at once to form her government and issue proclamations. She reduced the size of the Privy Council, in part to purge some of its Catholic members and to make it more efficient as an advisory body. Elizabeth carefully balanced the need for substantial administrative and judicial continuity with the desire for change, and she assembled a core of experienced and trustworthy advisers, including William Cecil, Nicholas Bacon, Francis Walsingham, and Nicholas Throckmorton. Chief among these was Cecil (afterward Lord Burghley), whom Elizabeth appointed her principal secretary of state on the morning of her accession. He was to serve her (first in this capacity and after 1571 as lord treasurer) with remarkable sagacity and skill for 40 years.

Elizabeth restored England to Protestantism. The Act of Supremacy, passed by Parliament and approved in 1559, revived the antipapal statutes of Henry VIII and declared the queen supreme governor of the church. The Act of Uniformity established a slightly revised version of the second Edwardian prayer book as the official order of worship. Although she restored the Protestant service, she retained many features of Catholicism, including bishops and archbishops. She hoped this compromise would produce unity in the state, but the Catholics, who formed a majority of her subjects, were not reconciled; neither were hardline Protestants. Elizabeth's government moved cautiously but steadily to transfer these structural and liturgical reforms from the statute books to the local parishes throughout the kingdom.

From time to time, some Catholics plotted with Spain or France to put Elizabeth's cousin, Mary, Queen of Scots, on the throne. France and Spain were rivals, and Elizabeth was usually able to play one against the other. She even used courtship as part of her diplomatic game. She refused to marry Philip II of Spain but held out hopes to more than one of his royal relatives when France appeared to be a threat to England. Later, when Philip turned against England, Elizabeth encouraged French princes to pursue her. To cut Scotland's ties with France, she gave secret help to the Scottish Presbyterians. She also aided the Protestant Netherlands when they revolted against Spain.

The alarming increase in religious tension, political intrigue, and violence was not only an internal, English concern. In 1570 Pope Pius V excommunicated Elizabeth and absolved her subjects from any oath of allegiance that they might have taken to her. Elizabeth was under great pressure to become more involved in the continental struggle between Roman Catholics and Protestants, in particular to aid the rebels fighting the Spanish armies in the Netherlands. But she was very reluctant to become involved, in part because she detested rebellion—even rebellion undertaken in the name of Protestantism—and in part because she detested expenditures. Eventually, after doubts that drove her councillors to despair, she agreed first to provide some limited funds and then, in 1585, to send a small expeditionary force to the Netherlands.

In 1586, Mary, Queen of Scots—who had been driven from her own kingdom in 1568 and had taken refuge in England—was implicated in a plot against Elizabeth's life. She was tried and sentenced to death, with Parliament requesting that the sentence be carried out without delay. For three months the queen hesitated and then, with every sign of extreme reluctance, signed the death warrant. When the news was brought to her that on February 8, 1587, Mary had been beheaded, Elizabeth responded with an impressive show of grief and rage. She had not, she wrote to Mary's son, James VI of Scotland, ever intended that the execution actually take place.

For years Elizabeth had cannily played a complex diplomatic game with the rival interests of France and Spain. But by the mid-1580s, it became increasingly clear that England could not avoid a direct military confrontation with Spain. Word reached London that the Spanish king, Philip II, had begun to assemble an enormous fleet that would sail to the Netherlands, join forces with a waiting Spanish army led by the duke of Parma, and then proceed to an invasion and conquest of Protestant England. Always reluctant to spend money, the queen had nonetheless authorized sufficient funds during her reign to maintain a fleet of maneuverable, well-armed fighting ships, to which could be added other vessels from the merchant fleet. In July 1588 when the Invincible Armada reached English waters, the queen's ships, in one of the most famous naval encounters of history, defeated the enemy fleet. Then, while attempting to return to Spain, the fleet was all but destroyed by terrible storms. Having reportedly indicated James VI of Scotland. as her successor, Elizabeth died quietly in 1603.

TOKUGAWA IEYASU

(b. Jan. 31, 1543, Okazaki, Japan—d. June 1, 1616, Sumpu)

Tokugawa Ieyasu was the founder of the last shogunate in Japan—the Tokugawa shogunate, which lasted from 1603 to 1867.

Ieyasu was born as Matsudaira Takechiyo into the family of a local warrior situated several miles east of modern Nagoya, one of many such families struggling to survive in a brutal age of endemic civil strife. In 1547 military adversity compelled his father to send him away as a hostage to the Imagawa family, powerful neighbours headquartered at Sumpu (now the city of Shizuoka) to the east. In the late 1550s he took a wife, fathered the first of several sons, and began to acquire military experience by leading forces on behalf of Imagawa Yoshimoto, the clan leader.

In 1560 Imagawa Yoshimoto was slain during a battle with Oda Nobunaga, who was rapidly gaining power. Within months young Ieyasu took steps to ally himself with Nobunaga, at the same time pacifying the new and inept leader of the Imagawa house long enough to recall his wife and son from Sumpu. During the later 1560s the Imagawa domain disintegrated, and Ieyasu expanded to the east as opportunity permitted. Relying heavily on his alliance with the now-mighty Nobunaga, Ieyasu survived the challenges of endemic war and slowly extended his territory until, by the early 1580s, he had become an important daimyo (feudal baron), in control of the fertile and populous area stretching from Okazaki eastward to the mountain barrier at Hakone.

In 1582 Nobunaga was wounded by a rebellious subordinate and committed suicide. Toyotomi Hideyoshi, his most brilliant general, quickly avenged the death and

moved to assume Nobunaga's preeminent political position. Ieyasu, then in the prime of life, emerged as his
principal rival. After a few bloody but indecisive skir-
mishes, however, the cautious Ieyasu offered a vow of
fealty, and Hideyoshi left Ieyasu's domain intact. During
the rest of the 1580s, while Hideyoshi busily extended his
control over the daimyo of southwestern Japan, Ieyasu
strengthened himself as best he could. He continued to
enlarge his vassal force, increase his domain's productivity,
and improve the reliability of his administration.

During the 1590s Ieyasu avoided involvement in
Hideyoshi's two disastrous military expeditions to Korea.
Instead, he grasped the opportunity to secure his domain
and make it as productive as possible. He stationed his
most powerful vassals on the perimeter of his territory and
along main access routes, keeping the least powerful—and
least dangerous to himself—nearer Edo. He then placed
large tracts of land near the town under direct administration by appointed officials. This assured his castle
inhabitants easy access to the largest possible supply of
foodstuffs, and made detailed land and property surveys
in order to regularize taxation. He also confiscated the
weapons of all villagers, thereby reducing the likelihood of
peasant rebellion, and moved vigorously to attract skilled
artisans and businessmen to his new castle town. He
undertook engineering projects to enlarge his castle, facilitate urban growth, and assure a water supply for the town
populace. By the end of the decade, Ieyasu had the largest,
most reliable army and the most productive and best organized domain in all Japan.

Hideyoshi's death in 1598 precipitated another power
struggle among the daimyo, and Ieyasu, as the most powerful and most respected of Hideyoshi's former vassal
advisers, became the head of one faction in that struggle.
A battle ensued in the autumn of 1600 at Sekigahara,

some 50 miles (80 km) northeast of Kyōto, and Ieyasu was victorious.

This triumph left Ieyasu the undisputed master of Japan, and he moved swiftly to make his mastery permanent. He confiscated his enemies' lands and gave them new domains away from Japan's heartland, much of which became Tokugawa property. He placed a number of his allies in strategic locations near surviving enemies, and secured for himself and his most faithful vassals direct control of much of central Japan.

In 1603 the powerless but prestigious imperial court appointed him shogun (generalissimo), thereby acknowledging that this most powerful daimyo in Japan was the man officially authorized to keep the peace in the emperor's name. Two years later Ieyasu formally retired and had the shogunal title assigned to his son Hidetada, intending thereby to assure that the title was recognized as a hereditary Tokugawa prerogative.

Ieyasu's daimyo transfers and political reforms of the years after Sekigahara had greatly strengthened his position, but he remained wary of the daimyo. From 1604 until 1614 he had Hidetada keep them at work building and enlarging the castle at Edo, which became the largest in the world at the time. Thousands of ships and tens of thousands of men were employed for years on end hauling huge stones and great logs from distant points to Edo.

By the time of his death, Ieyasu had brought enduring preeminence to his own family and a lasting peace to Japan.

OLIVER CROMWELL

(b. April 25, 1599, Huntingdon, Huntingdonshire, Eng.—d. Sept. 3, 1658, London)

English soldier and statesman Oliver Cromwell led parliamentary forces in the English Civil Wars and served

Oliver Cromwell, *painting by Robert Walker, in the National Portrait Gallery, London.* Courtesy of the National Portrait Gallery, London

as lord protector of England, Scotland, and Ireland from 1653 to 1658 during the Commonwealth.

Cromwell's father had been a member of one of Queen Elizabeth's parliaments. Oliver went to the local grammar school and then for a year attended Sidney Sussex College, Cambridge. In August 1620 he married Elizabeth Bourchier, and the couple had five sons and four daughters.

Cromwell was elected to Parliament in 1628, but King Charles I dissolved that Parliament in 1629 and did not call another for 11 years. By then, Cromwell had already become known as a fiery Puritan, launching an attack on Charles I's bishops. Cromwell, in fact, distrusted the whole hierarchy of the Church of England.

In 1640 Cromwell was elected to the Short and the Long Parliament. Differences between Charles and Parliament, however, eventually erupted into the English Civil Wars, in which Cromwell became a leading military figure on the Parliamentary side. During 1643 he acquired a reputation both as a military organizer and a fighting man. He made it a point to find loyal and well-behaved men regardless of their religious beliefs or social status. Although he would not allow Roman Catholics in his army, he accepted devout God-fearing believers from all the Protestant churches. Appointed a colonel in February, he began to recruit a first-class cavalry regiment. While he demanded good treatment and regular payment for his troopers, he exercised strict discipline. If they swore, they were fined; if drunk, put in the stocks; and if they deserted, they were whipped.

The quality of Cromwell's generalship was first proved at Marston Moor, near York, in July 1644. Prince Rupert drove the right wing of the Parliamentarians before him, but Cromwell's forces on the left restored the balance and won the battle. After the battle, Prince Rupert gave the name "Ironsides" to Cromwell's troops. As the civil war dragged on, Cromwell became more and more prominent. He even led a movement for remaking the parliamentary army as a whole on the model of his own Ironsides. He again won an important and decisive victory over the king's forces at Naseby in June 1645. King Charles, left almost defenseless, gave himself up early in the following year to the Scots. Because Charles was a Scot, he thought he could come to some agreement with them. The Scots, however, turned Charles over to the English.

England was now ruled by the army, its great leader, and the part of the Parliament of 1640 that was loyal to the Puritan ideals. This remnant, the "sitting" members of Parliament, was jokingly called the "Rump." Both the Rump and the army came to feel that Charles was so untrustworthy and autocratic that he must be eliminated. Cromwell was finally won over to this belief, and the king was tried and beheaded in 1649. The Rump thereupon proclaimed the whole of the British Isles a republic under the name of the Commonwealth. The Scots, however, now wanted Stuart rule and crowned Charles II, the young son of Charles I. The Irish, who were largely Roman Catholic, also resisted Parliament's authority.

Cromwell served as the first chairman of the Council of State, Parliament's executive body. During the first three years following Charles I's execution, however, he was chiefly absorbed in campaigns against the Royalists in Ireland and Scotland. He also had to suppress a mutiny—inspired by a group known as Levellers, an extremist Puritan party said to be aiming at a "levelling" between rich and poor—in the Commonwealth army. As commander in chief and lord lieutenant, he waged a ruthless campaign against the Irish. In June 1650 Cromwell led an army into Scotland, where Charles II had been acknowledged its new king. The campaign proved difficult, but he defeated the Scots with an army inferior in numbers at Dunbar on September 3, 1650. A year later, when Charles II and the Scots advanced into England, Cromwell destroyed that army at Worcester, the battle that ended the civil wars.

Cromwell became lord protector, ruling the three nations of England, Scotland, and Ireland with the advice and help of a council of state and a Parliament. Before Cromwell summoned his first Protectorate Parliament on Sept. 3, 1654, he and his Council of State passed more than 80 ordinances embodying a constructive domestic policy. His aim was to reform the law, to set up a Puritan Church, to permit toleration outside it, to promote education, and to decentralize administration. In spite of resistance from some members of his council, Cromwell readmitted Jews into the country. He concerned himself with education, founded a college at Durham, and saw to it that grammar schools flourished as they had never done before. In foreign affairs, Cromwell raised his country's status once more to that of a leading European power and concluded the Anglo-Dutch War.

When Cromwell's first Parliament met, he had justified the establishment of the Protectorate as providing for "healing and settling" the nation after the civil wars. A radical in some directions, Cromwell now adopted a conservative attitude because he feared that the overthrow of the monarchy might lead to political collapse. Vociferous republicans, who became leaders of this newly elected Parliament, were unwilling to concentrate on legislation, questioning instead the whole basis of Cromwell's government. He required all members of Parliament, if they wished to keep their seats, to sign an engagement to be faithful to a protector and Parliament and to promise not to alter its basic character. Except for 100 convinced republicans, the members agreed to do so.

Cromwell dissolved Parliament in 1655 and faced a Royalist insurrection. The uprising, however, fizzled out. In the spring of 1657 Parliament voted to invite Cromwell to become king, but he refused. Ever since the campaign in Ireland, Cromwell's health had been poor, and on September 3, 1658, he died.

LOUIS XIV

(b. Sept. 5, 1638, Saint-Germain-en-Laye, France—d. Sept. 1, 1715, Versailles)

Louis XIV (also known as Louis the Great or the Sun King) was king of France from 1643 to 1715 during one of its most brilliant periods. He remains the symbol of absolute monarchy of the classical age.

Louis was the son of Louis XIII and his Spanish queen, Anne of Austria. He succeeded his father on May 14, 1643, at the age of four years and eight months. Louis was nine years old when the nobles and the Paris Parlement (a powerful law court), driven by hatred of the prime minister Cardinal Jules Mazarin, rose against the crown in 1648. This marked the beginning of the long civil war known as the Fronde, in the course of which Louis suffered poverty, misfortune, fear, humiliation, cold, and hunger. These trials shaped the future character, behaviour, and mode of thought of the young king. He would never forgive either Paris, the nobles, or the common people. In 1653 Mazarin was victorious over the rebels and then proceeded to construct an extraordinary administrative apparatus with Louis as his pupil. The young king also acquired Mazarin's partiality for the arts, elegance, and display. Although he had been proclaimed of age, the king did not dream of disputing the cardinal's absolute power.

In 1660 Louis married Marie-Thérèse of Austria (1638–83), daughter of Philip IV of Spain, in order to ratify peace between their two countries. When Mazarin died in 1661, Louis assumed responsibility for ruling the kingdom. A believer in dictatorship by divine right, he viewed himself as God's representative on Earth. For 54 years Louis devoted himself to his task eight hours a day; not the smallest detail escaped his attention. To deal with the potential threat posed by the nobles, who had started 11 civil wars in

Louis XIV and His Family, *oil painting by Nicolas de Largillière, 1711; in the Wallace Collection, London.* Reproduced by permission of the trustees of the Wallace Collection, London; photograph, J.R. Freeman & Co. Ltd.

40 years, Louis lured them to his court, corrupted them with gambling, and ultimately weakened their power by making them dependent on the crown. From that time, the nobility ceased to be an important factor in French politics, which in some respects weakened the nation.

During his reign, an economic revolution aimed at making France economically self-sufficient while maximizing export occurred. Manufacturers, the navy and merchant marines, a modern police organization, roads, ports, and canals all emerged at about the same time. Louis attended to every detail. As a patron of the arts, Louis protected writers and devoted himself to building splendid palaces, including the extravagant Versailles, where he kept most of the nobility under his watchful eye. At the same time, he carried on a tumultuous love affair with Louise de La Vallière, the daughter of a military governor.

In 1667 Louis invaded the Spanish Netherlands (War of Devolution), which he regarded as his wife's inheritance, thus beginning a series of wars that lasted for a good part of his reign. After a brilliant campaign, the king had to retreat in 1668 in the face of English and especially Dutch pressure. He never forgave the Dutch and swore to destroy their Protestant mercantile republic. To this end he allied himself with his cousin Charles II of England and invaded the Netherlands in 1672 (Third Dutch War). The long war that ensued ended in 1678, with the first treaty of Nijmegen. Louis was triumphant.

At the same time, great changes were occurring in his private life. In 1680 the Marquise de Montespan, who had replaced Louise de La Vallière as Louis's mistress in 1667, was implicated in the Affair of the Poisons, a scandal in which a number of prominent people were accused of sorcery and murder. Fearful for his reputation, the King dismissed Mme de Montespan and imposed piety on his entourage. In 1682 he had the seat of government transferred to Versailles. The following year, the queen died, and the king secretly married his latest mistress, the pious Mme de Maintenon.

Meanwhile, Louis's expansionism alarmed England, the Dutch, and the Holy Roman Emperor, who united in opposition to him. The resulting War of the Grand Alliance lasted from 1688 to 1697. Despite many victories, Louis gave up part of his territorial acquisitions when he signed the Treaty of Rijswijk, for which the public judged him harshly. He reconciled himself to another painful sacrifice when he recognized William of Orange as William III of England, in violation of his belief in the divine right of the Stuart king James II to William's throne.

Three years later, in 1700, Charles II, the last Habsburg king of Spain, died, bequeathing his kingdoms to Louis's grandson, Philip of Anjou (Philip V). Louis, who desired nothing more than peace, hesitated but finally accepted the inheritance. He has been strongly criticized for his decision, but he had no alternative. With England against him, he had to try to prevent Spain from falling into the hands of the equally hostile Holy Roman Emperor Leopold I, who disputed Philip's claim. In the ensuing War of the Spanish Succession (1701–14), the anti-French alliance was reactivated by William of Orange before his death. The disasters of the war were so great that, in 1709, France came close to losing all the advantages gained over the preceding century. Finally, a palace revolution in London, bringing the pacific Tories to power, and a French victory over the imperial forces at the Battle of Denain combined to end the war. The treaties of Utrecht, Rastatt, and Baden, signed in 1713–14, cost France its hegemony but left its territory intact. Louis XIV died in 1715, ending the longest reign in European history.

PETER I

(b. June 9 [May 30, Old Style], 1672, Moscow, Russia—d. Feb. 8 [Jan. 28], 1725, St. Petersburg)

The founder of the Russian Empire was Peter I, also known as Peter the Great. As tsar of Russia, he reigned jointly with his half-brother Ivan V (1682–96) and alone thereafter (1696–1725). In 1721 he was proclaimed emperor. He was one of his country's greatest statesmen, organizers, and reformers.

Peter (in full, Pyotr Alekseyevich) was the son of Tsar Alexis by his second wife, Natalya Kirillovna Naryshkina. When Alexis died in 1676, Peter was only four years old. Peter's half-brother Fyodor, who then became tsar, died in 1682. Peter and another half-brother, Ivan, were to rule jointly, but because Ivan was sickly and feebleminded, his sister Sophia served as regent. Sophia, clever and influential, excluded Peter from the government, and he grew up in a village outside Moscow.

Early in 1689 his mother arranged Peter's marriage to the beautiful Eudoxia (Yevdokiya Fyodorovna Lopukhina). The marriage did not last long. Peter soon began to ignore his wife and eventually relegated her to a convent. Later that year, Peter removed Sophia from power. Though Ivan V remained nominally joint tsar with Peter, the administration was now largely given over to Peter's kinsmen, the Naryshkins, until Ivan's death in 1696.

At the beginning of Peter's reign, Russia was territorially a huge power, but had no access to the Black Sea, the Caspian, or to the Baltic. To win such an outlet became the main goal of Peter's foreign policy. He engaged in war with the Ottoman Empire (1695–96) with the goal of capturing Azov, which he did.

In 1697 Peter went with the so-called Grand Embassy to western Europe. Comprising about 250 people, its chief purposes were to examine the international situation and to strengthen the anti-Turkish coalition (to no avail), but also to gather information on the economic and cultural life of Europe. Peter pretended to be a ship's carpenter named Peter Mikhailov and worked in English and Dutch shipyards. He also visited factories, schools, and museums and studied everything from anatomy and engraving to European industrial techniques.

When Peter could not secure anti-Turkish alliances, he abandoned his plans for pushing forward from the Sea of Azov to the Black Sea. He now turned his attention to the Baltic instead, which led to the long-running Northern War (1700–21) with Sweden. At the war's end, the eastern shores of the Baltic were ceded to Russia. In the middle of the Northern War, Turkey declared war on Russia (1710–13), which ended with Azov left to the Turks. From that time on, Peter's military effort was concentrated on winning his war against Sweden. In 1722, hearing that the Ottoman Turks would take advantage of Persia's weakness and invade the Caspian region, Peter himself invaded Persian territory. In 1723 Persia ceded the western and southern shores of the Caspian to Russia in return for military aid.

Despite being occupied with several wars for many years, Peter managed to make many widespread reforms and changes in Russia. At the beginning of Peter's reign, Russia was less developed by comparison with the countries of western Europe. This inhibited foreign policy and even put Russia's national independence in danger. Peter's aim, therefore, was to overtake the developed countries of western Europe as soon as possible, in order both to promote the national economy and to ensure victory in his wars for access to the seas. He initiated a series of reforms that affected, in the course of 25 years, every field of the national life—administration, industry, commerce, technology, and culture. He modernized the calendar, making it conform to European usage with regard to the year. Peter simplified the alphabet, unified the currency, and introduced universal taxation. He encouraged the rise of private industry and the expansion of trade. Peter was the first ruler of Russia to sponsor education on secular lines and to bring an element of state control into that field. Various secular schools were opened and the children of soldiers, officials, and churchmen were admitted to them. The translation of books from western European languages was actively promoted. Peter built Russia's first modern hospitals and medical schools. He also began construction of the city of St. Petersburg in 1703 and established it as the new capital of Russia in 1712.

Peter had a son, the tsarevich Alexis, by his discarded wife Eudoxia. Although Alexis was his natural heir, the two were not close, and Alexis did not agree with Peter's policies. Peter, meanwhile, had formed a lasting liaison with a peasant woman, the future empress Catherine I, who bore him other children and whom he married in 1712. In 1718 Alexis was tried on charges of high treason and condemned to death. He died in prison before the formal execution of the sentence.

In the autumn of 1724, seeing some soldiers in danger of drowning in the Gulf of Finland, Peter characteristically plunged himself into the icy water to help them. Catching a chill, he became seriously ill in the winter but even so continued to work. He died early in the following year, leaving an empire that stretched from Arkhangelsk (Archangel) on the White Sea to Mazanderan on the Caspian and from the Baltic Sea to the Pacific Ocean. Although he had in 1722 issued a decree reserving to himself the right to nominate his successor, he did not in fact nominate anyone. His widow Catherine, whom he had crowned as empress in 1724, succeeded him to the temporary exclusion of his grandson, the future Peter II.

CATHERINE II

(b. April 21 [May 2, New Style], 1729, Stettin, Prussia [now Szczecin, Poland]—d. Nov. 6 [Nov. 17], 1796, Tsarskoye Selo [now Pushkin], near St. Petersburg, Russia)

German-born empress of Russia (1762–96), Catherine II the Great, born Sophie Friederike Auguste, Prinzessin von Anhalt-Zerbst, led her country into full participation in the political and cultural life of Europe.

ORIGINS AND EARLY EXPERIENCE

At age 14, Sophie Friederike Auguste von Anhalt-Zerbst, the daughter of an obscure German prince, was chosen to be the wife of Karl Ulrich, duke of Holstein-Gottorp, grandson of Peter the Great and heir to the throne of Russia as the grand duke Peter. In 1744 Catherine assumed the title of Grand Duchess Catherine Alekseyevna and married her young cousin the following year. The marriage was a complete failure, and the following 18 years were filled with deception and humiliation for Catherine.

Catherine would not have become empress if her husband had been at all normal. He was extremely neurotic, rebellious, obstinate, nearly alcoholic, and, most seriously, a fanatical worshipper of Frederick II of Prussia, the foe of the empress Elizabeth—Russia's then ruler and Peter the Great's daughter. Catherine, by contrast, was clear-headed and ambitious, intelligent, possessed considerable charm, and had a great love of Russia, which gained her much support. During her husband's lifetime, she had at least three lovers, and it is possible that none of her three children, not even the heir apparent Paul, was fathered by her husband. Her true passion, however, was ambition; she saw quite early the possibility of eliminating him and governing Russia herself.

The empress Elizabeth died on Dec. 25, 1761. Shortly after Elizabeth's death, Peter, now emperor, ended Russia's participation in the Seven Years' War against Prussia and concluded an alliance with Frederick II of Prussia. He made no attempt to hide his hatred of Russia and his love of his native Germany. Peter discredited himself endlessly by his foolish actions. Catherine had only to strike. She had the support of the army, "enlightened" elements of aristocratic society (she was known for her liberal opinions), and the public in both Moscow and St. Petersburg. On June 28, 1762, she had herself proclaimed empress. Peter III abdicated and was assassinated eight days later.

EARLY YEARS AS EMPRESS

Catherine's most pressing practical problem was to replenish the state treasury. She did this in 1762 by secularizing the property of the clergy, who owned one-third of the land and serfs in Russia. She preserved friendly relations with Prussia, Russia's old enemy, as well as with the country's traditional allies, France and Austria. In 1764 she installed one of her old lovers, Stanisław Poniatowski, as king of Poland.

Catherine's attempts at reform were less than satisfying. A commission she convened in 1767 for the purpose of framing a constitution came to nothing. Catherine's Instruction to the commission, a draft of a constitution and a code of laws, was considered too liberal for Russia.

Catherine seized the pretext of war with Turkey in 1768 to emphasize national grandeur. The war with the Ottoman Empire fired the patriotism and zeal of Catherine's subjects. Naval victory at Çeşme in 1770 brought military glory to the empress. But Russia soon encountered unforeseen difficulties, including a plague that broke out in Moscow and a great uprising in 1773 led by Yemelyan Pugachov, a former Cossack officer pretending to be the dead emperor Peter III. In June 1774 Pugachov's Cossack troops prepared to march on Moscow, but when war against Turkey ended in a Russian victory, Catherine sent her crack troops to crush the rebellion.

Before her accession to power, Catherine had planned to emancipate the serfs. Catherine saw very quickly, however, that emancipation would never be tolerated by the owners, whom she depended upon for support. She reconciled herself to serfdom and turned her attention to organizing and strengthening the system, even imposing serfdom on the Ukrainians who had until then been free.

INFLUENCE OF POTEMKIN

In 1774 Grigory Potemkin, who had distinguished himself in the war, became Catherine's lover, and he was to play an extensive political role. In Potemkin Catherine found an extraordinary man whom she could love and respect and with whom she could share her power. He had unlimited powers, even after the end of their liaison, which lasted only two years. Potemkin must be given part of the credit for the somewhat extravagant splendour of Catherine's reign. He was treated as an equal by the empress up to the time of his death in 1791.

The annexation of the Crimea from the Turks in 1783 was Potemkin's work. Through that annexation and others, Russia was in a position to threaten the existence of the Ottoman Empire and to establish a foothold in the Mediterranean. Catherine also sought to renew the alliance with Austria, Turkey's neighbour and enemy, and renounced the alliance with Prussia and England. Yet, during Catherine's reign, the country did not become involved in a European war.

THE FINAL YEARS

Catherine felt seriously threatened by the French Revolution. In 1790 the writer A.N. Radishchev, who attempted to publish a work openly critical of the abuses of serfdom, was tried, condemned to death, then pardoned and exiled. Ironically, the sentiments Radishchev expressed were very similar to Catherine's Instruction of 1767. Next, Poland, encouraged by the example of France, began agitating for a liberal constitution. In 1792, under the pretext of forestalling the threat of revolution, Catherine sent in troops to Poland and the next year annexed most of the western Ukraine, while Prussia helped itself to large territories of western Poland. After the national uprising led by Tadeusz Kościuszko in Poland in 1794, Catherine wiped Poland off the map of Europe by dividing it between Russia, Prussia, and Austria in 1795.

Catherine's last years were darkened by the execution of Louis XVI, the advance of the revolutionary armies, and the spread of radical ideas. The empress realized, moreover, that she had no suitable successor. She considered her son Paul an incompetent and unbalanced man, and her grandson Alexander was too young yet to rule. In 1796 she died unexpectedly from a stroke.

Russians, even Soviet Russians, continue to admire Catherine and regard her as a source of national pride. Non-Russian opinion of Catherine is less favourable. She figured in the Western imagination as the incarnation of the immense, backward, yet forbidding country she ruled. Yet, her many achievements—including the expansion of Russian territory and trade, together with the glory of military victories and the fame of a brilliant court—have won her a distinguished place in history.

GEORGE WASHINGTON

(b. Feb. 22 [Feb. 11, Old Style], 1732, Westmoreland County, Va., U.S.—d. Dec. 14, 1799, Mount Vernon, Va.)

A general and the commander in chief of the colonial armies in the American Revolution (1775–83), George Washington subsequently became the first president of the United States from 1789 to 1797. So great were his contributions to the founding of the United States that he is known simply as the Father of His Country.

CHILDHOOD AND YOUTH

Little is known of George Washington's early childhood, spent largely on the Ferry Farm on the Rappahannock River, opposite Fredericksburg, Virginia. Mason L. Weems's story of the hatchet and cherry tree is an apocryphal effort to fill an obvious gap. When Washington was 11, his father, Augustine, died, and he became the ward of his eldest half brother, Lawrence, on whose 2,500-acre (1,000-hectare) estate, Mount Vernon, he lived (though he spent some time near Fredericksburg with his other half brother, Augustine). Washington attended school irregularly and at age 16 became a surveyor. Upon the death of both Lawrence and his daughter in 1752, Washington inherited Mount Vernon, becoming, at age 20, head of one of the best estates in Virginia. For the next 20 years, his life revolved around the work and society of the estate. Although he strongly disapproved of slavery and hoped for some mode of abolishing it, at the time of Washington's death, more than 300 slaves were housed in the quarters on his property—although he is said to have given them exemplary treatment.

PREREVOLUTIONARY MILITARY CAREER AND LIFE

Washington began his military career in 1752 as adjutant for the southern district of Virginia. He participated in the first action of the French and Indian War (1754–63) when a force he led engaged the French in western Pennsylvania. Besieged by a force of 700 French soldiers, Washington's troops were forced to surrender Fort Necessity on July 3, 1754. As the aide-de-camp to British General Edward Bradock, Washington distinguished himself when a British and colonial force en route to attack Fort Duquesne was overwhelmed by the French on July 9, 1755. In August of that year, Washington, at age 23, was named commander of all Virginia forces. He resigned his commission in 1758 with the honorary rank of brigadier general. Frustrated in his attempts to gain a regular commission in the British army, Washington returned to Mount Vernon somewhat disillusioned. Immediately upon resigning his commission, Washington married the well-borne Martha Dandridge, widow of Daniel Parke Custis, on January 6, 1759. In the process he gained two stepchildren and thousands of acres of additional valuable land. Until the eve of the Revolution, he devoted himself to the duties of a great landholder, varied by several weeks' attendance every year in the House of Burgesses in Williamsburg.

REVOLUTIONARY LEADERSHIP

Washington's contented life was interrupted by the rising storm in imperial affairs. The British ministry, facing a heavy postwar debt, high home taxes, and continued military costs in America, decided in 1764 to obtain revenue from the colonies, resulting in the imposition of the Stamp Act. Up until that time, Washington had shown limited interest in state affairs. However, over the next few years, he transformed from a moderate into a radical. He served as a delegate to both the First Continental Congress in Philadelphia in September 1774, which he attended in full military uniform, and the Second Congress in March 1775.

Recognizing Washington's military experience and leadership, the Continental Congress made him commander in chief of all colonial military forces in June 1775. In March 1776 his army staged a siege and eventually expelled British troops from Boston. Washington fared less well in his subsequent defense of New York. However, in December 1776, Washington's forces pulled off stunning victories at Trenton and Princeton, stealing across the Delaware River in the midst of a raging snowstorm to surprise the British in formal battle. Washington's army suffered losses against the British forces in Pennsylvania at the battles of Brandywine and Germantown in the fall of 1777. In December 1777 Washington withdrew to Valley Forge, Pennsylvania, where he set up winter quarters and reorganized his army despite the bitter cold. By 1778 France recognized American independence and sent military support to help Washington's forces fight the British. In July 1778 a French naval fleet blockaded the British troops in New York City, leaving the British isolated from reinforcements. After 1779 the theatre of war shifted to the south. On Oct. 19, 1781, Washington's army—combined with the French naval fleet and ground troops—staged a siege at Yorktown, Virginia, forcing the surrender of the British under General Charles Cornwallis. The Treaty of Paris was signed on Sept. 3, 1783, officially ending the American Revolution.

It is unquestionable that Washington's strength of character, his ability to hold the confidence of the army and people and to diffuse his own courage among them, his unremitting activity, and his strong common sense constituted the chief factors in achieving American victory. He was not a great tactician, but he did succeed in keeping a strong army in existence and maintaining the flame of national spirit. When the auspicious moment arrived, he planned the rapid movements that ended the war.

CONSTITUTIONAL CONVENTION TO PRESIDENCY

With the war over, Washington returned to Mount Vernon, but he was a delegate to and presiding officer of the Constitutional Convention (1787). His weight of character did more than any other single force to bring the convention to an agreement and obtain ratification of the Constitution afterward. He did not believe it perfect, but his support gave it victory in Virginia

When the state electors met to select the first president in 1789, Washington was the unanimous choice. Slowly feeling his way, Washington defined the style of the first president of a country in the history of the world. The people, too, had to adjust to a government without a king. Even the question of how to address a president had to be discussed. It was decided that in a republic the simple salutation "Mr. President" would do.

During Washington's administration, the authority of the federal government was greatly strengthened. Washington and Alexander Hamilton chartered the Bank of the United States in 1791, and the federal government assumed responsibility for both national and state debts. Taxes were placed on imported goods and certain private property within the states, and money was deposited into the national treasury for paying debts. Also in 1791 the states ratified the Bill of Rights—the first 10 amendments to the Constitution—which granted U.S. citizens their basic rights. Elected to a second term, Washington followed a middle course between the political factions that later became the Federalist Party and the Democratic Party. He proclaimed a policy of neutrality in the war between Britain and France in 1793 and sent troops to suppress the Whiskey Rebellion in 1794. He declined to serve a third term (thereby setting a 144-year precedent) and retired in 1797 after delivering his "Farewell Address." He devoted himself for the last two and a half years of his life to his family, farm operations, and care of his slaves.

THOMAS JEFFERSON

(b. April 2 [April 13, New Style], 1743, Shadwell, Va., U.S.—d. July 4, 1826, Monticello, Va.)

Thomas Jefferson was the third president of the United States (1801–09). He also drafted the Declaration of Independence and was the nation's first secretary of state (1789–94) and its second vice president (1797–1801).

EARLY YEARS AND THE DECLARATION OF INDEPENDENCE

Jefferson entered the political arena in 1769 as a Virginia state legislator. In 1774 he wrote *A Summary View of the Rights of British America*, which catapulted him into visibility beyond Virginia as an early advocate of American independence from Parliament's authority. The Virginia legislature appointed him a delegate to the Second Continental Congress in 1775. Jefferson's chief role was as a draftsman of resolutions. In that capacity, on June 11, 1776, he was appointed to a five-person committee, which also included John Adams and Benjamin Franklin, to draft a formal statement of the reasons why a break with Great Britain was justified. This became the Declaration of Independence, and Jefferson was its primary author.

Jefferson returned to Virginia in October 1776 and immediately launched a project for the reform of the state's legal code, to bring it in line with the principles of the American Revolution. He was elected governor of the state in 1779. He was later criticized for being caught off-guard by a surprise British invasion in 1780, against which the state was defenseless.

AMERICAN IN PARIS

Jefferson agreed, albeit reluctantly, to serve as a delegate to the Continental Congress in December 1782, where he drafted the first of the Northwest Ordinances for dividing and settling the Northwest Territory. Then, in 1784, he agreed to replace Franklin as American minister to France.

During his five-year sojourn in Paris, Jefferson accomplished very little in any official sense. Several conditions rendered his best diplomatic efforts futile. The United States was heavily in debt because of the recent war, so few European nations were interested in signing treaties of amity and commerce with the infant American republic. Additionally, France was drifting toward a cataclysmic political crisis of its own, so relations with the upstart new nation across the Atlantic were hardly a high priority. And an alleged love affair with Sally Hemings, one of his slaves whom he summoned to Paris, sparked a paternity debate that persisted long after his death.

PARTY POLITICS

Jefferson returned to the United States in 1789 to serve as the first secretary of state under President George Washington. During his tenure as secretary of state, foreign policy was his chief responsibility. Within the cabinet a three-pronged division soon emerged over American policy toward the European powers. Washington and Adams, who was serving as vice president, insisted on complete neutrality. Alexander Hamilton pushed for a pro-English version of neutrality, while Jefferson favoured a pro-French version of neutrality.

Serving as vice president during the Adams presidency from 1797 to 1801, Jefferson worked behind the scenes to undermine Adams's efforts to sustain strict neutrality. Jefferson's foreign-policy vision was resolutely moralistic and highly ideological, dominated by a dichotomous view of England as a corrupt and degenerate engine of despotism and France as the enlightened wave of the future. Jefferson's position on domestic policy during the 1790s was a variation on the same ideological dichotomy, and he came to regard the consolidation of power at the federal level as a diabolical plot to subvert the true meaning of the American Revolution. By the middle years of the decade, two distinctive political camps had emerged, calling themselves Federalists and Republicans (later Democratic-Republicans). Jefferson, assisted and advised by James Madison, established the rudiments of the first opposition party in American politics under the Republican banner.

The highly combustible political culture of the early republic reached a crescendo in the election of 1800, one of the most fiercely contested campaigns in American history. Jefferson ran for the presidency with Aaron Burr as his vice presidential candidate. A quirk in the Constitution, subsequently corrected in the Twelfth Amendment, prevented electors from distinguishing between their choice of president and vice president, so Jefferson and Burr tied for the top spot, even though voter preference for Jefferson was incontestable. The decision was thrown into the House of Representatives, which chose Jefferson for president after several weeks of debate.

PRESIDENCY

Jefferson was inaugurated into office on March 4, 1801. He delegated all executive messages in writing rather than through public speeches. Initially, at least, his policies as president reflected his desire for decentralization, which meant dismantling the embryonic federal government, the army and navy, and all federal taxation programs, as well as eradicating the national debt. These reforms enjoyed considerable success.

The major achievement of his first term was what would become known as the Louisiana Purchase. In 1803 Napoleon decided to consolidate his resources for a new round of conflict with England by selling the vast Louisiana region, which stretched from the Mississippi Valley to the Rocky Mountains. Although the asking price, $15 million, was a stupendous bargain, the cost meant substantially increasing the national debt. But Jefferson never wavered, reasoning that the opportunity to double the national domain was too good to miss.

In 1804 Jefferson was easily reelected over Federalist Charles Cotesworth Pinckney, winning 162 electoral votes to Pinckney's 14. George Clinton replaced Aaron Burr as vice president.

Meanwhile, the resumption of the Napoleonic Wars resulted in naval blockades in the Atlantic and Caribbean that severely curtailed American trade. Jefferson's response was the Embargo Act (1807), which essentially closed American ports to all foreign imports and American exports. The embargo assumed that the loss of American trade would force England and France to alter their policies, but it did not. The embryonic American economy lacked the size to generate such influence and was itself wrecked by Jefferson's action. Moreover, the enforcement of the Embargo Act required the exercise of precisely those coercive powers by the federal government that Jefferson had previously opposed. By the time he left office in March 1809, Jefferson was weary and eager to return to private life.

RETIREMENT

During the last 17 years of his life, Jefferson maintained a crowded and active schedule. He continued to serve as president of the American Philosophical Society (1797–1815), and in 1819 he founded and designed the University of Virginia. In 1812 he began to correspond with his former friend and more recent rival John Adams. Their genuine differences of opinion made Adams and Jefferson the odd couple of the American Revolution and were the primary reasons why they had drifted to different sides of the divide during the party wars of the 1790s. The exchange of 158 letters between 1812 and 1826 created what is arguably the most intellectually impressive correspondence between statesmen in all of American history.

One issue that even Adams and Jefferson could not discuss candidly was slavery. Jefferson's mature position on that subject represented a further retreat from any leadership role in ending the "peculiar institution." In 1819, during the debate in Congress over the Missouri Compromise, he endorsed the expansion of slavery into all the western territories, precisely the opposite of his position in the 1780s. Although he continued to insist that slavery was a massive anomaly, he insisted even more strongly that it was wrong for the federal government to attempt any effort at emancipation. His letters to fellow Virginians during his last years reflect a conspiratorial mentality toward the national government and a clear preference for secession if threatened with any mandatory plan for abolition.

Apart from slavery, the other shadow that darkened Monticello during Jefferson's twilight years was debt. Jefferson was chronically in debt throughout most of his life, in part because of obligations inherited from his father-in-law in his wife's dowry, but mostly because of his own lavish lifestyle.

MAXIMILIEN DE ROBESPIERRE
(b. May 6, 1758, Arras, France — d. July 28, 1794, Paris)

Maximilien de Robespierre was one of the principal figures in the French Revolution. He was part of the Committee of Public Safety, the principal organ of the Revolutionary government during the Reign of Terror.

Robespierre received a law degree in 1781 and became a lawyer in Arras, where he was noted for his ability and honesty. In March 1789 the citizens of Arras chose him as one of their representatives to the National Assembly. In April 1790 he presided over the Jacobins, a political club promoting the ideas of the French Revolution, and in October he was appointed a judge of the Versailles tribunal. Robespierre nevertheless decided to devote himself fully to his work in the National Assembly, where a new constitution was being drawn up. Grounded in ancient history and the works of the French philosophers of the Enlightenment, he welcomed the Declaration of the Rights of Man and of the Citizen, which formed the preamble of the French constitution of Sept. 3, 1791, and he insisted that all laws should conform to it. He became notorious as an outspoken radical in favour of individual rights. When the National Assembly dissolved itself, the people of Paris organized a triumphal procession for

Robespierre. Although he had excluded himself and his colleagues from the new Legislative Assembly, Robespierre continued to be politically active. Henceforth, he spoke only at the Jacobin Club, where he was to be heard about 100 times, until August 1792.

That year, Paris mobs stormed the palace of the Tuileries and dethroned King Louis XVI and his queen, Marie Antoinette. Robespierre helped organize the new revolutionary governing body, the National Convention. From the first sessions of the new body, a faction known as the Girondins, who favoured political but not social democracy and who controlled the government and the civil service, accused Robespierre of dictatorship. Robespierre was a leading member of the faction known as the Montagnards, the deputies of the extreme left. On May 26, 1793, Robespierre called on the people "to rise in insurrection." Five days later he supported a decree of the National Convention indicting the Girondin leaders. On June 2 the decree was passed against many of them.

After the fall of the Girondins, the Montagnards were left to deal with the country's desperate position. In April 1793 the Committee of Public Safety had taken over the rule of the country to suppress royalist uprisings and to repel the Prussian-Austrian invaders on its borders. The committee employed harsh measures against those suspected of being enemies of the Revolution. The bloody three-year rule of this body was known as the Reign of Terror, during which some 300,000 suspects were arrested. About 17,000 were executed, and many others died in prison. Robespierre took his place on the committee in June.

Robespierre was not entirely to blame for the excesses of the Committee of Public Safety. He was not a man of action. He rarely attended its sessions and had almost no part in its routine work. His love of power and narrow self-righteousness, however, made him feared and hated by many of his associates.

A deist, Robespierre disapproved of the anti-Christian movement. In a report to the National Convention in May 1794, he affirmed the existence of God and the immortality of the soul and strove to rally the revolutionaries around a civic religion and the cult of the Supreme Being. The National Convention elected him president June 4, 1794.

Political opposition to Robespierre grew. Meanwhile, unremitting work and frequent speeches in the Legislative Assembly and at the Jacobin Club had undermined Robespierre's health, and he became irritable and distant. He stayed away from the National Convention and then, after June, from the Committee of Public Safety, confining his denunciations of counterrevolutionary intrigues to the Jacobin Club. At the same time, he began to lose the support of the people, whose hardships continued despite the recent French victories.

Weary of the mounting executions (1,300 in June alone), on July 27 deputies in the National Convention decreed the arrest of Robespierre and other members of the Committee of Public Safety. Robespierre was taken to the Luxembourg prison, but the warden refused to jail him. Later he went to the Hôtel de Ville (City Hall). The soldiers of the National Convention attacked there and easily seized Robespierre and his followers. In the evening of July 28, Robespierre and others were guillotined before a cheering mob on the Place de la Révolution (now the Place de la Concorde).

NAPOLEON I

(b. Aug. 15, 1769, Ajaccio, Corsica—d. May 5, 1821, St. Helena Island)

One of the most celebrated personages in the history of the West is Napoleon. He was a French general, first consul (1799–1804), and emperor of the French (1804–1814/15). Known as the Little Corporal because of his short stature, Napoleon revolutionized military organization and training. He also sponsored the Napoleonic Code, the prototype of later civil-law codes; reorganized education; and established the long-lived concordat with the papacy.

Napoleon was born on Corsica shortly after the island's cession to France by the Genoese. He was the fourth, and second surviving, child of Carlo Buonaparte, a lawyer, and his wife, Letizia Ramolino. His father's family, of ancient Tuscan nobility, had emigrated to Corsica in the 16th century.

The Emperor Napoleon in His Study at the Tuileries, *oil on canvas by Jacques-Louis David, 1812; in the National Gallery of Art, Washington, D.C.* © Photos.com/ Jupiterimages

Napoleon attended the École Militaire in Paris in 1784–85. There he received training as an artilleryman and as an officer. When his course was completed he joined the French army as a second lieutenant of artillery at age 16. He fought during the French Revolution and was promoted to brigadier general in 1793. The threat of revolt brought him the command of the army of the interior in 1795; he then

Bonaparte on the Bridge at Arcole, 17 November 1796, *oil on canvas by Antoine-Jean Gros, 1796; in the Versailles Museum.* © Photos.com/ Jupiterimages

commanded the army of Italy in several victorious campaigns.

In 1798 Napoleon persuaded the willing French government to send him and a large army to Egypt. He won the Battle of the Pyramids in July 1798, but his fleet was destroyed by the British in the Battle of the Nile at Aboukir Bay that same year. Napoleon then decided to invade Syria. At Acre, English troops fighting alongside those of Turkey held out, and Napoleon retreated to Egypt. In July 1799 he defeated 10,000 Turks in the Battle of Aboukir. Shortly after, unrest at home forced him to return.

Napoleon in His Imperial Robes, *by François Gérard, 1805; in the National Museum of Versailles and Trianons.* © Photos.com/Jupiterimages

The unrest turned out to be a coup that brought Napoleon to supreme power in 1799, and he instituted a military dictatorship, with himself as First Consul. Napoleon introduced numerous reforms in government. He established the University of France and reformed the educational system. He founded the Bank of France and the Legion of Honor. Most significantly, he created the Napoleonic Code, the first clear, compact statement of French law in centuries, which became a model for law

Napoleon on the Battlefield at Eylau, February 1807, *oil painting by Antoine-Jean Gros, 1808; in the Louvre, Paris.* © Photos.com/Jupiterimages

reformers throughout the world. He negotiated the Concordat of 1801, which restored friendly relations with the papacy.

After victory against the Austrians at the Battle of Marengo (1800), he embarked on the Napoleonic Wars, which lasted from 1799 to 1815. This series of conflicts pitted France against shifting alliances of European powers. The formation of coalitions of European countries against him led Napoleon to declare France a hereditary empire and to crown himself emperor in 1804. His greatest victory, the Battle of Austerlitz, against Austria and Russia, came in 1805. In 1807 Napoleon was able to impose the Treaty of Tilsit on Russia and Prussia.

Napoleon led the French army into Austria and defeated the Austrians at the Battle of Wagram in 1809, signing the Treaty of Vienna. Thereafter, except for temporary setbacks in Spain, he was successful, consolidating most of Europe as his empire by about 1810. In 1812, to enforce the Treaty of Tilsit, he led an army of about 600,000 into Russia. Napoleon's forces won the Battle of Borodino, but were forced to retreat from Moscow with disastrous losses. His army greatly weakened, he was met by a strong coalition of Allied powers, who defeated him at the Battle of Leipzig in 1813.

On March 30, 1814, the Allies captured Paris itself. Napoleon's generals refused to continue the hopeless

1814, the Campaign of France, *by Ernest Meissonier, 1864; in the Louvre, Paris.* © Photos.com/Jupiterimages

struggle despite all the emperor's pleading, and he was forced to abdicate on April 6, 1814. Napoleon was exiled to Elba. However, he remained on Elba for only 10 months. In March 1815 he escaped and landed in France. Escorted by a thousand of his old guard, he began a triumphant march on Paris, picking up support along the way. Hundreds rallied to his side. For a brief time, known as the Hundred Days, Napoleon enjoyed a return to his former glory, but it ended at the Battle of Waterloo on June 18, 1815, where he suffered his final defeat by a combined English and Prussian force. He was forced to abdicate once again. He was sent into final exile to St. Helena Island, where he died in 1821.

SIMÓN BOLÍVAR

(b. July 24, 1783, Caracas, New Granada [now in Venezuela]—d. Dec. 17, 1830, near Santa Marta, Colom.)

S imón Bolívar, known as the Liberator (El Libertador), was a soldier and statesman who led the revolutions against Spanish rule in the Viceroyalty of New Granada in South America. He was president of Gran Colombia (1819–30) and dictator of Peru from 1823 to 1826. Bolívar is still honoured as a hero and liberator in Latin America.

EARLY YEARS AND INDEPENDENCE MOVEMENT

The son of a Venezuelan aristocrat of Spanish descent, Bolívar was born to wealth and position in 1783. At the age of 16, Bolívar was sent to Europe to complete his education. Influenced by European rationalism, he joined Venezuela's independence movement (Venezuela was part of the Viceroyalty of New Granada, under Spanish rule) and became a prominent political and military leader. In

March 1811 a national congress met in Caracas to draft a constitution. After long deliberation it declared Venezuela's independence on July 5, 1811, although the young republic was defeated by the Spanish in 1812. Determined to continue the struggle, Bolívar led an expeditionary force to retake Venezuela. In a sweeping, hard-fought campaign, he vanquished the royalists in six pitched battles and on August 6, 1813, entered Caracas. He was given the title of Liberator and assumed political dictatorship. However, Venezuela was once more defeated by the Spanish, in 1814, and Bolívar went into exile.

It was during this exile that Bolívar wrote the greatest document of his career: *La Carta de Jamaica* ("The Letter from Jamaica"), in which he outlined a grandiose panorama from Chile and Argentina to Mexico. He proposed constitutional republics throughout Hispanic America, and for the former Viceroyalty of New Granada he envisioned a government modeled on that of Great Britain, with a hereditary upper house, an elected lower house, and a president chosen for life. The last provision, to which Bolívar clung throughout his career, constituted the most dubious feature of his political thinking.

LIBERATION OF NEW GRANADA

In spring 1819 Bolívar conceived his master plan of attacking the Viceroyalty of New Granada, considered one of the most daring attacks in military history. The route of his small army led through flood-swept plains and icy mountains, over routes that the Spanish considered nearly impassable. The Spaniards were taken by surprise, and in the crucial Battle of Boyacá on August 7, 1819, the bulk of the royalist army surrendered to Bolívar. Three days later he entered Bogotá. This was the turning point in the history of northern South America. La República de Colombia was established, comprising the three departments of Cundinamarca (New Granada), Venezuela, and Quito (Ecuador). Since most of this territory was still under royalist control, however, it was largely a paper achievement. In 1821 Bolívar defeated the Spanish forces in Venezuela. The Battle of Carabobo in June 1821 opened the gates of Caracas, and Bolívar's Venezuelan homeland was at last free. In the autumn of the same year, a congress convened in Cúcuta to draft a constitution for Gran Colombia. Its provisions disappointed Bolívar. Although he had been elected president, he thought the constitution too liberal in character to guarantee the survival of his creation. Leaving the administration to others, he asked permission to continue his military campaign. At the end of a year, with the help of one of his officers, Antonio José de Sucre, Ecuador was liberated. It was in Quito that the Liberator met the great passion of his life, Manuela Sáenz, an ardent revolutionary who freely admitted her love for Bolívar and accompanied him first to Peru and ultimately to the presidential palace in Bogotá.

LIBERATION OF PERU AND THE CREATION OF BOLIVIA

The territory of Gran Colombia—comprising present-day Colombia, Venezuela, Ecuador, and Panama—had now been completely recovered from Spain, and its new government was recognized by the United States. Only Peru and Upper Peru remained in the hands of the Spaniards. Bolívar completed the revolutionary work started by the Argentine revolutionary José de San Martín, freeing Peru in 1824.

Bolívar was now president of Gran Colombia and dictator of Peru. Only a small section of the continent—Upper Peru—was still defended by royalist forces. The liberation of this region fell to Sucre, and in April 1825 he reported that the task had been accomplished. The new nation chose to be called Bolivia after the name of the Liberator.

A League of Hispanic American States

One of Bolívar's favourite projects, a league of Hispanic American states, came to fruition in 1826. He had long advocated treaties of alliance between the American republics, whose weakness he correctly apprehended. By 1824 such treaties had been signed and ratified by the republics of Colombia, Peru, Mexico, Central America, and the United Provinces of the Río de la Plata. In 1826 a general American congress convened in Panama under Bolívar's auspices. Compared with Bolívar's original proposals, it was a fragmentary affair, with only Colombia, Peru, Central America, and Mexico sending representatives. The four nations that attended signed a treaty of alliance and invited all other American nations to adhere to it. A common army and navy were planned, and a biannual assembly representing the federated states was projected. All controversies among the states were to be solved by arbitration. Only Colombia ratified the treaty, yet the congress in Panama provided an important example for future hemispheric solidarity and understanding in South America.

Civil War

But Bolívar was aware that his plans for hemispheric organization had met with only limited acceptance. His contemporaries thought in terms of individual nation-states, Bolívar in terms of continents. In the field of domestic policy, he continued to be an authoritarian republican. He thought of himself as a rallying point and anticipated civil war as soon as his words should no longer be heeded. Such a prophecy, made in 1824, was fulfilled in 1826, when civil war broke out. Bolívar was determined to preserve the unity of Gran Colombia, but his efforts were to no avail. Less successful at ruling countries than at liberating them, he exiled himself in 1830 and died of tuberculosis later that year.

GIUSEPPE GARIBALDI

(b. July 4, 1807, Nice, French Empire [now in France]—d. June 2, 1882, Caprera, Italy)

An Italian patriot and soldier of the Risorgimento, Giuseppe Garibaldi contributed to the achievement of Italian unification.

Initially, Garibaldi was a sailor. By 1833–34, when he served in the navy of the kingdom of Piedmont-Sardinia, he had come under the influence of the revolutionary Giuseppe Mazzini. In 1834 Garibaldi took part in a mutiny intended to provoke a republican revolution in Piedmont, but the plot failed. He escaped to France and in his absence was condemned to death by a Genoese court.

From 1836 to 1848, Garibaldi lived in exile in South America. There he took part in wars, first in Brazil and then in Uruguay, where he raised and commanded the Italian Legion. His South American experiences gave him invaluable training in the techniques of guerrilla warfare, which he later used with great effect against French and Austrian armies, not trained in how to counter them.

Revolution and insurrection raged throughout the Italian peninsula in 1848, and in April Garibaldi returned with 60 members of his Italian Legion to fight for the Risorgimento, or resurrection, of Italy in the war of independence against the Austrians. He was given command of the forces of the short-lived Roman Republic, which Mazzini had set up. After a desperate defense, he was forced to flee with his followers across the peninsula. Garibaldi was in exile again.

When Pius IX, threatened by liberal forces within the Papal States, fled from Rome toward the end of 1848, Garibaldi led a group of volunteers to that city. In 1849 they defended Rome from the French, who were attempting to reinstate papal rule, but Garibaldi's men were ultimately forced to retreat.

The retreat through central Italy, coming after the defense of Rome, made Garibaldi a well-known figure. Soon he was in exile again, first in Tangier, then on Staten Island, and finally in Peru. Only in 1854 was he allowed to return to Italy. The Conte di Cavour, the prime minister of Piedmont, believed that by permitting Garibaldi's repatriation, he could pry him away from the republican Mazzini. In the following year, Garibaldi bought part of the island of Caprera off the Sardinian coast, which remained his home for the rest of his life. In 1858 he received an invitation from Cavour to help prepare for another war against Austria, and he was given the rank of major general in the Piedmontese army. When war broke out in April 1859, he led his Cacciatori delle Alpi (Alpine Huntsmen) in the capture of Varese and Como and reached the frontier of the south Tirol. This war ended with the acquisition of Lombardy by Piedmont.

In May 1860 Garibaldi set out on the greatest venture of his life, the conquest of Sicily and Naples. This time he had no government backing, but Cavour and King Victor Emmanuel II of Piedmont-Sardinia did not dare to stop him, for he had become a popular hero. They stood ready to assist, but only if he proved successful, and he accepted this. Sailing from near Genoa on May 6 with about 1,000 men, he reached Marsala in Sicily on May 11 and in the name of Victor Emmanuel proclaimed himself dictator.

In August he crossed over the Strait of Messina and landed on the mainland in Calabria. After a lightning campaign, he moved up through Calabria and on September 7, 1860, entered Naples, Italy's largest city. He then fought the biggest battle of his career, on the Volturno River north of Naples. After his victory, he held plebiscites in Sicily and Naples, which allowed him to hand over the whole of southern Italy to King Victor Emmanuel. In 1861 a new kingdom of Italy came into existence.

Garibaldi was determined to seize Rome, which was still under the rule of the pope, and make it Italy's capital. Such action would have brought both France and Austria against Italy, though, so the Italian government was forced to intervene and take the radical Garibaldi prisoner after his attempts in 1862 and 1867. In between his attempts on Rome, the Italian government called on Garibaldi for assistance when war broke out with Austria in 1866, and once again he emerged from the war with a good deal more credit than any of the regular soldiers. In 1870–71, Garibaldi led one final campaign, when he assisted the French Republic against Prussia. When the war was over, Garibaldi retired to Caprera, where he spent the rest of his life.

Garibaldi was recognized as a champion of the rights of labour and of women's emancipation. Moreover, he showed himself to be a religious freethinker and ahead of his time in believing in racial equality and the abolition of capital punishment.

ABRAHAM LINCOLN

(b. Feb. 12, 1809, near Hodgenville, Ky., U.S.—d. April 15, 1865, Washington, D.C.)

The 16th president of the United States (1861–65), Abraham Lincoln preserved the Union during the American Civil War and brought about the emancipation of the slaves. His extraordinary ongoing appeal for Americans and also for people of other lands derives from his engaging life story, his distinctively human and humane personality, as well as from the huge shadow he casts on history. His experiences at different points of his life generated the well-known bynames of Honest Abe, the Rail-Splitter, and the Great Emancipator.

Abraham Lincoln, 1863. Library of Congress, Washington, D.C.

EARLY LIFE

Born in a backwoods cabin in Kentucky, Lincoln moved with his family to southwestern Indiana in 1816, then on to Illinois in 1830. A tall and lanky but muscular young man, Lincoln settled in the village of New Salem, working a variety of jobs and serving during the Black Hawk War in 1832, though he saw no real action. Lincoln had little formal education but he loved reading. Having taught himself law, he passed the bar examination in 1836 and soon after moved to Springfield, Illinois.

Abraham Lincoln's boyhood home, Knob Creek, Kentucky, originally built early 19th century. Wettach/ Shostal

In addition to his practice in the capital, he followed the court as it made the rounds of its circuit and handled cases for railroads and other businesses, becoming one of the most distinguished and successful lawyers in Illinois.

Although stories were told of a grand romance in New Salem between Lincoln and Ann Rutledge, who died at age 22, in 1835, they are not supported by sound historical evidence. So far as can be known, the first and only real love of Lincoln's life was Mary Todd, a woman from a distinguished Kentucky family whom he married in 1842. Of their four sons, only Robert, the eldest, survived to

Lincoln Home National Historic Site, Springfield, Illinois. © James P. Rowan

adulthood. During the White House years, Mary, who was emotionally unstable, became deeply disturbed by the death of son Willie at age 11 (she was officially declared insane in 1875).

THE ROAD TO THE PRESIDENCY

Lincoln served as a Whig member of the Illinois State Assembly four times from 1834 to 1840. Although he demonstrated that he opposed slavery, he was no abolitionist. With his "spot resolutions" during his single term in Congress from 1847 to 1849, Lincoln challenged President James K. Polk's claim that the Mexican-

Photo of Abraham Lincoln, 1846. Library of Congress, Washington, D.C.

American War had begun with the shedding of American blood upon American soil. His criticisms of the war were not popular with his constituents, however, and he was not reelected.

Lincoln took little part in politics until 1854, when Stephen A. Douglas maneuvered through Congress the Kansas-Nebraska Act, reopening the Louisiana Purchase to slavery and allowing settlers of Kansas and Nebraska to decide for themselves whether to permit slaveholding. Opposition to the act sped the disintegration of the Whig Party but gave rise to the Republican Party, which Lincoln joined in 1856. He challenged the incumbent Douglas for the Senate seat in 1858, and the series of debates they engaged in throughout Illinois was political oratory of the highest order. In one of his most famous speeches, Lincoln said, "A house divided against itself cannot stand . . . I believe the government cannot endure permanently half slave and half free." Yet he agreed with Thomas Jefferson and other founding fathers that slavery should be merely contained, not directly attacked. In the end, Lincoln lost the election to Douglas but gained national recognition that led to his nomination as the Republic Party's candidate for president in 1860. With the Republicans united, the Democrats divided, and a total of four candidates in the field, he carried the election on November 6.

LEADERSHIP IN WAR

After Lincoln's election, South Carolina withdrew from the Union, followed by six additional states, which joined to form the Confederate States of America (four more states joined later). When Confederate batteries fired on Fort Sumter, a federal installation in Charleston Bay, South Carolina, on April 12, 1861, the Civil War began. Lincoln

Election poster of the Abraham Lincoln and Hannibal Hamlin campaign of 1860, lithograph. Library of Congress, Washington, D.C.

called upon the state governors for troops and proclaimed a blockade of the Southern ports.

As a war leader, he employed the style that had served him as a politician. He preferred to react to problems and to the circumstances that others had created rather than to originate policies and lay out long-range designs. It was not that he was unprincipled; rather, he was a practical man, mentally nimble and flexible. If one action or decision proved unsatisfactory in practice, he was willing to experiment with another. From 1861 to 1864 Lincoln struggled to find a leader for the Union army, passing through a succession of generals before giving command of all of the federal armies to Gen. Ulysses S. Grant, who had won a huge victory in capturing Vicksburg, Mississippi, in July 1863. At last Lincoln had found a man who could execute large-scale, coordinated offensives that Lincoln had conceived. As commander in chief, Lincoln combined statecraft and the overall direction of armies with an effectiveness that increased year by year. His achievement is all the more remarkable in view of his lack of training and experience in the art of warfare.

As president, he was at first reluctant to adopt an abolitionist policy. He especially feared that an abolitionist program might drive the border states to the Confederacy, but on Jan. 1, 1863, Lincoln issued the Emancipation Proclamation. Although it applied only to those parts of the country actually under Confederate control and brought freedom to fewer than 200,000 slaves, it indicated that the Lincoln government had added freedom to reunion as a war aim. However, it took the Thirteenth Amendment to the U.S. Constitution—which Lincoln had seen become a part of the Republican Party's platform of the 1864 election—to end slavery completely.

To win the war, Lincoln had to have popular support from a variety of divergent interest groups in the North, not just in the opposition party—divided among peace Democrats, often referred to as Copperheads, and war Democrats—but within his own Republican Party. Considering the dangers and provocations of the time, he was quite liberal in his treatment of political opponents and the opposition press. He was by no means the dictator critics often accused him of being, though his suspension of the writ of habeas corpus disturbed many.

Two main factions arose among the Republicans regarding the conduct of the war: the "Radicals" and the "Conservatives." Lincoln was inclined toward the Conservatives but strove to maintain his leadership over both. In appointing his cabinet, he chose his several rivals

President Abraham Lincoln (seated centre) and his cabinet, with Lieutenant General Winfield Scott, in the council chamber at the White House, lithograph, 1866. Library of Congress, Washington, D.C.

for the 1860 nomination and, all together, gave representation to every important party group. Lincoln had to deal with even more serious factional uprisings in Congress over the Reconstruction of the South. Lincoln's proposal that new state governments might be formed when 10 percent of the qualified voters had taken an oath of future loyalty to the United States was rejected by the Radicals. They had carried through Congress the Wade-Davis Bill, which would have permitted the remaking and readmission of states only after a majority had taken the loyalty oath. When Lincoln pocket-vetoed that bill, its authors published a "manifesto" denouncing him. Despite this

The Assassination of President Lincoln at Ford's Theatre—After the Act, *wood engraving from* Harper's Weekly, *April 29, 1865.* Library of Congress, Washington, D.C.

dissension, the party united behind the president for the 1864 election, which Lincoln won with a large popular majority over his Democratic opponent, General George B. McClellan.

On the question of Reconstruction, Lincoln and the extremists of his own party stood farther apart in early 1865 than a year before. However, in April 1865 Lincoln began to modify his own stand in some respects to narrow the gap between himself and the Radicals. On the evening of April 14, 1865, John Wilkes Booth—an actor and a rabid advocate of slavery—shot Lincoln as he sat in Ford's Theatre in Washington. Early the next morning, Lincoln died.

OTTO VON BISMARCK

(b. April 1, 1815, Schönhausen, Altmark, Prussia [Germany]—d. July 30, 1898, Friedrichsruh, near Hamburg)

Otto von Bismarck served as prime minister of Prussia from 1862–73 and 1873–90 and was founder and first chancellor (1871–90) of the German Empire.

EARLY YEARS AND CAREER

Bismarck was born in 1815 at Schönhausen, a family estate in Prussia. He studied law at universities in Göttingen and Berlin and then entered the Prussian civil service. After leaving the service, he helped manage the family estates. In 1847 he attended the Prussian United Diet, where his speeches against Jewish emancipation and contemporary liberalism gained him the reputation of a backwoods conservative.

In 1849 Bismarck was elected to the Prussian Chamber of Deputies (the lower chamber of the Prussian Diet) and moved his family to Berlin. At this stage he was far from a German nationalist. In 1851 Frederick William IV appointed Bismarck as the Prussian representative to the federal Diet in Frankfurt, a clear reward for his loyalty to the monarchy. It was in Frankfurt that Bismarck began to reassess his view of German nationalism and the goals of Prussian foreign policy, which he felt relegated Prussia to a status of a second-rate power in central Europe.

PRIME MINISTER

After serving as ambassador to Russia from 1859 to 1862 and France in 1862, he became prime minister and foreign minister of Prussia (1862–71). In 1864 Bismarck led Prussia to ally with Austria in order to provoke war with Denmark. The victorious allies won the duchies of Schleswig and Holstein, but two years later quarrels over the duchies led to war between Prussia and Austria. The defeat of Austria gave Prussia control over the states north of the Main River. In 1867 Bismarck formed them into the North German Confederation, with Prussia as its matrix.

Bismarck set about tying the southern states to the north almost immediately, but all of his efforts failed because of popular opposition in the south. Bismarck then sought to seek conflict with France. If he could not bring the south into a united German nation by reason, he would rely on the passions aroused by war.

He did not have to work too hard to produce a conflict, as relations between Prussia and its age-old enemy France were already tense. France declared war on Prussia on July 19, 1870. The Prussian army, with the armies of the other German states, attacked and defeated the disorganized French. The German states were then united, and Prussia's king, William I, became kaiser (emperor) of the new German Empire. Bismarck, raised to the rank of prince, became chancellor. Bismarck also remained prime minister of Prussia until 1890, apart from a brief period in 1872–73.

IMPERIAL CHANCELLOR

FOREIGN POLICY

After three successful wars, Bismarck saw his task as promoting peace and gaining time so that the powerful German Empire would come to be accepted as natural. In 1873 he embraced a pacific foreign policy when he negotiated the Dreikaiserbund (Three Emperors' League) with Russia and Austria-Hungary. But the alliance did not survive the Russo-Turkish War of 1877. When the Austrians and British threatened war over a Carthaginian peace imposed on Turkey by the Russian victors, Bismarck called for a peace congress in Berlin. The German chancellor succeeded in getting the Russians to moderate their gains, and peace was preserved.

Soon after the conference, Bismarck negotiated a defensive alliance with Austria-Hungary, which remained in effect through World War I. Although in the mid-1860s he had rejected such an alliance as harmful, he now considered it advantageous. Having a solid ally, Bismarck demonstrated his virtuosity by negotiating a revived Dreikaiserbund in 1881. In 1882 Italy, fearing French hostility, joined the Dual Alliance, making it into the Triple Alliance.

But the ephemeral nature of all these alliances soon became apparent. A crisis in Bulgaria inflamed Russo-Austrian relations, leading to a breakup of the revived league. Once again a war was avoided with Bismarck's intervention, but his efforts could not reconstitute the league. He then negotiated a separate secret treaty with Russia, while maintaining the 1879 accord with Austria-Hungary.

DOMESTIC POLICY

From the defeat of Austria in 1866 until 1878 Bismarck was allied primarily with the National Liberals. Liberals now viewed him as a comrade, a man who had rejected his conservative roots. Many conservative leaders agreed with this assessment. Their fears were further enhanced when he joined liberals in a campaign against political Catholicism (Kulturkampf) in 1873. The Kulturkampf failed to achieve its goals and, if anything, convinced the Catholic minority that their fear of persecution was real. Bismarck gradually relented in his campaign, especially after the death of the activist pope, Pius IX, in 1878.

Bismarck had not counted on the emergence of new parties such as the Catholic Centre or the Social Democratic Party, both of whom began participating in imperial and Prussian elections in the early 1870s. Along with the left liberal Progressive Party, he labeled them all enemies of the empire (*Reichsfeinde*) and worked to halt the spread of social democracy.

In 1878–79 Bismarck initiated a significant change in economic policy, which coincided with a new alliance with the conservative parties at the expense of the liberals. Part of Bismarck's strategy to destroy social democracy was the introduction of social legislation to woo the workers away from political radicalism. During the 1880s, accident and old-age insurance as well as a form of socialized medicine were introduced and implemented by the government. But Bismarck did not succeed, and support for the Social Democrats increased with each election.

In 1888 William I was succeeded by his son Frederick III, a sick man who ruled only three months, and Frederick's son became Kaiser William II. Because William II wanted sole power, he forced Bismarck to resign in 1890. Bismarck retired to his estate at Friedrichsruh, where he resided until his death.

During Bismarck's rule, the map of Europe changed immeasurably. However, the German Empire, his greatest achievement, survived him by only 20 years because he had failed to create an internally unified people.

FREDERICK DOUGLASS

(b. February 1818?, Tuckahoe, Md., U.S.—d. Feb. 20, 1895, Washington, D.C.)

Frederick Douglass was one of the most eminent human-rights leaders of the 19th century. His oratorical and literary brilliance thrust him into the forefront of the U.S. abolition movement, and he became the first black citizen to hold high rank in the U.S. government.

Born Frederick Augustus Washington Bailey around 1818, he was separated as an infant from his slave mother and never knew his white father. Frederick lived with his grandmother on a Maryland plantation until, at age eight, his owner sent him to Baltimore to live as a house servant with the family of Hugh Auld, whose wife defied state law by teaching the boy to read. Auld, however, declared that learning would make him unfit for slavery, and Frederick was forced to continue his education surreptitiously with the aid of schoolboys in the street. After the death of his master, he was returned to the plantation as a field hand at 16. Later, he was hired out in Baltimore as a ship caulker. Frederick tried to escape with three others in 1833, but the plot was discovered before they could get away. Five years later, however, he fled to New York City and then to New Bedford, Massachusetts, where he worked as a labourer for three years, eluding slave hunters by changing his surname to Douglass.

At a Nantucket, Massachusetts, antislavery convention in 1841, Douglass was invited to describe his feelings and experiences under slavery. These extemporaneous remarks were so poignant and naturally eloquent that he was unexpectedly catapulted into a new career as agent for the Massachusetts Anti-Slavery Society. From then on, despite heckling and mockery, insult, and violent personal attack, Douglass never flagged in his devotion to the abolitionist cause.

To counter skeptics who doubted that such an articulate spokesman could ever have been a slave, Douglass felt impelled to write his autobiography in 1845, revised and completed in 1882 as *Life and Times of Frederick Douglass*. Douglass's account became a classic in American

Frederick Douglass. Courtesy of the Holt-Messer Collection, Schlesinger Library, Radcliffe College, Cambridge, Mass.

literature as well as a primary source about slavery from the bondsman's viewpoint. To avoid recapture by his former owner, whose name and location he had given in the narrative, Douglass left on a two-year speaking tour of Great Britain and Ireland. Abroad, Douglass helped to win many new friends for the abolition movement and to cement the bonds of humanitarian reform between the continents.

Douglass returned with funds to purchase his freedom and also to start his own anti-slavery newspaper, the *North Star* (later *Frederick Douglass's Paper*), which he published from 1847 to 1860 in Rochester, New York. The abolition leader William Lloyd Garrison disagreed with the need for a separate, black-oriented press, and the two men broke over this issue as well as over Douglass's support of political action to supplement moral influence. Thus, after 1851 Douglass allied himself with the faction of the movement led by James G. Birney. He did not countenance violence, however, and specifically counseled against the raid on Harpers Ferry, Virginia in October 1859.

During the Civil War (1861–65) Douglass became a consultant to President Abraham Lincoln, advocating that former slaves be armed for the North and that the war be made a direct confrontation against slavery. Throughout Reconstruction (1865–77), he fought for full civil rights for freedmen and vigorously supported the women's rights movement.

After Reconstruction, Douglass served as assistant secretary of the Santo Domingo Commission in 1871, and in the District of Columbia he was marshal (1877–81) and recorder of deeds (1881–86). Finally, he was appointed U.S. minister and consul general to Haiti (1889–91).

VICTORIA

(b. May 24, 1819, Kensington Palace, London, Eng. — d. Jan. 22, 1901, Osborne, near Cowes, Isle of Wight)

Alexandrina Victoria was queen of the United Kingdom of Great Britain and Ireland from 1837 to 1901 and empress of India from 1876 to 1901. She gave her name to an era, the Victorian Age.

ACCESSION TO THE THRONE AND EARLY YEARS OF REIGN

EARLY LIFE AND DOMESTIC AFFAIRS

The only child of Edward, duke of Kent, Victoria succeeded her uncle, William IV, in 1837. Initially Queen Victoria was guided by her first prime minister, Lord Melbourne, with whom she had a romantic friendship. In 1839, Victoria met and fell in love with Prince Albert of Saxe-Coburg-Gotha, her first cousin; they were married the next year. Marriage to Albert lessened the queen's enthusiasm for the influence of Melbourne, who had resigned in 1839. Albert shifted Victoria's political sympathies. He also became the dominant figure and influence in her life.

For both the queen and the prince consort, the highlight of their reign came in 1851, with the opening of the Great Exhibition. Albert poured himself into the task of organizing the international trade show that became a symbol of the Victorian Age. Housed in the architectural marvel of the Crystal Palace, a splendid, greenhouse-inspired glass building erected in Hyde Park, the Great Exhibition displayed Britain's wealth and technological achievements to a wondering world.

FOREIGN AFFAIRS

Albert and Victoria felt that the sovereign had a special part to play in foreign affairs and could conduct them alone with a secretary of state. They had relatives throughout Europe whom they visited and were visited by other monarchs as well. They often had their own opinions on international affairs, and, as a result, were known to clash with Lord Palmerston, the foreign secretary, who already had a long career that began before the royal couple was born.

Nonetheless, the foreign secretary continued to follow policies disapproved of by both Albert and Victoria. Finally, after Palmerston expressed his approval of the coup d'état of Louis Napoleon (later Napoleon III) in 1851 without consulting the queen, the prime minister, Lord John Russell, dismissed him. Within a few months the immensely popular Palmerston was back in office, however, as home secretary. He would serve twice as prime minister. After Albert's death Victoria's disapproval of Palmerston would diminish, as his conservative domestic policy and insistence that Britain receive its due in world affairs accorded with her own later views.

On the eve of the Crimean War (1854–56) the royal pair encountered a wave of unpopularity, and Albert was suspected, without any foundation, of trying to influence the government in favour of the Russian cause. There was, however, a marked revival of royalist sentiment as the war wore on. The queen personally superintended the committees of ladies who organized relief for the wounded and eagerly seconded the efforts of Florence Nightingale. She visited crippled soldiers in the hospitals and instituted the Victoria Cross for gallantry.

With the death of Prince Albert on Dec. 14, 1861, the Albertine monarchy came to an end, although Albert's influence on the queen was lasting. He had changed her personal habits and her political sympathies. From him she had received training in orderly ways of business, in hard work, in the expectation of royal intervention in ministry making at home, and in the establishment of a private intelligence service abroad.

WIDOWHOOD

After Albert's death Victoria descended into deep depression. Even after climbing out of depression, she remained in mourning and in partial retirement. After an initial period of respect and sympathy for the queen's grief, the public grew increasingly impatient with its absent sovereign. No one, however, could budge the stubborn Victoria.

Victoria was frequently at odds with Prime Minister William Gladstone, and welcomed his replacement, Benjamin Disraeli, in 1874. Disraeli, Gladstone's political rival, was able to enter into the queen's grief, flatter her, restore her self-confidence, and make the lonely crown an easier burden. Disraeli, moreover, had told the queen in 1868 that it would be "his delight and duty, to render the transaction of affairs as easy to your Majesty, as possible." Since the queen was only too ready to consider herself overworked, this approach was especially successful.

One of the bonds shared by Victoria and Disraeli was a romantic attachment to the East and the idea of empire. She was entranced by his imperialism and by his assertive foreign policy. She applauded his brilliant maneuvering, which led to the British purchase of slightly less than half of the shares in the Suez Canal in 1875 (a move that prevented the canal from falling entirely under French control). The addition of "Empress of India" in 1876 to the royal title thrilled the queen even more.

Disraeli's fall from power in 1880 was a blow to the queen, even more so because Gladstone was once again prime minister. She made no secret of her hostility. The queen abhorred Gladstone's lack of Disraelian vision of Britain's role in the world, and convinced herself that Gladstone's government, which she believed to be dominated by radicals, threatened the stability of the nation. Nevertheless, Victoria did act as an important mediating influence between the two houses to bring about the compromise that resulted in the third parliamentary Reform Act in 1884.

LAST YEARS AND LEGACY

In the administration of Lord Robert Salisbury (1895–1902), during which time her long reign ended, Victoria was to find not only the sort of ministry with which she felt comfortable but one which lent a last ray of colour to her closing years by its alliance with the mounting imperialism that she had so greatly enjoyed in Disraeli's day.

The queen died after a short and painless illness. She was buried beside Prince Albert in the mausoleum at Frogmore near Windsor.

Victoria's essential achievement was simple. By the length of her reign (64 years), the longest in English history, she had restored both dignity and popularity to a tarnished crown—an achievement of character, as well as of longevity. It was during her reign that the English monarchy took on its modern ceremonial character.

She and Albert had nine children, through whose marriages were descended many of the royal families of Europe. By the end of the 19th century, Victoria had so many royal relatives that she was called the "grandmother of Europe."

SITTING BULL

(b. *c.* 1831, near Grand River, Dakota Territory [now in South Dakota], U.S.—d. Dec. 15, 1890, on the Grand River in South Dakota)

S itting Bull was the Teton Dakota Indian chief under whom the Sioux tribes united in their struggle for survival on the North American Great Plains. He is remembered for his lifelong distrust of white men and his stubborn determination to resist their domination.

Sitting Bull was born into the Hunkpapa division of the Teton Sioux. His Indian name was Tatanka Iyotake. He joined his first war party at age 14 and soon gained a reputation for fearlessness in battle. He became a leader of the powerful Strong Heart warrior society and, later, was a participant in the Silent Eaters, a select group concerned with tribal welfare. As a tribal leader, Sitting Bull helped extend the Sioux hunting grounds westward into what had been the territory of the Shoshone, Crow, Assiniboin, and other Indian tribes. His first skirmish with white soldiers occurred in June 1863 during the U.S. Army's retaliation against the Santee Sioux after the Minnesota Massacre, in which the Teton Sioux had no part. For the next five years, he was in frequent hostile contact with the army, which was invading the Sioux hunting grounds and bringing ruin to the Indian economy. In 1866 he became principal chief of the northern hunting Sioux, with Crazy Horse— leader of the Oglala Sioux—as his vice-chief. Respected for his courage and wisdom, Sitting Bull was made principal chief of the entire Sioux nation about 1867.

In 1868 the Sioux accepted peace with the U.S. government on the basis of the Second Treaty of Fort Laramie, which guaranteed the Sioux a reservation in what is now southwestern South Dakota. But when gold was discovered in the Black Hills in the mid-1870s, a rush of white prospectors invaded lands guaranteed to the Indians by the treaty. Late in 1875 those Sioux who had been resisting the whites' incursions were ordered to return to their reservations by Jan. 31, 1876, or be considered hostile to the United States. Even had Sitting Bull been willing to comply, he could not possibly have moved his village 240 miles (390 km) in the bitter cold by the specified time.

In March General George Crook took the field against the hostiles, and Sitting Bull responded by summoning the Sioux, Cheyenne, and certain Arapaho to his camp in Montana Territory. There on June 17, Crook's troops were forced to retreat in the Battle of the Rosebud. The Indian chiefs then moved their encampment into the valley of the Little Bighorn River. At this point Sitting Bull performed the Sun Dance, and when he emerged from a trance induced by self-torture, he reported that he had seen soldiers falling into his camp like grasshoppers from the sky. His prophecy was fulfilled on June 25, when Lieutenant Colonel George Armstrong Custer rode into the valley, and he and all the men under his immediate command were annihilated in the Battle of the Little Bighorn.

Strong public reaction among whites to the Battle of the Little Bighorn resulted in stepped-up military action. The Sioux emerged the victors in their battles with U.S. troops, but while they might win battle after battle, they could never win the war. They depended on the buffalo for their livelihood, and the buffalo, under the steady encroachment of whites, were rapidly becoming extinct.

Hunger led more and more Sioux to surrender, and in May 1877, Sitting Bull led his remaining followers across the border into Canada. But the Canadian government could not acknowledge responsibility for feeding a people whose reservation was south of the border and, after four years during which his following dwindled steadily, famine forced Sitting Bull to surrender. After 1883 he lived at the Standing Rock Agency, where he vainly opposed the sale of tribal lands. In 1885, partly to get rid of him, the Indian agent allowed him to join Buffalo Bill's Wild West show, in which he gained international fame.

The year 1889 saw the spread of the Ghost Dance religious movement, which prophesied the advent of an Indian messiah who would sweep away the whites and restore the Indians' former traditions. The Ghost Dance movement augmented the unrest already stirring among the Sioux by hunger and disease. Out of fear that Sitting Bull would use his influence to promote the movement, Indian police and soldiers were sent to arrest the chief. Seized on Grand River, December 15, 1890, Sitting Bull was killed while his warriors were trying to rescue him. He was buried at Fort Yates, but his remains were moved in 1953 to Mobridge, South Dakota, where a granite shaft marks his resting place.

THEODORE ROOSEVELT

(b. Oct. 27, 1858, New York, N.Y., U.S.—d. Jan. 6, 1919, Oyster Bay, N.Y.)

Theodore Roosevelt, also known as Teddy or TR, was the 26th president of the United States, from 1901 to 1909. He was also a writer, naturalist, and soldier. He won the Nobel Prize for Peace in 1906 for mediating an end to the Russo-Japanese War.

Portrait of Theodore Roosevelt. Encyclopædia Britannica, Inc.

The Early Years

In frail health as a boy, Roosevelt was educated by private tutors. He graduated from Harvard College, where he was elected to Phi Beta Kappa, in 1880. He then studied briefly at Columbia Law School but soon turned to writing and politics as a career.

Elected as a Republican to the New York State Assembly at 23, Roosevelt quickly made a name for himself as a foe of corrupt machine politics. In 1884, overcome by grief by the deaths of both his mother and his first wife, Alice, on the same day, he left politics to spend two years on his cattle ranch in the badlands of the Dakota Territory, where he became increasingly concerned about environmental damage to the West and its wildlife.

Roosevelt attempted to return to politics in 1886 with an unsuccessful run for New York City mayor. In 1897, Roosevelt was appointed assistant secretary of the navy by President William McKinley, and he vociferously championed a bigger navy and agitated for war with Spain. When war was declared in 1898, he organized the 1st Volunteer Cavalry, known as the Rough Riders, who were sent to fight in Cuba. The charge of the Rough Riders, who were on foot, up Kettle Hill during the Battle of Santiago made Roosevelt the biggest national hero to come out of the Spanish-American War.

Upon his return, Roosevelt was elected governor of New York, and was an energetic reformer. His actions irked the Republican Party's bosses so much that they conspired to get rid of him by drafting him for the Republican vice presidential nomination in 1900, assuming that his would be a largely ceremonial role. He became vice president when William McKinley was re-elected.

Theodore Roosevelt as a young man. Encyclopædia Britannica, Inc.

On September 14, 1901, McKinley died after being shot by an assassin, and Roosevelt became president. He was the youngest person ever to enter the presidency, and he transformed the public image of the office at once. He renamed the executive mansion the White House, and his young children from his second wife, Edith, romped on the White House lawn. From what he called the presidency's "bully pulpit," Roosevelt gave speeches aimed at raising public consciousness about various issues. His refusal to shoot a bear cub on a 1902 hunting trip inspired a toy maker to name a stuffed bear after him, and the teddy bear fad soon swept the nation.

THE SQUARE DEAL

In 1902 Roosevelt cajoled Republican conservatives into creating the Bureau of Corporations with the power to investigate businesses engaged in interstate commerce but without regulatory powers. He also resurrected the nearly defunct Sherman Antitrust Act by bringing a successful suit to break up a huge railroad conglomerate. Roosevelt pursued this policy of trust-busting by initiating suits against 43 other major corporations during the next seven years.

Also in 1902 Roosevelt intervened in the anthracite coal strike, when he publicly asked representatives of capital and labour to meet in the White House and accept his mediation. His tactics worked to end the strike and gain a modest pay hike for the miners. Roosevelt characterized his actions as striving toward a Square Deal between capital and labour, and those words became his campaign slogan in the 1904 election.

After he was reelected, Roosevelt pushed Congress to grant powers to the Interstate Commerce Commission to regulate interstate railroad rates. The Hepburn Act of 1906 conveyed those powers and created the federal government's first true regulatory agency. Also in 1906, Roosevelt pressed Congress to pass the Pure Food and Drug and Meat Inspection acts, which created agencies to assure protection to consumers.

Roosevelt's boldest actions came in the area of natural resources. At his urging, Congress created the Forest Service (1905) to manage government-owned forest reserves. Simultaneously, Roosevelt exercised existing presidential authority to designate public lands as national forests, setting aside almost five times as much land as all of his predecessors combined.

The end of Roosevelt's presidency was tempestuous. His already strained relations with Republican conservatives

Theodore Roosevelt photographed in Colorado in 1905. Library of Congress, Washington, D.C.

in Congress degenerated into a spiteful stalemate that blocked any further domestic reforms.

Foreign Policy

Every year Roosevelt asked for bigger appropriations for the army and navy. By the end of his presidency, he had built the U.S. Navy into a major force at sea and reorganized the army along efficient, modern lines.

Several times during Roosevelt's first years in office, European powers threatened to intervene in Latin America. As a result, in 1904, he issued the Roosevelt Corollary to the Monroe Doctrine. It stated that the United States would not only bar outside intervention in Latin American affairs but would also police the area and guarantee that countries there met their international obligations.

Quoting an African proverb, Roosevelt claimed that the right way to conduct foreign policy was to "speak softly and carry a big stick." Roosevelt resorted to big-stick diplomacy most conspicuously in 1903, when he helped Panama to secede from Colombia and give the United States the Canal Zone. Roosevelt showed the soft-spoken, sophisticated side of his diplomacy in dealing with major powers outside the Western Hemisphere as well. In 1904–05 he worked to end the Russo-Japanese War by bringing both nations to the Portsmouth Peace Conference and mediating between them. For his efforts, he won the Nobel Peace Prize in 1906.

During his second term Roosevelt increasingly feared a general European war. In 1906, when France and Germany were ready to fight over their interests in Morocco, Roosevelt took the lead in arranging a conference of the powers in Algeciras, Spain. This meeting temporarily settled the differences.

LATER YEARS

Immediately upon leaving office in 1909, Roosevelt embarked on a 10-month hunting safari in Africa and toured Europe. Upon his return, he was once again drawn to politics. Both policy differences and personal animosity eventually impelled Roosevelt to run against William Howard Taft for the Republican nomination in 1912. When that quest failed, he formed the Progressive Party, nicknamed the Bull Moose Party. In the presidential campaign as the new party's candidate, Roosevelt espoused a New Nationalism that would inspire greater government regulation of the economy and promotion of social

Theodore Roosevelt riding a horse. Encyclopædia Britannica, Inc.

welfare. He lost the election to the Democratic candidate, Woodrow Wilson.

Roosevelt died in early January 1919, less than three months after his 60th birthday.

MOHANDAS KARAMCHAND GANDHI
(b. Oct. 2, 1869, Porbandar, India—d. Jan. 30, 1948, Delhi)

M ohandas Karamchand Gandhi was the leader of the Indian nationalist movement against British rule and is considered to be the father of his country. Known as Mahatma ("Great-Souled"), he is internationally esteemed for his doctrine of nonviolent protest to achieve political and social progress.

EARLY YEARS AND EDUCATION IN ENGLAND

Gandhi was born in Porbandar, near Bombay (Mumbai) in 1869. His family belonged to the Hindu merchant caste Vaisya, and his father had been prime minister of several small native states. Gandhi grew up in a home steeped in Vaishnavism—worship of the Hindu god Vishnu—with a strong tinge of Jainism, a morally rigorous Indian religion, whose chief tenets are nonviolence and the belief that everything in the universe is eternal. Thus he took for granted *ahimsa* (noninjury to all living beings), vegetarianism, fasting for self-purification, and mutual tolerance between adherents of various creeds and sects.

Gandhi was married when he was only 13 years old. When he was 19, he went abroad to study law at University College London. Gandhi took his studies seriously. But, during the three years he spent in England, his main preoccupation was with personal and moral issues rather than with academic ambitions. The transition from the half-rural atmosphere of his home in India to the cosmopolitan life of London was not easy for him. As he struggled painfully to adapt himself to Western food, dress, and etiquette, he felt awkward. During this time he took solace in reading philosophical tomes, and he discovered the principle of nonviolence as enunciated in Henry David Thoreau's "Civil Disobedience."

South African Activist

In 1891 Gandhi returned to India. Unsuccessful in Bombay due to the overcrowded legal profession there, in 1893 he accepted an offer of a year's contract from an Indian law firm in the British colony of Natal in South Africa. At Natal he built a large practice. His interest soon turned to the problem of fellow Indians who had come to South Africa as labourers. He had seen how they were treated as inferiors in India, in England, and then in South Africa. In 1894 he founded the Natal Indian Congress to agitate for Indian rights. Yet he remained loyal to the British Empire. In 1899, during the South African War, he raised an ambulance corps and served the South African government. Later in 1906, however, Gandhi began his peaceful revolution. Thousands of Indians joined him in this civil disobedience campaign. He was imprisoned twice. Yet in World War I he again organized an ambulance corps for the British before returning home to India in 1914.

Emergence as Leader of Nationalist India

From 1915 to 1918, Gandhi seemed to hover uncertainly on the periphery of Indian politics. Not until February 1919, provoked by the British insistence on pushing through the Rowlatt Bills—which empowered the authorities to

Mohandas K. Gandhi (front left) *and other delegates attending the Round Table Conference in London, 1931.* Encyclopædia Britannica, Inc.

imprison without trial those suspected of sedition—did Gandhi reveal a sense of estrangement from the British Raj. He announced a *satyagraha* struggle, or nonviolent resistance. The result was a virtual political earthquake that shook the subcontinent in the spring of 1919. The violent outbreaks that followed—leading, among other incidents, to the killing by British-led soldiers of nearly 400 Indians and the enactment of martial law—prompted him to stay his hand for the time being.

By the autumn of 1920, Gandhi was the dominant figure on the political stage. He refashioned the 35-year-old Indian National Congress into an effective political instrument of Indian nationalism. Gandhi launched a nonviolent non-cooperation campaign against Britain, urging Indians to spin their own cotton and to boycott British goods, courts, and government. This program electrified the country, broke the spell of fear of foreign rule, and led to arrests of thousands of *satyagrahis*, who defied laws and cheerfully lined up for prison. Gandhi himself was arrested on March 10, 1922, tried for sedition, and sentenced to six years' imprisonment. He was released in February 1924, after an operation for appendicitis. The political landscape had changed in his absence. The Congress Party had split into two factions, one under Chitta Ranjan Das and Motilal Nehru favouring the entry of the party into legislatures and the other under C. Rajagopalachari and Vallabhbhai Jhaverbhai Patel opposing it.

Gandhi later came back to the helm of the Congress Party. In March 1930, he launched the *satyagraha* against the tax on salt, which affected the poorest section of the community. He led thousands of Indians on a 200-mile (320-kilometer) march to the sea to make their own salt. One of the most spectacular and successful campaigns in Gandhi's nonviolent war against the British, it resulted in the imprisonment of more than 60,000 persons. A year later, Gandhi accepted a truce, called off civil disobedience, and agreed to attend the Round Table Conference in London as the sole representative of the Indian National Congress. The conference, which concentrated on the problem of the Indian minorities rather than on the transfer of power from the British, was a great disappointment to the Indian nationalists. Moreover, when Gandhi returned to India in December 1931 he found his party facing an all-out offensive, as the colonial administration unleashed the sternest repression in the history of the nationalist movement. Gandhi was once more imprisoned for a time, and the government tried to insulate him from the outside world and destroy his influence.

In 1934 Gandhi retired as head of the party but remained its actual leader. Gradually he became convinced that India would receive no real freedom as long as it remained in the British Empire. Early in World War II he demanded immediate independence as India's price for aiding Britain in the war. He was imprisoned for the third time, from 1942 to 1944.

Gandhi's victory came in 1947 when India won independence. However, the subcontinent was split into two countries (India and Pakistan) and incited Hindu-Muslim riots. On January 30, 1948, while on his way to an evening prayer meeting, Gandhi was killed by Nathuram Godse, a young Hindu fanatic who had been maddened by the Mahatma's efforts to reconcile Hindus and Muslims.

VLADIMIR ILICH LENIN

(b. April 10 [April 22, New Style], 1870, Simbirsk, Russia—d. Jan. 21, 1924, Gorki [later Gorki Leninskiye], near Moscow)

Vladimir Ilich Lenin was the founder of the Russian Communist Party (Bolsheviks), inspirer and leader of the Bolshevik Revolution in 1917, and the first head of the Soviet state.

Early Life

Born Vladimir Ilich Ulyanov into a middle-class family, Lenin nevertheless became an advocate of Marxism in 1889. In 1891 he received a degree in law from St. Petersburg University. He moved to St. Petersburg in August 1893 and, while working as a public defender, associated with revolutionary Marxist circles. His comrades sent him abroad to make contact with Russian exiles in western Europe, and, upon his return in 1895, Lenin and other Marxists succeeded in unifying the Marxist groups of the capital. In December 1895 he and other Marxist leaders were arrested. Lenin was jailed for 15 months and thereafter was sent into exile in Siberia for three years.

After 1900, Lenin lived mostly in western Europe. While in Germany, he and other comrades developed the newspaper *Iskra* ("The Spark"), which they hoped would unify the Russian Marxist groups into a cohesive Social-Democratic party.

Iskra's success in recruiting Russian intellectuals to Marxism led Lenin and his comrades to believe that the time was ripe for a revolutionary Marxist party. In 1903 an organizing committee for the Russian Social-Democratic Workers' Party (RSDWP) was convened in London, where Lenin emerged as the leader of the Bolshevik faction. He put forth his theory of the party as the vanguard of the proletariat, a centralized body organized around a core of professional revolutionaries. His ideas, later known as Leninism, would be joined with Karl Marx's theories to form Marxism-Leninism.

Challenges of the Revolution of 1905 and World War I

With the outbreak of the Russian Revolution of 1905, Lenin returned to Russia. By then, clear differences had emerged between Lenin and Mensheviks ("minoritarians") within the RSDWP. The Mensheviks argued that the bourgeois revolution must be led by the bourgeoisie, or middle class, with whom the proletariat, or working class, must ally itself in order to make the democratic revolution. Lenin defiantly rejected this kind of alliance. Hitherto he had spoken of the need for the proletariat to win hegemony in the democratic revolution. Now he flatly declared that the proletariat was the driving force of the revolution and that its only reliable ally was the peasantry. The bourgeoisie he branded as hopelessly counterrevolutionary and too cowardly.

The 1905 revolution failed, and in 1907 Lenin was forced again into exile. When World War I broke out, socialist parties throughout Europe rallied behind their governments, despite being obliged by the resolutions of prewar congresses to resist or even overthrow their respective governments if they plunged their countries into an imperialist war. Lenin denounced the prowar socialists, arguing that the real enemy of the worker was not the worker in the opposite trench but the capitalist at home.

By 1917 it seemed to Lenin that the war would never end and that the prospect of revolution was receding. But in March, the starving, freezing, war-weary workers and soldiers of Petrograd—St. Petersburg until 1914—succeeded in deposing the tsar. Lenin and his closest lieutenants hastened home from Germany, as German officials believed that their return would undermine the Russian war effort.

By the time Lenin arrived in Petrograd in April, a provisional government had been formed by leaders of the bourgeois liberal parties. Lenin believed this government incapable of satisfying the desires of the workers, soldiers, and peasants and that only a soviet government—that is, direct rule by workers, soldiers, and peasants—could fulfill these demands. The Bolsheviks, Lenin exhorted, must persuade these people to retrieve state power for the soviets from the provisional government.

Leadership in the Russian Revolution

From March to September 1917, the Bolsheviks remained a minority in the soviets. By autumn, however, the provisional government had lost popular support. Lenin had gone underground in July after he was accused of being a "German agent." Around October 20, Lenin slipped into Petrograd. A few days later, he attended a secret meeting of the Bolshevik Central Committee. After heated debate he convinced the majority to prepare for an armed takeover.

On November 7 and 8, the Bolshevik-led Red Guards and revolutionary soldiers and sailors deposed the provisional government. Lenin was elected chairman of the Council of People's Commissars, heading the revolutionary government of the largest country in the world.

Opposition groups were banned, and newspapers and journals of other political groups were shut down. Banks and industries throughout the country were placed under the control of the new government. The Bolshevik government outlawed trade and the ownership of most private property. Lenin argued that the severe measures would facilitate the immediate transition to socialism in Russia.

Lenin immediately opened negotiations with Germany to end the war between the two countries. The German government demanded exorbitant concessions from Lenin's government, including the Russian territories of Poland, the Caucasus, and Ukraine. When the terms of the proposed peace agreement became known, Lenin's political opponents accused the Bolsheviks of outright treason. Nevertheless, in March 1918 the Bolshevik government hesitatingly signed the Brest-Litovsk peace agreement, ending the war with Germany. The treaty sparked civil war in Russia, which raged for three years.

Lenin instituted drastic measures known as War Communism, designed to aid the Red Army war effort against the Whites. Groups of armed brigades were sent to the countryside to appropriate by force food from the peasantry. A new secret police, named the Cheka, was formed by Lenin to weed out criminals, political opponents, and counterrevolutionary agitators. In July 1918, the Bolshevik government issued the most notorious of its edicts when, fearing a promonarchist backlash, it ordered Red Army troops to carry out the murder of Russian emperor Nicholas II and his entire family.

The civil war exacted its toll on Russia and on Lenin. By the time of the final Bolshevik victory in 1921, the country lay in absolute ruin. Lenin then instituted the New Economic Policy, which allowed for a modest resumption of capitalist relations. Other restrictions were gradually reduced but never repealed. Lenin suffered two strokes in 1922 and a third in 1923 that severely impaired his ability to function. A final stroke on January 21, 1924, ended his life.

SIR WINSTON CHURCHILL

(b. Nov. 30, 1874, Blenheim Palace, Oxfordshire, Eng. — d. Jan. 24, 1965, London)

S tatesman, orator, and author Sir Winston Leonard Spencer Churchill twice served as prime minister of

Winston Churchill, photographed by Yousuf Karsh, 1941. Karsh/Woodfin Camp and Associates

the United Kingdom (1940–45, 1951–55), rallying the British people during World War II and leading his country from the brink of defeat to victory.

POLITICAL CAREER BEFORE 1939

After graduation from the Royal Military College at Sandhurst and service as a subaltern (1895–99) and war correspondent in Cuba, India, and South Africa, Churchill entered politics as a Conservative and won a seat in Parliament in 1900. In 1904, however, he broke with his party, joined the Liberals, and in 1906 became undersecretary of state for the colonies in a Liberal government. In 1908 Churchill became a member of the Cabinet, first holding the post of president of the Board of Trade and later that of home secretary. Transferred to the Admiralty in 1911, he strengthened the British navy. But after World War I broke out, and after the failure of the Dardanelles expedition he had promoted, Churchill resigned from his post with the Admiralty and served as an active military officer from 1915 to 1916. He returned to Parliament as a private member in 1916, then as minister of munitions (1917–18).

After the war, Churchill, while serving as secretary of war (1919–21), as head of the Colonial Office (1921–22), and chancellor of the Exchequer (1924–29), became increasingly conservative. By 1931, when a national government was formed, Churchill had arrived at a point where he was distrusted by every party. He was thought to lack judgment and stability and was regarded as a guerrilla fighter impatient of discipline.

In this situation Churchill found relief, as well as profit, in writing. But he had mounting anxiety about the growing menace of Adolf Hitler's Germany. Before a passive government and a doubting opposition, Churchill persistently argued the case for taking the German threat seriously. When Stanley Baldwin became prime minister in 1935, he excluded Churchill from office but gave him the exceptional privilege of membership in the secret committee on air-defense research.

When Neville Chamberlain succeeded Baldwin, the gulf between the Churchill and the Conservative leaders widened. Repeatedly the accuracy of Churchill's information on Germany's aggressive plans and progress was confirmed by events. His warnings were ignored. As German pressure mounted on Czechoslovakia, Churchill unsuccessfully urged the government to effect a joint declaration of purpose by Great Britain, France, and the Soviet Union. When the Munich Agreement with Hitler was made in September 1938, sacrificing Czechoslovakia to the Nazis, Churchill laid bare its implications, insisting that it represented "a total and unmitigated defeat." In March 1939 Churchill pressed for a truly national coalition, and, at last, sentiment in the country, recognizing him as the nation's spokesman, began to push for his return to office.

Leadership during World War II

On September 3, 1939, Britain declared war on Germany, and Chamberlain appointed Churchill to his old post in charge of the Admiralty. Following the German invasion of the Low Countries, on May 10, 1940, Chamberlain resigned. It was obvious that Churchill alone could unite and lead the nation, since the Labour Party, for all its old distrust of Churchill's anti-Socialism, recognized the depth of his commitment to the defeat of Hitler. A coalition government, which included all elements save the far left and right, was formed. Churchill concentrated on the actual conduct of the war. He delegated freely but also probed and interfered continuously, regarding nothing as too large or too small for his attention.

At the moment Churchill took office, Germany was sweeping Europe. Yet Churchill stood firm before the British people and declared, "I have nothing to offer but blood, toil, tears, and sweat." He promised "to wage war against a monstrous tyranny, never surpassed in the dark, lamentable catalogue of human crime." His thundering defiance and courage heartened Britain, and his two fingers raised in the "V for Victory" sign became an international symbol for determination and hope.

After the Allied defeat and the evacuation of the battered British forces from Dunkirk in 1940, Churchill warned Parliament that invasion was a real risk to be met with total and confident defiance. Faced with the swift collapse of France, Churchill made repeated personal visits to the French government in an attempt to keep France in the war, culminating in the celebrated offer of Anglo-French union on June 16, 1940. When all this failed, the Battle of Britain began. Here Churchill was in his element, in the firing line—at fighter headquarters, inspecting coast defenses or antiaircraft batteries, visiting scenes of bomb damage or victims of the blitz, smoking his cigar, giving his V sign, and broadcasting frank reports to the nation, which were laced with touches of grim Churchillian humour and splashed with Churchillian rhetoric. The nation took him to its heart; he and they were one in "their finest hour."

Before the United States entered the war, Churchill obtained American destroyers and lend-lease aid and met with President Roosevelt in 1941 to draw up the Atlantic Charter. Later he helped plan overall Allied strategy. Although Churchill held that international communism was a threat to peace, he worked with Soviet Premier Joseph Stalin for the defeat of the common enemy—Nazi Germany.

Ultimately, the Allies turned the war in their favour. Churchill's focus on military matters did not mean indifference to its political implications. In 1944 he flew to Moscow to try to conciliate the Russians and the Poles and to get an agreed division of spheres of influence in the Balkans, which would protect as much of them as possible from communism. In Greece Churchill used British forces to thwart a communist takeover, and at Christmas, he flew to Athens to effect a settlement. Much of what passed at the Yalta Conference in February 1945, including the Far East settlement, concerned only Roosevelt and Stalin, and Churchill did not interfere. He fought to save the Poles but saw clearly enough that there was no way to force the Soviets to keep their promises. Realizing this, he urged the United States to allow the Allied forces to thrust as far into eastern Europe as possible before the Russian armies should fill the vacuum left by German power, but he could not win over the Americans. He went to Potsdam in July 1945 in a worried mood. But in the final decisions of the conference he had no part. Halfway through, news came of his government's defeat in parliamentary elections, and he returned to England to tender his resignation.

POSTWAR POLITICAL CAREER

Churchill then entered the House of Commons as "leader of His Majesty's loyal opposition." His flair for colourful speech endured. During a visit to the United States, at Fulton, Missouri, on March 5, 1946, he declared: "From

Stettin in the Baltic to Trieste in the Adriatic an iron curtain has descended over the Continent." "Iron curtain" soon became the term for the barrier between the West and areas under Soviet control.

In 1951 Churchill was again chosen as prime minister, and he resigned in 1955. In 1953 he was knighted by Queen Elizabeth II and received the Nobel Prize for Literature. By an act of Congress, Churchill was made an honourary citizen of the United States in 1963.

MOHAMMED ALI JINNAH

(b. Dec. 25, 1876, Karachi, India [now in Pakistan]—d. Sept. 11, 1948, Karachi)

Mohammed Ali Jinnah was the founder and first governor-general of Pakistan from 1947 to 1948, and is known in Pakistan as Qaid-i-Azam, or Great Leader.

EARLY YEARS

Born in 1876, Jinnah was the first of seven children of Jinnahbhai, a prosperous merchant. After being taught at home, Jinnah was sent to the Sind Madrasat al-Islam in 1887. Later he attended the Christian Missionary Society High School in Karachi, where at the age of 16 he passed the matriculation examination of the University of Bombay (now University of Mumbai). He studied law in London, England, from 1892 to 1896. He practiced law for 10 years before entering politics.

ENTRY INTO POLITICS

Jinnah was elected to India's Imperial Legislative Council in 1910. Committed to home rule for India and to maintaining Hindu-Muslim unity, he held off on joining the

Muslim League until 1913 and worked to ensure its collaboration with the Hindu Indian National Congress.

Jinnah's endeavours to bring about the political union of Hindus and Muslims earned him the title of "the best ambassador of Hindu-Muslim unity." It was largely through his efforts that the Congress and the Muslim League began to hold their annual sessions jointly, to facilitate mutual consultation and participation. In 1915 the two organizations held their meetings in Bombay (later Mumbai) and in 1916 in Lucknow, where the Lucknow Pact was concluded. Under the terms of the pact, the two organizations put their seal to a scheme of constitutional reform that became their joint demand vis-à-vis the British government. There was a good deal of give and take, but the Muslims obtained one important concession in the shape of separate electorates, already conceded to them by the government in 1909 but previously resisted by the Congress.

The emergence of Mahatma Gandhi and a series of Hindu revivalist movements drove a wedge between the two religious factions in the 1920s and 1930s. Frustrated, Jinnah moved to London in 1930. He remained there until 1935, when constitutional changes were in progress, and he was persuaded to return home to head a reconstituted Muslim League.

Soon preparations started for the elections under the Government of India Act of 1935. Jinnah was still thinking in terms of cooperation between the Muslim League and the Hindu Congress and with coalition governments in the provinces. But the elections of 1937 proved to be a turning point in the relations between the two organizations. The Congress obtained an absolute majority in six provinces, and the League did not do particularly well. The Congress decided not to include the League in the formation of provincial governments, resulting in an exclusive all-Congress government. Relations between Hindus and Muslims started to deteriorate, and soon Muslim discontent became boundless.

CREATOR OF PAKISTAN

Jinnah had originally been dubious about the practicality of Pakistan, an idea that Sir Muḥammad Iqbāl had propounded to the Muslim League conference of 1930. But before long he became convinced that a Muslim homeland on the Indian subcontinent was the only way of safeguarding Muslim interests and the Muslim way of life. He converted the Muslim League into a powerful instrument for unifying the Muslims into a nation.

At this point, Jinnah emerged as the leader of a rising Muslim nation. Events began to move fast. On March 22–23, 1940, in Lahore, the league adopted a resolution to form a separate Muslim state, Pakistan. The Pakistan idea was at first ridiculed and then tenaciously opposed by the Congress. But it captured the imagination of the Muslims. Many influential Hindus were pitted against Jinnah, including Gandhi and Jawaharlal Nehru. And the British government seemed to be intent on maintaining the political unity of the Indian subcontinent. But Jinnah led his movement with such skill and tenacity that ultimately both the Congress and the British government had no option but to agree to the partitioning of India. Pakistan emerged as an independent state in 1947.

Jinnah became the first head of the new state. Faced with the serious problems of a young nation, he tackled Pakistan's problems with authority. He was not regarded as merely the governor-general but as the father of the nation. He worked hard until he was overpowered by age and disease in Karachi, the place of his birth, in 1948.

JOSEPH STALIN

(b. Dec. 21 [Dec. 9, Old Style], 1879, Gori, Georgia, Russian Empire—d. March 5, 1953, Moscow, Russia, U.S.S.R.)

Joseph Stalin was the secretary-general of the Communist Party of the Soviet Union (1922-53) and premier of the Soviet state (1941-53), who for a quarter of a century dictatorially ruled the Soviet Union and transformed it into a major world power.

THE YOUNG REVOLUTIONARY AND RISE TO POWER

Born in Georgia as Ioseb Dzhugashvili, Stalin was the son of a cobbler. He studied at a seminary but was expelled for revolutionary activity in 1899. He joined an underground Georgian revolutionary organization in 1900 and the Bolshevik faction of the Russian Social Democratic Workers' Party in 1903. A disciple of Vladimir Lenin, he served in minor party posts and was appointed to the first Bolshevik Central Committee in 1912. In the following year he published, at Lenin's behest, an important article on Marxism and the national question. By now he had adopted the name Stalin, deriving from Russian *stal* ("steel"), and he also briefly edited the newly founded Bolshevik newspaper *Pravda* before undergoing a long period of exile in Siberia from July 1913 to March 1917.

Until the Russian Revolution of 1917 brought the Bolsheviks to power, Stalin was a relatively minor figure in the party. Active as a politico-military leader on various fronts during the Civil War of 1918–20, Stalin held two ministerial posts in the new Bolshevik government, being commissar for nationalities (1917–23) and for state control (1919–23). But it was his position as secretary general of

Joseph Stalin. Library of Congress, Washington, D.C. (neg. no. LC-USW33- 019081-C)

the party's Central Committee, from 1922 until his death, that provided the power base for his dictatorship. Besides heading the secretariat, he was also member of the powerful Politburo. Because Stalin was unintellectual, his rivals thought him unintelligent—a gross error, and one literally fatal in their case.

LENIN'S SUCCESSOR

From 1921 onward Stalin flouted the ailing Lenin's wishes, until, a year before his death, Lenin wrote a political "testament" calling for Stalin's removal from the secretary generalship. Coming from Lenin, this document was potentially ruinous to Stalin's career, but Stalin's usual luck and skill enabled him to have it discounted during his lifetime. After Lenin died in 1924, Stalin overcame his rivals, including Leon Trotsky, Grigory Zinovyev, Lev Kamenev, Nikolay Bukharin, and Aleksey Rykov, and took control of Soviet politics. Stalin expelled Trotsky, his main rival, from the Soviet Union in 1929 and had him assassinated in Mexico in 1940.

In 1928 Stalin inaugurated the five-year plans that radically altered Soviet economic and social structures—including intensive industrialization that forced collectivization of agriculture and resulted in the deaths of many millions. Among those who vainly sought to moderate Stalin's policies was his young second wife, Nadezhda Alliluyeva, whom he had married in 1919. She committed suicide in 1932.

In late 1934—just when the worst excesses of Stalinism seemed to have spent themselves—Stalin launched a new campaign of political terror against the very Communist Party members who had brought him to power. Widespread secret executions and persecution of not only party members but also military leaders, industrial managers, a large number of people in the arts, academic, and legal worlds, and foreign communists on Soviet soil.

ROLE IN WORLD WAR II

In August 1939, Stalin concluded a pact with Adolf Hitler, which encouraged the German dictator to attack Poland and begin World War II. Stalin annexed eastern Poland, Estonia, Latvia, Lithuania, and parts of Romania; he also attacked Finland and extorted territorial concessions. In May 1941 Stalin recognized the growing danger of a German attack on the Soviet Union by appointing himself chairman of the Council of People's Commissars or head of the government, his first governmental office since 1923.

Stalin's prewar measures were exposed as incompetent by the German blitzkrieg that surged deep into Soviet territory after Hitler's attack on the Soviet Union of June 22, 1941. Stalin allied with the United States and the United Kingdom and took control of military operations, directing the Soviet armies as they repulsed the German invaders and occupied the eastern European lands. When the Germans threatened Moscow in the winter of 1941, he remained in the capital, helping to organize a great counteroffensive. The Battle of Stalingrad, in the following winter, and the Battle of Kursk, in the summer of 1943, were also won by the Soviet army under Stalin's direction, turning the tide of invasion against the Germans, who capitulated in May 1945.

Stalin participated in high-level Allied meetings, including those of the Big Three with British prime minister Winston Churchill and U.S. president Franklin D. Roosevelt at Tehrān (1943) and Yalta (1945). A formidable negotiator, he outwitted these statesmen, extracting great concessions for the Soviet Union. After the war, Stalin imposed on eastern Europe a new kind of colonial control based on native communist regimes, nominally independent but in fact subservient to himself. In 1948 the defection of Yugoslavia, led by Josip Broz Tito, from the Soviet camp, struck a severe blow to world Communism as a Stalin-dominated monolith. To prevent others from following Tito's example, Stalin instigated local show trials, in which satellite Communist leaders confessed to Titoism, and many were executed.

LAST YEARS

Far from continuing his wartime alliance, Stalin now regarded as enemies the United Kingdom and, especially,

(Left to right) *Soviet leader Joseph Stalin, U.S. president Franklin D. Roosevelt, and British prime minister Winston Churchill at the Tehrān Conference, December 1943.* Encyclopædia Britannica, Inc.

Joseph Stalin, 1950. Sovfoto

the United States, against whom he embarked on the Cold War. At home, the primacy of Marxist ideology was harshly reasserted, and Stalin's chief ideological hatchet man, Andrey Zhdanov, a secretary of the Central Committee, began a reign of terror in the Soviet artistic and intellectual world. Hopes for domestic relaxation, widely aroused in the Soviet Union during the war, were thus sadly disappointed.

Increasingly suspicious and paranoid in his later years, Stalin ordered the arrest, announced in January 1953, of certain—mostly Jewish—Kremlin doctors on charges of medically murdering various Soviet leaders, including Zhdanov. The dictator was evidently preparing to make this Doctors' Plot the pretext for yet another great terror menacing all his senior associates, but he died suddenly on March 5.

Noted for bringing the Soviet Union into world prominence, at terrible cost to his own people, Stalin left a legacy of repression and fear as well as industrial and military power. In 1956 Stalin and his personality cult were denounced by Nikita Khrushchev.

IBN SA'ŪD

(b. *c.* 1880, Riyadh, Arabia—d. Nov. 9, 1953, Al-Ṭā'if, Saudi Arabia)

I bn Sa'ūd was the tribal and Muslim religious leader who formed the modern state of Saudi Arabia and initiated the exploitation of its oil.

The Sa'ūds ruled much of Arabia from 1780 to 1880; but, while Ibn Sa'ūd was still an infant, his family was driven out by their rivals, the Rashīds, and became penniless exiles in Kuwait. In 1901 Ibn Sa'ūd, then 21, set out from Kuwait with 40 camelmen in a bold attempt to regain his family's lands. A daring raid into Riyadh in January 1902 succeeded in rousing the former supporters of his dynasty, and within two years Ibn Sa'ūd had won over much of central Arabia. Turkish forces summoned by the Rashīds opposed him until 1912 with little success and then withdrew for lack of supplies.

Ibn Sa'ūd decided, in the years before World War I, to revive his dynasty's support for Wahhābism, an extremist Muslim puritan revival. Ibn Sa'ūd was in fact a devoted puritan Muslim, yet he was also aware that religious fanaticism could serve his ambition, and he deliberately fostered it, founding a militantly religious tribal organization known as the Ikhwān (brethren). This fanatical brotherhood encouraged his followers to fight and to massacre their Arab rivals, and it helped him to bring many nomadic tribesmen under more immediate control.

During World War I, Ibn Sa'ūd entered into a treaty with the British (December 1915), accepting protectorate status and agreeing to make war against Ibn Rashīd, who was being supported by the Turks. But despite British arms and a subsidy of £5,000 a month from the British government (which continued until 1924), he was inactive until 1920, arguing that his subsidy was insufficient. During

1920–22, however, he marched against Ibn Rashīd and extinguished Rashīdī rule, doubling his own territory.

Ibn Sa'ūd now ruled central Arabia except for the Hejaz region along the Red Sea. This was the territory of Sharīf Ḥusayn of Mecca. In 1924 the Ikhwān took Mecca, and the Hejaz was added to Ibn Sa'ūd's dominions. In the late 1920s, the Ikhwān turned against him when he forbade further raiding on their part. He defeated them at the Battle of Sibilla in March 1929.

This battle opened a new era; thereafter Ibn Sa'ūd's task was government, not conquest. In 1932 he formally unified his domains into the Kingdom of Saudi Arabia. An absolute monarch, he had no regular civil service or professional administrators. All decisions were made by him or by those he personally delegated for a particular task. There was little money, and he himself was not interested in finance. In May 1933 Ibn Sa'ūd signed his first agreement with an American oil company. Not until March 1938 did the company strike oil, and work virtually ceased during World War II, so that Ibn Sa'ūd was again nearly penniless.

Saudi Arabia took no part in the war, but toward its end the exploitation of oil was resumed. By 1950 Ibn Sa'ūd had received a total of about $200,000. Three years later, he was getting some $2,500,000 a week. The effect was disastrous on the country and on Ibn Sa'ūd. He had no idea of what to do with all the money, and he watched helplessly the triumph of everything he hated. His austere religious views were offended. The secluded, penurious, hard, but idealistic life of Arabia was vanishing. Such vast sums of money drew half the swindlers in the Middle East to this puritan religious sanctum. Ibn Sa'ūd was unable to cope with financial adventurers. His last years were marked by severe physical and emotional deterioration.

KEMAL ATATÜRK

(b. 1881, Salonika [now Thessaloníki], Greece—d. Nov. 10, 1938, Istanbul, Turkey)

Kemal Atatürk (Turkish: Kemal, Father of Turks) was a soldier, statesman, and reformer who was the founder and first president of the republic of Turkey from 1923 to 1938.

Atatürk was born in Salonika, then a thriving port of the Ottoman Empire, and was given the name Mustafa. Early in life he decided on a military career. He attended a military secondary school, and for his excellent work in mathematics, he took the name Kemal, an Arabic word meaning "the perfect one." He entered the military academy in Constantinople (now Istanbul) in 1899 and in 1902 the General Staff College. He served in the Italo-Turkish War in 1911–12 and in the Balkan Wars in 1912–13. These wars undermined the 400-year-old Ottoman Empire.

During World War I (1914–18), Kemal opposed Turkey's alliance with Germany. He nevertheless fought for Turkey, achieving great success against Allied forces during the Dardanelles campaign. His outstanding military abilities and widely circulated political opinions calling for an independent Turkish state won him a popular following. He opposed the presence of foreign powers in Turkey and desired an end to the Ottoman Empire. The eventual Allied victory brought British, French, and Italian troops to Anatolia.

Modern Turkish history may be said to begin on the morning of May 19, 1919, the day Mustafa Kemal landed at Samsun, on the Black Sea coast of Anatolia. Abandoning his official reason for being in Anatolia—to restore order—he headed inland for Amasya. There he told a cheering crowd that he had come to prevent the nation from

Mustafa Kemal (Atatürk) in 1923. UPI/Bettmann Newsphotos

slipping through the fingers of its people. This became his message to the Turks of Anatolia.

In 1920, as leader of a national resistance movement, he set up a rival government in Ankara, 300 miles (480 kilometres) from Istanbul. He expelled Greek forces from Asia Minor in 1921–22, and in 1922 he proclaimed the end of the Ottoman Empire. He became president of Turkey in 1923. On October 29, 1923, the Turkish republic was proclaimed. Turkey was now in complete control of its territory and sovereignty.

Mustafa Kemal then embarked upon the reform of his country, his goal being to bring it into the 20th century. His program was embodied in the party's "Six Arrows": republicanism, nationalism, populism, statism (state-owned and state-operated industrialization aimed at making Turkey self-sufficient), secularism, and revolution.

The caliphate—a religious title of leadership controlled by Ottoman sultans since the early 16th century—was abolished on March 3, 1924. The religious schools were dismantled at the same time. Abolition of the religious courts followed on April 8. In the same year, the religious brotherhoods, strongholds of conservatism, were outlawed.

The emancipation of women was set in motion by a number of laws. In December 1934, women were given the vote for parliamentary members and were made eligible to hold parliamentary seats. Almost overnight the whole system of Islamic law was discarded. From February to June 1926 the Swiss civil code, the Italian penal code, and the German commercial code were adopted wholesale. As a result, women's emancipation was strengthened by the abolition of polygamy. Marriage was made a civil contract, and divorce was recognized as a civil action.

One reform of truly revolutionary proportions was the replacement of the Arabic script—in which the Ottoman Turkish language had been written for centuries—by the Latin alphabet. This took place officially in November 1928. Education benefited from this reform, as the youth of Turkey were encouraged to take advantage of new educational opportunities that gave access to the Western scientific and humanistic traditions.

This ambitious program of forced modernization was not accomplished without strain and bloodshed. In February 1925 the Kurds of southwestern Anatolia raised the banner of revolt in the name of Islam. It took two months to put the revolt down; its leader Şeyh Said was then hanged. In June 1926, a plot by several disgruntled politicians to assassinate Atatürk was discovered, and the 13 ringleaders were tried and hanged.

In his later years Atatürk grew more remote from the Turkish people. He had the Dolmabahçe Palace in Istanbul, formerly a main residence of the sultans, refurbished and spent more time there. Always a heavy drinker who ate little, he began to decline in health. His illness, cirrhosis of the liver, was not diagnosed until too late. He bore the pain of the last few months of his life with great character and dignity.

FRANKLIN D. ROOSEVELT

(b. Jan. 30, 1882, Hyde Park, N.Y., U.S.—d. April 12, 1945, Warm Springs, Ga.)

Franklin Delano Roosevelt, known simply as FDR, was the 32nd president of the United States, serving from 1933 to 1945. The only president elected to the office four times, Roosevelt led the United States through two of the greatest crises of the 20th century: the Great Depression and World War II.

Early Life and Political Activities

Roosevelt was the only child of James and Sara Delano Roosevelt. Young Roosevelt was educated privately at home until age 14, when he entered Groton Preparatory School in Groton, Massachusetts. In 1900 Roosevelt entered Harvard University. It was during his Harvard years that he fell in love with Eleanor Roosevelt, the niece of Theodore Roosevelt and a distant cousin. They were married on March 17, 1905. Roosevelt attended Columbia University Law School. After passing the New York bar exam, he went to work as a law clerk .

Motivated by his cousin, former president Theodore Roosevelt, Franklin looked for an opportunity to launch a career in politics. He served in the New York senate from 1910 to 1913 and as U.S. assistant secretary of the navy from 1913 to 1920. Although he was stricken with polio in 1921, he remained active in Democratic politics and was elected governor of New York State in 1928. Roosevelt was then reelected in 1930.

Economic Depression and the Presidency

Amidst the background of economic depression, Roosevelt won the Democratic presidential nomination in 1932 and went on to be elected president over the incumbent Herbert Hoover. By inauguration day—March 4, 1933—most banks had shut down, industrial production had fallen to just 56 percent of its 1929 level, at least 13 million wage earners were unemployed, and farmers were in desperate straits. In his inaugural address, Roosevelt promised prompt, decisive action, and he conveyed some of his own unshakable self-confidence to millions of Americans listening on radios throughout the land. "This great nation will endure as it has endured, will revive and prosper," he asserted, adding, "the only thing we have to fear is fear itself."

THE FIRST TERM

THE HUNDRED DAYS

Roosevelt followed up on his promise of prompt action with the Hundred Days — the first phase of the New Deal, in which his administration presented Congress with a broad array of measures intended to achieve economic recovery, to provide relief to the millions of poor and unemployed, and to reform aspects of the economy that Roosevelt believed had caused the collapse.

Two key recovery measures of the Hundred Days were the Agricultural Adjustment Act (AAA) and the National Industrial Recovery Act (NIRA), which included the Public Works Administration (PWA) and the National Recovery Administration (NRA). Another important recovery measure was the Tennessee Valley Authority (TVA), a public corporation created in 1933 to build dams and hydroelectric power plants and to improve navigation and flood control in the vast Tennessee River basin.

The Hundred Days also included relief and reform measures. The Federal Emergency Relief Administration (FERA) and the Civilian Conservation Corps (CCC) were created. The Home Owners' Refinancing Act provided mortgage relief for millions of unemployed Americans in danger of losing their homes. Reform measures included the Federal Securities Act and the Glass-Steagall Banking Reform Act, the latter prohibiting commercial banks from making risky investments and established the Federal Deposit Insurance Corporation (FDIC) to protect depositors' accounts.

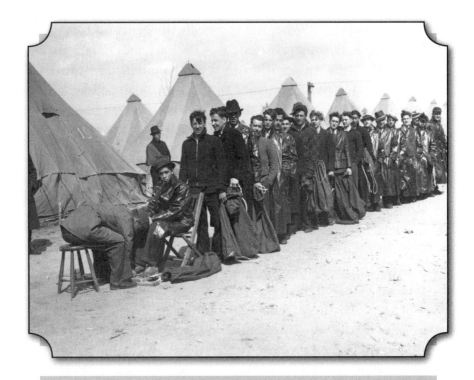

New members of the Civilian Conservation Corps wait to be fitted for shoes at Camp Dix, N.J., 1935. Encyclopædia Britannica, Inc.

THE SECOND NEW DEAL

By the fall of 1934, the measures passed during the Hundred Days had produced a limited degree of recovery; more important, they had regenerated hope that the country would surmount the crisis. Although the New Deal had alienated conservatives, including many businessmen, most Americans supported Roosevelt's programs.

Roosevelt asked Congress to pass additional New Deal legislation—sometimes called the Second New Deal—in 1935. The key measures of the Second New Deal were the Social Security Act, the Works Progress Administration

(WPA), and the Wagner Act (officially the National Labor Relations Act), which created the National Labor Relations Board (NLRB). In addition to these hallmark measures, Congress also passed a major tax revision—labeled by its opponents as a "soak-the-rich" tax—that raised tax rates for persons with large incomes and for large corporations.

THE SECOND TERM

Roosevelt was reelected in 1936 with the firm support of farmers, labourers, and the poor. He faced the equally firm opposition of conservatives. After his victory, Roosevelt was determined to push forward with further New Deal reforms. With large Democratic majorities in both houses of Congress, there remained only one obstacle to his objectives: the Supreme Court. To solve legal challenges to the New Deal, he proposed enlarging the Supreme Court by appointing six new justices (giving the court a liberal majority), but his court-packing plan aroused strong opposition and had to be abandoned.

By 1939 foreign policy was overshadowing domestic policy. When World War II broke out in Europe in September 1939, Roosevelt called Congress into special session to permit belligerents such as Britain and France to buy American arms on a "cash-and-carry" basis. When France fell to the Germans in the spring and early summer of 1940 and Britain was left alone to face the Nazi war machine, Roosevelt convinced Congress to intensify defense preparations and to support Britain with "all aid short of war."

THE THIRD AND FOURTH TERMS

In 1940 the Democrats had nominated Roosevelt for a third term, which he won. In March 1941, after a bitter debate in

Congress, Roosevelt obtained passage of the Lend-Lease Act, which enabled the United States to accept noncash payment for military and other aid to Britain and its allies. Later that year he authorized the U.S. Navy to provide protection for lend-lease shipments, and in the fall he instructed the navy to "shoot on sight" at German submarines. All these actions moved the United States closer to actual belligerency with Germany.

(From left, seated) *Canadian prime minister W. L. Mackenzie King, U.S. president Franklin D. Roosevelt, and British prime minister Winston Churchill at an Allied conference in Quebec, 1943.* Encyclopædia Britannica, Inc.

Yet it was in the Pacific rather than the Atlantic that war came to the United States. The Japanese bombed Pearl Harbor, Hawaii, on Dec. 7, 1941, destroying nearly the entire U.S. Pacific fleet and hundreds of airplanes and killing about 2,500 military personnel and civilians. On December 8, at Roosevelt's request, Congress declared war on Japan; on December 11 Germany and Italy declared war on the United States.

From the start of American involvement in World War II, Roosevelt took the lead in establishing a grand alliance among all countries fighting the Axis powers. He, Joseph Stalin, and Winston Churchill seemed to get along well when they met at Tehrān in November 1943. The Big Three met again at the Yalta Conference in the Crimea, U.S.S.R., in February 1945.

Declining Health and Death

Roosevelt had been suffering from advanced arteriosclerosis for more than a year before the Yalta Conference. His political opponents had tried to make much of his obviously declining health during the campaign of 1944, when he ran for a fourth term against Governor Thomas E. Dewey of New York. But Roosevelt campaigned actively and won the election. By the time of his return from Yalta, however, he was weak. On the afternoon of April 12, he suffered a massive cerebral hemorrhage, and he died a few hours later.

EAMON DE VALERA

(b. Oct. 14, 1882, New York, N.Y., U.S. — d. Aug. 29, 1975, Dublin, Ire.)

E amon de Valera was a Irish politician and patriot who served as prime minister of Ireland in the years 1932–48, 1951–54, and 1957–59, and president from 1959 to 1973. An active revolutionary from 1913, he became president of the Sinn Féin political party in 1918 and founded the Fianna Fáil Party in 1924. In 1937 he took the Irish Free State out of the British Commonwealth and made his country a "sovereign" state, renamed Ireland, or Éire. His academic attainments also inspired wide respect; he became chancellor of the National University of Ireland in 1921.

Born Edward de Valera to a Spanish father and Irish mother in the United States, he was sent to his mother's family in County Limerick, Ireland, when he was two, after his father's death. He studied at the local national school and at Blackrock College, Dublin; he graduated from the Royal University, Dublin, and became a teacher of mathematics and an ardent supporter of the Irish language revival. In 1913 he joined the Irish Volunteers, which had been organized to resist opposition to Home Rule for Ireland. In the anti-British Easter Rising in Dublin in 1916, he commanded an occupied building and was the last commander to surrender. Because of his American birth, he escaped execution by the British but was sentenced to penal servitude.

Released in 1917 but arrested again and deported to England in May 1918, de Valera was acclaimed by the Irish as the chief survivor of the uprising and was elected president of the revolutionist Sinn Féin ("We Ourselves") Party, which won three-quarters of all the Irish constituencies in December 1918. After a dramatic escape from Lincoln Jail in February 1919, he went in disguise to the United States, where he collected funds. He returned to Ireland before military repression ended with the truce of 1921 and appointed plenipotentiaries—diplomats with full power to represent their government—to negotiate in London. He rejected the treaty that they signed to form the Irish

Free State, however, because it accepted the exclusion of Northern Ireland and imposed an oath of allegiance to the British crown.

When Dáil Éireann (the assembly of Ireland) ratified the treaty by a small majority in 1922, de Valera supported the republican resistance in the ensuing civil war. William Thomas Cosgrave's Irish Free State ministry imprisoned him; but he was released in 1924 and then organized a Republican opposition party that would not sit in the Dáil. In 1927, however, he persuaded his followers to sign the oath of allegiance as "an empty political formula," and his new Fianna Fáil ("Warriors of Ireland") Party then entered the Dáil, demanding abolition of the oath of allegiance, the governor-general, the Seanad (senate) as then constituted, and land-purchase annuities payable to Great Britain. The Cosgrave ministry was defeated by Fianna Fáil in 1932, and de Valera, as head of the new ministry, embarked quickly on severing connections with Great Britain. He withheld payment of the land annuities, and an economic war resulted. Increasing retaliation by both sides enabled de Valera to develop his program of austere national self-sufficiency in an Irish-speaking Ireland, while building up industries behind protective tariffs. In 1937 the Free State declared itself a sovereign state, as Ireland, or Éire, conceding voluntary allegiance to the British crown.

De Valera's prestige was enhanced by his success as president of the Council of the League of Nations in 1932 and of its assembly in 1938. The menace of war in Europe induced British prime minister Neville Chamberlain, in 1938, to conclude the "economic war" with mutual concessions. Britain relinquished the naval bases of Cobh, Berehaven, and Lough Swilly. In September 1939 de Valera proclaimed that Ireland would remain neutral and resist attack from any quarter. Besides avoiding the burdens and

Eamon de Valera. Encyclopædia Britannica, Inc.

destruction of war, he had brought temporary prosperity, and he retained office in subsequent elections.

In 1948 a reaction against the long monopoly of power and patronage held by de Valera's party enabled the opposition, with the help of smaller parties, to form an interparty government under John A. Costello. But this precarious coalition collapsed within three years, ironically, after declaring Ireland a republic by formal law, an act de Valera had avoided. De Valera resumed office until 1954, when he appealed unsuccessfully for a fresh mandate, and Costello formed his second interparty ministry. No clearly defined difference now existed between the opposing parties in face of rising prices, continued emigration, and underdeveloped agriculture. De Valera claimed, however, that a strong single-party government was indispensable and that all coalitions must be weak and insecure. On this plea he obtained, in March 1957, the overall majority that he demanded. In 1959 de Valera agreed to stand as a candidate for the presidency. He resigned his position as *taoiseach* (head of government) and leader of the Fianna Fáil Party. In June he was elected president and was reelected in 1966. He retired to a nursing home near Dublin in 1973 and died there in 1975.

BENITO MUSSOLINI

(b. July 29, 1883, Predappio, Italy—d. April 28, 1945, near Dongo)

B enito Mussolini was the Italian prime minister from 1922 to 1943 and the first of 20th-century Europe's Fascist dictators.

EARLY LIFE

Benito Amilcare Andrea Mussolini was an intelligent but restless and disobedient child. He became a socialist in his teens and worked, often as a schoolmaster, to spread the party doctrine. The newspaper he founded, *La Lotta di Classe* ("The Class Struggle"), won such recognition that in 1912 he was made editor of *Avanti!* ("Forward!"), the official socialist daily published in Milan. As its antimilitarist, antinationalist, and anti-imperialist editor, he thunderously opposed Italy's intervention in World War I.

Soon, however, he changed his mind about intervention. He began writing articles and making speeches in favour of war. He resigned from *Avanti!* and was expelled from the Socialist Party. He assumed the editorship of *Il Popolo d'Italia* ("The People of Italy") and served with the Italian army from 1915 to 1917.

RISE TO POWER

Wounded while serving with the *bersaglieri* (a corps of sharpshooters), he returned home a convinced antisocialist and a man with a sense of destiny. Advocating government by dictatorship, he formed a political group in 1919 that marked the beginning of Fascism, *fasci di combattimento* ("fighting bands"). It was comprised of groups of fighters bound together by ties as close as those that secured the fasces of the lictors—the symbols of ancient Roman authority. So Fascism was created and its symbol devised.

Mussolini was a dynamic and captivating orator. At rallies—surrounded by supporters wearing black shirts— he caught the imagination of the crowds. His attitudes were highly theatrical, his opinions were contradictory, his facts were often wrong, and his attacks were frequently malicious and misdirected; but his delivery was extraordinarily effective.

Fascist squads—militias inspired by Mussolini but often created by local leaders—swept through the countryside of the Po Valley and the Puglian plains, rounded up Socialists, burned down union and party offices, and terrorized the local population. By late 1921, the Fascists controlled large parts of Italy. As the Fascist movement built a broad base of support around the powerful ideas of nationalism and anti-Bolshevism, Mussolini began planning to seize power at the national level. He did so in 1922, when he organized the March on Rome to prevent a socialist-led general strike. Although it was far less orderly than Fascist propaganda later suggested, it was sufficiently threatening to bring down the government. The king, Victor Emmanuel III, was prepared to accept the Fascist alternative and named Mussolini prime minister, the youngest in Italian history at 39.

DICTATORSHIP

Mussolini obtained a law to establish the Fascists as the majority party and then became the dictator, known as Il Duce ("The Leader"). Many Italians, especially among the middle class, welcomed his authority. Soon a kind of order had been restored, and the Fascists inaugurated ambitious programs of public works. The costs of this order were, however, enormous. Italy's fragile democratic system was abolished.

Mussolini's dreams of empire led him to seek foreign conquests. Italy invaded Ethiopia in October 1935. A brutal campaign of colonial conquest followed, in which the Italians dropped tons of gas bombs upon the Ethiopian people. Europe expressed its horror but did nothing to stop Mussolini.

Italy had also found a new ally: Germany. Supported in his Fascist schemes by Adolf Hitler but wary of German power, Mussolini agreed to the Rome-Berlin Axis. In 1938, following the German example, Mussolini's government passed shameful anti-Semitic laws in Italy that discriminated against Jews in all sectors of public and private life and prepared the way for the deportation of some 20 percent of Italy's Jews to German death camps during the war.

ROLE IN WORLD WAR II

Mussolini watched the progress of Hitler's war with bitterness and alarm, becoming more and more bellicose with each fresh German victory. He frequently expressed hope that the Germans would be slowed down or would meet with some reverse that would satisfy his personal envy and give Italy breathing space. When Germany advanced westward, however, and France seemed on the verge of collapse, Mussolini felt he could delay no longer. So, on June 10, 1940, Italy declared war on the Allies.

From the beginning the war went badly for Italy, and Mussolini's opportunistic hopes for a quick victory soon dissolved. France surrendered before there was an opportunity for even a token Italian victory. Mussolini then decided to attack Greece through Albania in 1940 without informing the Germans. The result was an extensive and humiliating defeat, and the Germans were forced unwillingly to extricate Mussolini from its consequences. The 1941 campaign to support the German invasion of the Soviet Union also failed disastrously and condemned thousands of ill-equipped Italian troops to a nightmarish winter retreat. Hitler had to come to his ally's help once again in North Africa. After the Italian surrender in North Africa in 1943, the Germans began to take precautions against a likely Italian collapse. Mussolini had grossly exaggerated the extent of public support for his regime and for the war. When the Allies successfully invaded Sicily in July 1943, it was obvious that collapse was imminent.

On July 24, at a meeting of the Fascist Grand Council, an overwhelming majority passed a resolution that in effect dismissed Mussolini from office. Disregarding the vote as a matter of little concern, Mussolini appeared at his office the next morning as though nothing had happened. That afternoon, however, he was arrested and imprisoned. German commandos rescued him on Sept. 12, 1943, and provided for his escape by air to Munich. Rather than allow the Germans to occupy and govern Italy entirely in their own interests, Mussolini agreed to Hitler's suggestion that he return to Italy, establish a new Fascist government in the German-controlled north, and execute those members of the Grand Council who had dared to vote against him.

As German defenses in Italy collapsed and the Allies advanced rapidly northward, the Italian Communists of the partisan leadership decided to execute Mussolini. Disguised as a German soldier, Mussolini tried to escape from the Allied advance, but he and his mistress, Clara Petacci, were recognized and shot near Como by Italian partisans on April 28, 1945. Their bodies were hung, head downward, in the Piazza Loreto in Milan. Huge, jubilant crowds celebrated the fall of the dictator and the end of the war.

ELEANOR ROOSEVELT

(b. Oct. 11, 1884, New York, N.Y., U.S.—d. Nov. 7, 1962, New York)

Eleanor Roosevelt was one of the world's most widely admired and powerful women. She was the wife of Franklin D. Roosevelt, 32nd president of the United States, but was also a towering figure in her own right, a humanitarian, and a United Nations diplomat.

Born Anna Eleanor Roosevelt, she was the daughter of Elliott Roosevelt and Anna Hall Roosevelt and the niece of Theodore Roosevelt, 26th president of the United States. Eleanor grew up in a wealthy family that attached great value to community service. Both her parents died before she was 10, and she and her surviving brother (another brother died when she was 9) were raised by relatives. The death of Eleanor's father, to whom she had been especially close, was very difficult for her.

At age 15 Eleanor enrolled at Allenswood, a girls' boarding school outside London. She returned to New York in the summer of 1902 to prepare for her "coming out" into

Eleanor Roosevelt visiting with Children of the American Revolution at the White House, 1935. Encyclopædia Britannica, Inc.

society that winter. Following family tradition, she devoted time to community service, including teaching in a settlement house on Manhattan's Lower East Side. Soon after Eleanor returned, Franklin Roosevelt, her distant cousin, began to court her, and they were married on March 17, 1905, in New York City. Between 1906 and 1916 Eleanor gave birth to six children, one of whom died in infancy.

After Franklin won a seat in the New York Senate in 1911, the family moved to Albany, where Eleanor was initiated into the job of political wife. When Franklin was appointed assistant secretary of the navy in 1913, the family moved to Washington, D.C., and Eleanor spent the next few years performing the social duties expected of an "official wife."

With the entry of the United States into World War I in April 1917, Eleanor was able to resume her volunteer work. She visited wounded soldiers and worked for the Navy–Marine Corps Relief Society and in a Red Cross canteen.

In 1918 Eleanor discovered that Franklin had been having an affair with her social secretary, Lucy Mercer. Franklin refused Eleanor's offer of a divorce and agreed to stop seeing Mercer. The Roosevelts' marriage settled into a routine in which both of them kept independent agendas while remaining respectful of and affectionate toward each other. But their relationship had ceased to be an intimate one.

Eleanor's interest in politics later increased, partly as a result of her decision to help in her husband's political career after he was stricken with polio in 1921 and partly as a result of her desire to work for important causes. She joined the Women's Trade Union League and became active in the New York State Democratic Party. As a member of the Legislative Affairs Committee of the League of Women Voters, she began studying the *Congressional Record* and learned to evaluate voting records and debates.

When Franklin became governor of New York in 1929, Eleanor found an opportunity to combine the responsibilities of a political hostess with her own burgeoning career and personal independence. She continued to teach at Todhunter, a girls' school in Manhattan that she and two friends had purchased, making several trips a week back and forth between Albany and New York City.

She continued along these lines as First Lady during Franklin's 12 years as president. The unprecedented breadth of Eleanor's activities and her advocacy of liberal causes made her nearly as controversial a figure as her husband. She instituted regular White House press conferences for women correspondents. Therefore, wire services that had not formerly employed women were forced to do so in order to have a representative present in case important news broke. In deference to the president's infirmity, she helped serve as his eyes and ears throughout the nation, embarking on extensive tours and reporting to him on conditions, programs, and public opinion. Beginning in 1936 she wrote a daily syndicated newspaper column, "My Day." A widely sought-after speaker at political meetings and at various institutions, Eleanor showed particular interest in child welfare, housing reform, and equal rights for women and ethnic minorities.

In 1939, when the Daughters of the American Revolution (DAR) refused to let Marian Anderson, an African American opera singer, perform in Constitution Hall, Eleanor resigned her membership in the DAR and arranged to hold the concert at the nearby Lincoln Memorial. The event turned into a massive outdoor celebration attended by 75,000 people. Eleanor's defense of the rights of African Americans, youth, and the poor helped to bring groups into government that formerly had been alienated from the political process.

After President Roosevelt's death in 1945, President Harry S. Truman appointed Eleanor a delegate to the United Nations (UN), where she served as chairman of the Commission on Human Rights from 1946 to 1951 and played a major role in the drafting and adoption of the Universal Declaration of Human Rights (1948). In the last decade of her life, Eleanor continued to play an active part in the Democratic Party.

In 1961 President John F. Kennedy appointed her chair of his Commission on the Status of Women, and she continued with that work until shortly before her death. She had not initially favoured the Equal Rights Amendment (ERA), saying it would take from women the valuable protective legislation that they had fought to win and still needed, but she gradually embraced it.

An indefatigable traveler, Eleanor Roosevelt circled the globe several times, visiting scores of countries and meeting with most of the world's leaders. She continued to write books and articles, and the last of her "My Day" columns appeared just weeks before her death, from a rare form of tuberculosis, in 1962.

DAVID BEN-GURION

(b. Oct. 16, 1886, Płońsk, Pol., Russian Empire [now in Poland]—d. Dec. 1, 1973, Tel Aviv–Yafo, Israel)

David Ben-Gurion was a Zionist statesman and political leader who was the first prime minister and defense minister of Israel. It was Ben-Gurion who, on May 14, 1948, at Tel Aviv, delivered Israel's declaration of independence. He was revered as the father of the nation.

Ben-Gurion, born David Gruen, was the son of Victor Gruen, one of the leaders in Płońsk of the "Lovers of Zion," a movement that was disseminating among the oppressed Jews of eastern Europe the idea of the return to their original homeland of Israel. Zionism fascinated the young David Gruen, and he became convinced that the first step for the Jews who wanted to revive Israel as a nation was to immigrate to Palestine and settle there as farmers. In 1906 the 20-year-old Gruen arrived in Palestine and for several years worked as a farmer. There he adopted the ancient Hebrew name Ben-Gurion and joined the Zionist socialist party, Poale Zion ("Workers of Zion").

With the outbreak of World War I, the Turkish governors of Palestine—their suspicions aroused by his Zionist activity—arrested Ben-Gurion and expelled him from the Ottoman Empire. During the height of the war, he traveled to New York, where he met and eventually married the Russian-born Pauline Munweis. Following the issuance of the Balfour Declaration in 1917, which promised the Jews a national home in Palestine, he joined the British army's Jewish Legion and returned to the Middle East to join the war for the liberation of Palestine from Ottoman rule.

The British had already defeated the Turks when the Jewish Legion reached the battlefield, and, when Britain received the mandate over Palestine, the work of realizing the "Jewish national home" had begun. For Ben-Gurion, the "national home" was a step toward political independence. To implement it, he called for accelerated Jewish immigration to Palestine in the effort to create a Jewish nucleus that would serve as the foundation for the establishment of a Jewish state. In the 1920s and 1930s, Ben-Gurion led several political organizations, including Mapai (the Israeli Workers Party) and the Jewish Agency—world Zionism's highest directing body.

As the Jewish settlement strengthened and deepened its roots in Palestine, anxiety mounted among the Palestinian

Arabs, resulting in violent clashes between the two communities. In 1939 Britain changed its Middle East policy, abandoning its sympathetic stand toward the Jews and adopting a sympathetic attitude toward the Arabs, leading to severe restrictions on Jewish immigration and settlement in Palestine. At the end of World War II, Ben-Gurion again led the Jewish community in its successful struggle against the British mandate. In May 1948, in accordance with a decision of the United Nations General Assembly, with the support of the United States and the Soviet Union, the State of Israel was established.

Ben-Gurion became prime minister and minister of defense of the new country. He succeeded in breaking up the underground armies that had fought the British and in fusing them into a national army, which became an effective force against the invading Arab armies from Syria, Jordan, Iraq, and Egypt. Although the fighting ended with an Israeli victory, the Arab leaders refused to enter into formal peace negotiations with the Jewish state.

Ben-Gurion's stronghanded policy inspired little sympathy for him from the governments of the United States and Britain, but he found an ally in France—then embroiled in its own war in the Arab world. France helped arm Israel in the period leading up to the Suez Crisis in 1956, and it was French initiative that brought Israel to join the Franco-British military campaign against Egypt. On October 29, 1956, Ben-Gurion ordered the army to take over the Sinai Peninsula, while France and Britain were making an abortive attempt to seize the canal from Egyptian forces. Israel subsequently withdrew from Sinai after having been assured freedom of navigation in the Strait of Tiran and de facto peace along the Egyptian-Israeli border. Following the Sinai campaign, Israel entered a period of diplomatic and economic prosperity. During Ben-Gurion's last years of office, he initiated several plans for secret talks with Arab leaders with a view to establishing peace in the Middle East. The talks were unsuccessful.

In June 1963 Ben-Gurion unexpectedly resigned from the government for unnamed "personal reasons." His move apparently resulted in part from the bitter internal controversy between his supporters and his rivals in the party. Ben-Gurion left Mapai in 1965 with a number of his supporters and established a small opposition party, Rafi.

In 1970 Ben-Gurion retired from the Knesset and from all political activity, devoting himself to the writing of his memoirs in Sde-Boqer, a kibbutz in the Negev. He published a number of books, mostly collections of speeches and essays. Through most of his life he had also engaged in researches into the history of the Jewish community in Palestine and in the study of the Bible.

CHIANG KAI-SHEK

(b. Oct. 31, 1887, Chekiang Province, China—d. April 5, 1975, Taipei, Taiwan)

Chiang Kai-shek was a soldier and statesman who was head of the Nationalist government in China from 1928 to 1949 and subsequently head of the Chinese Nationalist government in exile on Taiwan.

Chiang was born into a moderately prosperous merchant and farmer family in the coastal province of Chekiang. He prepared for a military career first at the Paoting Military Academy in North China and subsequently in Japan. From 1909 to 1911, he served in the Japanese army, whose Spartan ideals he admired and adopted. More influential were the youthful compatriots he met in Tokyo, who wanted to overthrow the Qing (Manchu) dynasty—a group that had controlled China since the 17th century—and establish a republic. In 1911 Chiang returned to China and took part in the revolt that accomplished that goal.

In 1913, with the new republic in the hands of a would-be dictator, Yuan Shikai, Chiang joined in an unsuccessful revolt. This cost him his army post. After the death of Yuan in 1916, various leaders and warlords struggled for power in the country. Sun Yat-sen, as leader of the Kuomintang (Nationalist Party), tried to unify the country. In 1923 he sent Chiang to Moscow to study Soviet military and political institutions. On his return Chiang became the director of a military academy at Canton (Guangzhou), the southern stronghold of the revolutionaries.

After Sun's death in 1925, Chiang, supported by his well-trained cadets, rose to power in the Kuomintang. In 1926 he took command of the revolutionary army. The general then began advancing to the north of China, with Beijing, capital of the weak republic, as his goal. In a 1,200-mile (1,900-kilometer) march, he gained control of south and central China. During this period Chiang took two steps that were to have major consequences for the country and his own life. Alarmed by the growth of Communism, he dismissed his Soviet advisers and expelled the Communists from his party. He also married the American-educated Soong Mei-ling. Known as Madame Chiang, she became her husband's close adviser.

In 1928 Chiang's army entered Beijing and, as chief of the Kuomintang, he became the head of the Republic of China. Nanjing (Nanking), to the south, was made the new capital. China, however, was still far from unified. For years Chiang battled insurgent regional commanders and armed Communist forces. When Japan invaded Manchuria in 1931, Chiang decided not to resist the coming Japanese invasion until after he had crushed the Communists—a decision that aroused many protests, especially since a complete victory over the Communists continued to elude him.

Chiang accelerated his program for unifying and strengthening China. To give the nation more moral cohesion, Chiang revived the state cult of Confucius and in 1934 launched a campaign, the so-called New Life Movement—a program designed to improve the lot of the peasants through education, home industries, and self-help. Its goal was to halt the spread of Communism by teaching traditional Chinese values.

In December 1936 Chiang was seized by one of his generals who believed that Chinese forces should concentrate on fighting the Japanese instead of the Communists. Chiang was held captive for some two weeks, and the Xi'an (Sian) Incident, as it became known, ended after he agreed to form an alliance with the Communists against the Japanese invaders. In 1937 the mounting conflict between the two countries erupted into war. His forces kept most of China free of Japanese control and managed to move industries and schools to the interior. After the Allied forces declared war against Japan during World War II, Chiang became Allied commander in China. He became China's president in 1943. China received economic aid from the United States, but Chiang did not push economic or political reforms. Much of his Nationalist government was corrupt, and inflation brought increasing hardship to the masses. Civil war recommenced in 1946. By 1949 Chiang had lost continental China to the Communists, and the People's Republic of China was established. Chiang moved to Taiwan with the remnants of his Nationalist forces, established a relatively benign dictatorship over the island with other Nationalist leaders, and attempted to harass the Communists across the Formosa Strait. The chastened Chiang reformed the ranks of the once-corrupt Nationalist Party, and with the help of generous American aid he succeeded in the next two decades in setting Taiwan on the road to modern economic development. In 1955 the United States signed an agreement with Chiang's Nationalist government on Taiwan, guaranteeing its defense. Beginning in 1972, however, the value of this agreement and the future of Chiang's government were seriously called into question by the growing cordiality between the United States and the People's Republic of China. Chiang did not live to see the United States finally break diplomatic relations with Taiwan in 1979 in order to establish full relations with the People's Republic of China.

JEAN MONNET AND ROBERT SCHUMAN

Respectively (b. Nov. 9, 1888, Cognac, France—d. March 16, 1979, Houjarray); (b. June 29, 1886, Luxembourg—d. Sept. 4, 1963, Metz, France)

French statesmen Jean Monnet and Robert Schuman can, in some ways, be considered the fathers of Europe, having proposed the establishment of a common European market for coal and steel, resulting in the creation of the European Coal and Steel Community (ECSC), the forerunner of the European Union.

JEAN MONNET

Monnet was a French political economist and diplomat. During World War I, Monnet was the French representative on the Inter-Allied Maritime Commission, and after the war he was deputy secretary-general of the League of Nations from 1919 to 1923. Then, after reorganizing his family's brandy business, he became the European partner of a New York investment bank in 1925.

At the start of World War II, Monnet was made chairman of the Franco-British Economic Co-ordination Committee. In June 1940 it was he who suggested a Franco-British union to Winston Churchill. After the Franco-German armistice, he left for Washington, D.C., and in 1943 he was sent to Algiers to work with the Free French administration there.

After the liberation of France, Monnet headed a government committee to prepare a comprehensive plan for the reconstruction and modernization of the French economy. On Jan. 11, 1947, the Monnet Plan was adopted by the French government, and Monnet himself was appointed commissioner-general of the National Planning Board. In May 1950 he and Robert Schuman, then the French foreign minister, proposed the establishment of a common European market for coal and steel by countries willing to delegate their powers over these industries to an independent authority. Six countries—France, West Germany, Italy, Belgium, The Netherlands, and Luxembourg—signed the treaty in 1951 that set up the European Coal and Steel Community. From 1952 to 1955 Monnet served as the first president of the ECSC's High Authority. The ECSC inspired the creation of the European Economic Community, or Common Market, in 1957.

In 1955 Monnet organized the Action Committee for the United States of Europe and served as its president from 1956 to 1975. In 1976 the heads of the nine Common Market governments named Monnet a Citizen of Europe. In the same year, he published his memoirs.

Robert Schuman

Schuman, a member of the French National Assembly from 1919, was arrested by the German Gestapo in September

1940 after the German occupation of France. He escaped in 1942 and worked in the Résistance until France was liberated in 1944. A founder of the Popular Republican Movement (Mouvement Républicain Populaire; MRP), he served as minister of finance (July–November 1946), premier (November 1947–July 1948 and August–September 1948), foreign minister (July 1948–December 1952), and minister of justice (1955–56).

While serving as foreign minister, Schuman developed the Schuman Plan (1950) to promote European economic and military unity and a Franco-German rapprochement to prevent another war between the two nations. The economic aspects of his plan were realized in 1952 in the European Coal and Steel Community, the six-nation western European economic union, the first in a series of economic agreements leading to the formation of the European Economic Community (the Common Market) in 1957. He served as president of the Assembly, the consultative arm of the Common Market, from 1958 to 1960 and was an assembly member until February 1963.

ADOLF HITLER

(b. April 20, 1889, Braunau am Inn, Austria—d. April 30, 1945, Berlin, Ger.)

The leader of the National Socialist (Nazi) Party and dictator of Germany from 1933 to 1945, Adolf Hitler was responsible for both World War II and the Holocaust and, for many people, became the incarnation of evil.

EARLY LIFE AND RISE TO POWER

Hitler spent his early life in Linz, Austria, and in Vienna. He was a lonely, frustrated artist and moved to Munich,

Adolf Hitler reviewing troops on the Eastern Front, 1939. Heinrich Hoffmann, Munich

Germany, in 1913. While serving in the German army during World War I, he was wounded (1916) and gassed (1918). He began his political career as an army political agent in the German Workers' (later National Socialist, or Nazi) Party in 1919 and became head of its propaganda arm in 1920 and later its president. From the first he set out to create a mass movement, whose mystique and power would be sufficient to bind its members in loyalty to him. He engaged in unrelenting propaganda through the party newspaper and through meetings whose audiences soon grew from a handful to thousands. With his charismatic personality and dynamic leadership, he attracted a devoted cadre of Nazi leaders, men whose names today live in infamy—Alfred Rosenberg, Rudolf Hess, Hermann Göring, and Julius Streicher. Hitler was also aided by Ernst Röhm, whose "strong arm" squads, which evolved into the SA (Sturmabteilung), exploited violence for the impression of strength it gave. Conditions were ripe for the development of a party like the Nazis. Resentment at the loss of World War I and the severity of the peace terms added to the economic woes and brought widespread discontent. This was especially sharp in Bavaria, due to its traditional separatism and the region's popular dislike of the republican government in Berlin.

After the abortive Beer Hall Putsch of 1923, in which the Nazis tried to take over the government in Munich, Hitler was sentenced to prison for five years but served only nine months. He used the time to dictate the first volume of *Mein Kampf*, his political autobiography, which included his notions of inequality among races, nations, and individuals as part of an unchangeable natural order that exalted the "Aryan race" as the creative element of mankind. According to Hitler, the natural unit of mankind was the *Volk* ("the people"), of which the German people were the greatest. Beyond Marxism he believed the greatest enemy of all to be Jews, whom Hitler described as "a parasite within the nation."

The years 1924 to 1928 were prosperous for Germany, and from 1925 to 1927 Hitler was even forbidden to speak publicly in either Bavaria or Saxony. Then a worldwide depression plunged Germany again into poverty and unemployment, and the Nazis began to gain votes. By 1930 Hitler had the support of many industrialists and the military caste. He unsuccessfully opposed Paul von Hindenburg in the presidential election of 1932 but was appointed chancellor in 1933. After Hindenburg's death, Hitler merged the offices of chancellor and president in 1934 and adopted the title of Führer ("leader"). After establishing a totalitarian police state in Germany, Hitler then turned his attention to foreign policy, and his aggressively expansionist policies triggered World War II, which lasted from 1939 to 1945. At its height, Hitler's Germany briefly occupied most of Europe.

DICTATOR

Hitler sought to establish a "New Order" in Europe. From 1933 to 1939 and in some instances even during the first years of the war, Hitler's purpose was to expel the Jews from the Greater German Reich. In 1941 this policy changed from expulsion to extermination, resulting in the Holocaust. The concentration camps created under the Nazi regime were thereby expanded to include extermination camps, such as Auschwitz, and mobile extermination squads, the *Einsatzgruppen*. Although Catholics, Poles, homosexuals, Roma (Gypsies), and the handicapped were also targeted for persecution—if not outright extermination—the Jews of Germany, Poland, and the Soviet Union were by far the most numerous among the victims. In German-occupied Europe, some six million Jews were killed during the war.

The Allied invasion of Normandy on June 6, 1944, marked the beginning of the end for Hitler's Third Reich. Within a few months, eight European capitals were liberated by the Allies or surrendered to them. Hitler retreated to the chancellory in Berlin in January 1945 and, in the face of impending capture by advancing Soviet troops, committed suicide.

HITLER'S PLACE IN HISTORY

The popular view of Hitler often involves assumptions about his mental health. There has been a tendency to attribute madness to Hitler. Despite the occasional evidences of his furious outbursts, Hitler's cruelties and his most extreme expressions and orders suggest a cold brutality that was fully conscious. The attribution of madness to Hitler would of course absolve him from his responsibility for his deeds and words (as it also absolves the responsibility of those who are unwilling to think further about him). Extensive researches of his medical records also indicate that, at least until the last 10 months of his life, he was not profoundly handicapped by illness (except for advancing symptoms of Parkinson's disease). What is indisputable is that Hitler had such a certain tendency to hypochondria that he ingested vast amounts of medications during the war. It should also be noted that Hitler possessed mental abilities that were denied by some of his earlier critics. These included an astonishing memory for certain details and an instinctive insight into his opponents' weaknesses—talents that increase, rather than diminish, his responsibility for the many brutal and evil actions he ordered and committed.

Hitler's most amazing achievement was his uniting the great mass of the German and Austrian people behind him. Throughout his career his popularity was larger and deeper than the popularity of the Nazi Party. A great majority of Germans believed in him until the very end. In this respect he stands out among almost all of the dictators of the 19th and 20th centuries. There is no question that the overwhelming majority of the German people supported Hitler, though often only passively. Of course, what contributed to this support were the economic and social successes, for which he fully took credit, during his early leadership. These included the virtual disappearance of unemployment, the rising prosperity of the masses, the new social institutions, and the increase of German prestige in the 1930s.

By 1938 Hitler had made Germany the most powerful and feared country in Europe, and perhaps the world. He achieved all of this before the war. Hitler came very close to winning the war in 1940, but the resistance of Britain thwarted him. It took the overwhelming, and in many ways unusual, Anglo-American coalition with the Soviet Union to finally defeat the Third Reich; and there are reasons to believe that neither side would have been able to conquer him alone. At the same time, it was Hitler's brutality and some of his decisions that led to his destruction, binding the unusual alliance of capitalists and Communists together. Hitler thought he was a great statesman, but he did not realize the unconditional contemptibility of what he had unleashed; he thought that the coalition of his enemies would eventually break up and then he would be able to settle with one side or the other. In thinking this, he deceived himself.

JAWAHARLAL NEHRU

(b. Nov. 14, 1889, Allahabad, India—d. May 27, 1964, New Delhi)

Jawaharlal Nehru was the first prime minister of independent India, serving from 1947 to 1964. Known as Pandit (Teacher), he was also one of the principal leaders of India's independence movement in the 1930s and 1940s.

EARLY YEARS AND INTRODUCTION TO POLITICS

Nehru was born to a family of Kashmiri Brahmans that had migrated to India early in the 18th century. He was the son of Motilal Nehru, a renowned lawyer and one of Mahatma Gandhi's prominent lieutenants. When Jawaharlal was 16, he went to England to study at Harrow, Trinity College, and later Cambridge. He returned to India in 1912 and became a lawyer in Allahabad.

Nehru met Gandhi for the first time in 1916 at the annual meeting of the Indian National Congress (Congress Party) in Lucknow, and he later became absorbed in Gandhi's campaign for Indian independence. In 1923 he became general secretary of the party for two years and again, in 1927, for another two years. His interests and duties took him on journeys over wide areas of India, winning support for Gandhi's program of nonviolent resistance to British rule. Between 1921 and 1945, he would be jailed nine times for his political activity.

STRUGGLE FOR INDIAN INDEPENDENCE

In 1929 Nehru became president of the Congress Party, presiding over the historic Lahore session that proclaimed complete independence (rather than dominion status) as India's political goal. In 1935 India was granted limited self-government with the Government of India Act. Ultimately, it provided for a federal system composed of the autonomous provinces and princely states. Although federation never came into being, provincial autonomy was implemented.

When the elections following the introduction of provincial autonomy brought the Congress Party to power in a majority of the provinces, Nehru was faced with a dilemma. The Muslim League under Mohammed Ali Jinnah, who was to become the creator of Pakistan, had fared badly at the polls. Congress, therefore, unwisely rejected Jinnah's plea for the formation of coalition Congress-Muslim League governments in some of the provinces, a decision on which Nehru had not a little influence. The subsequent clash between the Congress and the Muslim League hardened into a conflict between Hindus and Muslims, which ultimately led to the partition of India and the creation of Pakistan.

WORLD WAR II AND INDEPENDENCE

When, at the outbreak of World War II in September 1939, the viceroy, Lord Linlithgow, committed India to war without consulting the autonomous provincial ministries, the Congress Party's high command withdrew its provincial ministries as a protest. Congress's action left the political field virtually open to Jinnah and the Muslim League.

When the Japanese carried their attack through Burma (now Myanmar) to the borders of India in the spring of 1942, the British government, faced by this new military threat, decided to make some overtures to India. Prime Minister Winston Churchill dispatched Sir Stafford Cripps, a member of the war cabinet who was politically close to Nehru and also knew Jinnah, with proposals for a settlement of the constitutional problem. Cripps's mission failed, however, for Gandhi would accept nothing less than independence.

The initiative in the Congress Party now passed to Gandhi, who called on the British to leave India. Nehru, though reluctant to embarrass the war effort, had no alternative but to join Gandhi. Following the Quit India resolution passed by the Congress Party in Bombay (now Mumbai) on August 8, 1942, the entire Congress working committee, including Gandhi and Nehru, was arrested and imprisoned. Nehru emerged from this—his ninth and last detention—only on June 15, 1945.

Within two years India was to be partitioned and free. A final attempt by the viceroy, Lord Wavell, to bring the Congress Party and the Muslim League together failed. The Labour government that had meanwhile displaced Churchill's wartime administration dispatched a Cabinet mission to India and later replaced Lord Wavell with Lord Mountbatten. The question was no longer whether India was to be independent but whether it was to consist of one or more independent states. While Gandhi refused to accept partition, Nehru reluctantly but realistically acquiesced. On August 15, 1947, India and Pakistan emerged as two separate, independent countries. Nehru became independent India's first prime minister.

ACHIEVEMENTS AS PRIME MINISTER AND LEGACY

Nehru attempted a foreign policy of nonalignment during the Cold War, drawing harsh criticism if he appeared to favour either camp. During his tenure, India clashed with Pakistan over the Kashmir region (1948) and with China over the Brahmaputra River valley (1962). He wrested Goa from the Portuguese in 1961, which raised a furor in many

Western countries; but in the hindsight of history, Nehru's action is justifiable. The Kashmir region remained a perennial problem throughout Nehru's term as prime minister.

Nehru's health showed signs of deteriorating not long after the clash with China. He suffered a slight stroke in 1963, followed by a more debilitating attack in January 1964. He died a few months later from a third and fatal stroke.

Nehru's only child, Indira Gandhi, served as India's prime minister from 1966 to 1977 and from 1980 to 1984. Her son, Rajiv Gandhi, was prime minister from 1984 to 1989.

HO CHI MINH

(b. May 19, 1890, Hoang Tru, Vietnam, French Indochina—d. Sept. 2, 1969, Hanoi, Vietnam)

Ho Chi Minh was the founder of the Indochina Communist Party and its successor, the Viet Minh (1941). From 1945 to 1969, he was president of the Democratic Republic of Vietnam (North Vietnam).

EARLY LIFE

Born Nguyen Sinh Cung, Ho was brought up in the village of Kim Lien. The son of a poor country scholar, he had a wretched childhood, but between the ages of 14 and 18 he was able to study at a grammar school in Hue. He is next known to have been a schoolmaster in Phan Thiet and then was apprenticed at a technical institute in Saigon.

In 1911, under the name of Ba, he found work as a cook on a French steamer. He was a seaman for more than three years, visiting various African ports and the American cities of Boston and New York. After living in London from 1915 to 1917, he moved to France, where he worked, in turn, as a gardener, sweeper, waiter, photo retoucher, and oven stoker. While in Paris he became a socialist, working under the name Nguyen Ai Quoc ("Nguyen the Patriot"), and organized a group of Vietnamese living there in a protest against French colonial policy.

Inspired by the successful Communist revolution in Russia, he went to Moscow in 1924 and took part in the fifth Congress of the Communist International. His anticolonial views kept him from returning to Vietnam until the end of World War II. Much of his time was spent in China, where he organized the Indochina Communist Party on Feb. 3, 1930. It was in about 1940 that he began to use the name Ho Chi Minh, meaning "he who enlightens."

WORLD WAR II AND THE FOUNDING OF THE VIETNAMESE STATE

After crossing over the border from China into Vietnam in January 1941, Ho Chi Minh and some of his comrades organized the Viet Nam Doc Lap Dong Minh Hoi (League for the Independence of Vietnam), or Viet Minh; this gave renewed emphasis to a peculiarly Vietnamese nationalism.

In 1945 two events occurred that paved the way to power for the Vietnamese revolutionaries. First, the Japanese completely overran Indochina and imprisoned or executed all French officials. Six months later the United States dropped the atomic bomb on Hiroshima, and the Japanese were totally defeated. Thus, the two strongest adversaries of the Viet Minh and Ho Chi Minh were eliminated.

Ho Chi Minh seized his opportunity. Within a few months, he contacted U.S. forces and began to collaborate with the Office of Strategic Services (a U.S. undercover operation) against the Japanese. Further, his Viet Minh guerrillas fought against the Japanese in the mountains of South China. After Japan's surrender to the Allies in 1945, Ho Chi Minh's forces entered Hanoi, and on September 2 Ho Chi Minh declared Vietnam independent.

All obstacles were not removed from the path of the Viet Minh, however. According to the terms of an Allied agreement, Chiang Kai-shek's troops were supposed to replace the Japanese north of the 16th parallel. More significantly, France refused to relinquish its former colony, and within three months French troops had control of South Vietnam. Ho had to choose between continuing the fight or negotiating. He chose negotiations, but not without preparing for an eventual transition to war.

THE FIRST INDOCHINA WAR

The agreement, reached in March 1946, was unsatisfactory to extremists on both sides, and the First Indochina War began on December 19. Using guerrilla tactics, the Viet Minh had control of most of the countryside, with the larger cities under a virtual state of siege by the end of 1953. The French were decisively defeated at Dien Bien Phu on May 7, 1954, and had no choice but to negotiate. At the Geneva Accords, it was decided that Vietnam was to be divided at the 17th parallel—creating a North Vietnam and South Vietnam—until elections, scheduled for 1956, after which the Vietnamese would establish a unified government.

THE SECOND INDOCHINA WAR

Ultimately, the elections that were to guarantee the country's reunification were postponed indefinitely by the

United States and by South Vietnam. North Vietnam, where Ho and his associates were established, was a poor country, cut off from the vast agricultural areas of the south. Its leaders were forced to ask for assistance from their larger Communist allies, China and the Soviet Union. In these adverse conditions, Ho Chi Minh's regime became repressive and rigidly totalitarian. Attempted agricultural reforms in 1955–56 were conducted with ignorant brutality and repression. However, "Uncle" Ho, as he had become known to the North Vietnamese, was able to preserve his immense popularity.

Beginning about 1959, North Vietnam again became involved in war. Guerrillas, popularly known as the Vietcong, were conducting an armed revolt against the U.S.-sponsored regime in South Vietnam. Their leaders, veterans of the Viet Minh, appealed to North Vietnam for aid. In July 1959, at a meeting of the central committee of Ho Chi Minh's Lao Dong (Worker's Party), it was decided that the establishment of socialism in the North was linked with the unification with the South. This policy was confirmed by the third congress of the Lao Dong, held shortly thereafter in Hanoi. During the congress, Ho Chi Minh ceded his position as the party's secretary-general to Le Duan. He remained chief of state, but, from this point on, his activity was largely behind-the-scenes. Still, Ho certainly continued to have enormous influence in the government.

American air strikes against the North began in 1965. On July 17, 1966, Ho sent a message to the people — "nothing is as dear to the heart of the Vietnamese as independence and liberation" — that became the motto of the North Vietnamese cause. On February 15, 1967, in response to a personal message from U.S. president Lyndon Johnson, he announced: "We will never agree to negotiate under the threat of bombing." Ho lived to see only the beginning of a long round of negotiations before he died. The removal of this powerful leader undoubtedly damaged chances for an early settlement.

CHARLES DE GAULLE

(b. Nov. 22, 1890, Lille, France—d. Nov. 9, 1970, Colombey-les-deux-Églises)

C harles de Gaulle was a French soldier, writer, and statesman. He was the architect of France's Fifth Republic.

EDUCATION AND EARLY CAREER

Charles André Joseph Marie de Gaulle was the second son of a Roman Catholic, patriotic, and nationalist upper-middle-class family. He attended the Military Academy of Saint-Cyr, and in 1913, as a young second lieutenant, he joined an infantry regiment commanded by Colonel Philippe Pétain.

In World War I he fought at Verdun, was three times wounded, and spent two years and eight months as a prisoner of war (during which time he made five unsuccessful attempts to escape). He was released after the 1918 armistice. After the war, de Gaulle served on a military mission to Poland and then taught military history at Saint-Cyr. He became Pétain's aide in 1927 and served in the army in Germany and the Middle East. During the 1920s and 1930s, de Gaulle wrote several books on military subjects.

WORLD WAR II

At the outbreak of World War II, de Gaulle commanded a tank brigade attached to the French Fifth Army. On June 6 he entered the government of Paul Reynaud as undersecretary of state for defense and war, and he under-took several missions to England to explore the possibilities of continuing the war. When the Reynaud government was replaced 10 days later by that of Marshal Pétain, who intended to seek an armistice with the Germans, de Gaulle left for England. On June 18 he broadcast from London his first appeal to his compatri-ots to continue the war under his leadership. He established a shadow government and had only a handful of haphazardly recruited political supporters and volun-teers for what were to become the Free French Forces. On August 2, 1940, a French military court tried and sen-tenced him in absentia to death, deprivation of military rank, and confiscation of property. In 1943 he moved his headquarters to Algiers.

EARLY POLITICAL CAREER

On Sept. 9, 1944, de Gaulle and his shadow government returned from Algiers to Paris on the heels of the retreat-ing Germans. There he headed two successive provisional governments, but on Jan. 20, 1946, he abruptly resigned, apparently because of his irritation with the political par-ties forming the coalition government.

In 1947, still working for a strong central government, de Gaulle organized a new political party—the Rally of the French People (Rassemblement du Peuple Français; RPF). His influence declined, however, and in 1953, he sev-ered his connection with it. In the years that followed, de Gaulle's warnings against unstable government were justi-fied. No French government was able to stay in power for more than a few months. A major cause of the political uproar was the civil war fought in Algeria over French attempts to preserve colonialism in North Africa.

RETURN TO PUBLIC LIFE

De Gaulle was popular with the French army, and in 1958 a group of officers in Algeria appealed to him to restore order to the French government. De Gaulle then went to Paris for an interview with Pres. René Coty, who asked him to try to form a new government. De Gaulle agreed but only if the National Assembly would grant him the executive powers that he had long sought. France's Fifth Republic was formed in December, and de Gaulle took office as its first president on January 8, 1959.

De Gaulle's greatest challenge in his early years as president was to find a way to resolve the bloody and extraordinarily divisive Algerian War. De Gaulle promoted peace negotiations in Algeria, and in a nationwide referendum, the voters of France overwhelmingly supported a cease-fire agreement he had announced in March 1962. De Gaulle attributed the attainment of peace to his broad presidential powers. He declared Algeria's independence on July 3.

In 1962, de Gaulle proposed that future presidents be chosen by popular election. His plan was approved in a national referendum. De Gaulle also increased his efforts to make France a leading world power. He moved to strengthen the country's economy, and, at his urging, the French developed a nuclear force and a space program.

From 1962 until his reelection as president in 1965, de Gaulle used the European Economic Community (EEC; now part of the European Union) to serve French interests. France's participation in the supranational North Atlantic Treaty Organization (NATO) was progressively withdrawn, because de Gaulle's policy for France was one of "national independence" and of international cooperation based only on agreements between nation-states. This was the main theme of his presidential campaign in 1965. On December 21 he was reelected, and on March 7, 1966, de Gaulle announced France's withdrawal from the integrated military command of NATO but not from the alliance.

During the remainder of his second term as president, de Gaulle turned his attention increasingly to wider fields. He had already begun a policy of "détente and cooperation" with countries behind the Iron Curtain by encouraging trade and cultural relations with the Soviet Union and the countries of eastern Europe and by recognizing the People's Republic of China in January 1964. As a solution for the Vietnam War, he advocated a policy of neutrality for all nations concerned, based on a negotiated peace of which a necessary preliminary was to be the withdrawal of all U.S. troops from Vietnam.

After civil unrest in May 1968 by students and workers, de Gaulle was defeated in a referendum on constitutional amendments. On April 28, 1969, he resigned and returned to Colombey-les-deux-Églises to retire permanently and to resume writing his memoirs. There he died of a heart attack the following year.

JOSIP BROZ TITO

(b. May 7, 1892, Kumrovec, near Zagreb, Croatia, Austria-Hungary [now in Croatia] — d. May 4, 1980, Ljubljana, Yugos. [now in Slovenia])

The chief architect of the "second Yugoslavia," a socialist federation that lasted from World War II until 1991, Josip Broz Tito, known simply by his pseudonym, Tito, was the first Communist leader in power to defy Soviet hegemony, a backer of independent roads to socialism, and a promoter of the policy of nonalignment between the two hostile blocs in the Cold War.

Early Life

Josip Broz was born to a large peasant family, of a Croat father and a Slovene mother. After working as an itinerant metalworker, he was drafted into the Austro-Hungarian army in 1913 to fight in World War I. As a prisoner-of-war of the Russians, he became acquainted with Bolshevik propaganda. In 1917 he participated in the July Days demonstrations in Petrograd (St. Petersburg) and, after the October Revolution, joined a Red Guard unit in Omsk, Siberia. In October 1920 he returned to his native Croatia—then part of the newly established Kingdom of the Serbs, Croats, and Slovenes—and soon joined the Communist Party of Yugoslavia (CPY). His rise in the party hierarchy was interrupted by a five-year prison sentence for possession of bombs. In 1934, after his release from prison, Broz assumed the pseudonym Tito. From February 1935 to October 1936, he worked in the Soviet Union in the Comintern, becoming its choice for the CPY's new secretary-general in 1939. Tito's leftist strategy for the CPY focused the party on armed insurrection and on a Soviet-style federalist solution to Yugoslavia's nationality conflict.

Partisan Leader

After Germany attacked Yugoslavia on April 6, 1941, Tito became the leader of Communist-dominated Partisan resistance. Its ultimate aim, carefully concealed in the rhetoric of "national liberation struggle," was the seizure of power. In Partisan-held territories Communist-dominated administrative organs were established that prefigured the future federal republics. As a result, Tito's Partisans threatened not only the occupiers and collaborators but also the royal government-in-exile and its domestic exponents, the Serbian Chetniks. In time, Communist pressure drove the Chetniks into tactical alliances with the Axis, thereby precipitating their isolation and defeat.

In 1943, the Western Allies recognized Tito as the leader of the Yugoslav resistance and obliged the London government-in-exile to come to terms with him. The Soviet army, aided by Tito's Partisans, liberated Serbia in October 1944, thereby sealing the fate of the Yugoslav dynasty. In the process of mop-up operations, the Yugoslav frontiers were extended to take in Istria and portions of the Julian Alps, where reprisals against fleeing Croat and Slovene collaborationists were especially brutal.

THE CONFLICT WITH STALIN

Tito consolidated his power in the summer and fall of 1945 by purging his government of noncommunists and by holding fraudulent elections that legitimated the jettisoning of the monarchy. The Federal People's Republic of Yugoslavia was proclaimed under a new constitution in November 1945. Tito's excesses in imitation of Soviet methods eventually became as irritating to Moscow as did his independent manner—especially in foreign policy. After a series of Stalin-initiated moves to purge the Yugoslav leadership failed, the CPY was expelled from the Cominform, the international organization of mainly ruling Communist parties. Yugoslavia, cut off from the Soviet bloc, steadily drew closer to the West.

THE POLICY OF NONALIGNMENT

By 1953 Western military aid to Yugoslavia had evolved into an informal association with NATO via a tripartite pact with Greece and Turkey. After the changes in the Soviet Union following Stalin's death in 1953, Tito was faced with a choice: continue the Westward course and give up one-party dictatorship or seek reconciliation with a somewhat reformed new Soviet leadership. The latter course became increasingly possible after a conciliatory state visit by Nikita Khrushchev to Belgrade in May 1955. However, the limits of reconciliation with the Soviets became obvious after the Soviet intervention in Hungary in 1956, which was followed by a new Soviet campaign blaming Tito for inspiring the Hungarian insurgents. Nevertheless, Stalin's departure lessened the pressures for greater integration with the West, and Tito came to conceive of his internal and foreign policy as being equidistant from both blocs. Negotiations with Gamal Abdel Nasser of Egypt and Jawaharlal Nehru of India in June 1956 led to a closer cooperation among states that were "nonengaged" in the East-West confrontation. From nonengagement evolved the concept of "active nonalignment"—that is, the promotion of alternatives to bloc politics, as opposed to mere neutrality. The first meeting of nonaligned states took place in Belgrade under Tito's sponsorship in 1961.

SELF-MANAGEMENT AND DECENTRALIZATION

The break with the Soviet Union also inspired a search for a new model of socialism in Yugoslavia, and Tito, never a theoretician, depended on the ideological formulations of his lieutenants, notably Edvard Kardelj. He supported the notion of workers' management of production, embodied in the formation of the first workers' councils in 1950. In the process, Soviet-style central planning was abandoned. As power steadily shifted from the federation to the republics, conservative centralist forces fought back, dividing the Communist elite between 1963 and 1972. During this period Tito purged first the Serbian centralists and then the leaders of the decentralizing and liberal forces in Croatia in 1971 and then in Serbia in 1972.

RETRENCHMENT OF THE 1970S

Tito's response to the crises of the 1960s and early 1970s was to fashion a system of "symmetrical federalism," in which various internal rules and rituals (including a rotating presidency to lead Yugoslavia after Tito's death) were supposed to formalize equality among the six republics and Serbia's two autonomous provinces, Kosovo and the Vojvodina. This system, enshrined in the constitution of 1974, promoted the weaker and smaller federal units at the expense of the big two—Serbia and Croatia. Serbia's displeasure at the independent role assigned to its autonomous provinces and the promotion of minority identity—especially that of the Albanians in Kosovo—was felt already in Tito's last years, but it became radicalized after his death in 1980. Serb resentment provided the opening for Slobodan Milošević and other promoters of recentralization, who contributed greatly to the undoing of Tito's federal system during the following decade.

FRANCISCO FRANCO

(b. Dec. 4, 1892, El Ferrol, Spain—d. Nov. 20, 1975, Madrid)

Francisco Franco was a general who led the Nationalist forces that overthrew the Spanish democratic republic during the Spanish Civil War, which lasted from 1936 to 1939. Thereafter, he led Spain as its dictator until his death in 1975.

LIFE

Francisco Paulino Hermenegildo Teódulo Franco Bahamonde was born at the coastal city and naval centre of El Ferrol in Galicia (northwestern Spain). Franco entered the Infantry Academy at Toledo in 1907 and graduated in July 1910 as a second lieutenant. At 17 he was in Spanish Morocco fighting the Rif. He rose in rank rapidly. He was a major at 23, commander of the Spanish foreign legion at 30, and a general at 33—the youngest in Europe at the time. After that Franco's fortunes rose and fell with the change of governments.

In May 1935, he was appointed chief of the Spanish army's general staff, and he began tightening discipline and strengthening military institutions. Later that year, following a number of scandals that weakened the Radicals—one of the parties of the governing coalition—parliament was dissolved, and new elections were announced for February 1936. By this time the Spanish political parties had split into two factions: the rightist National Bloc and the leftist Popular Front. The left proved victorious in the elections, but the new government was unable to prevent the accelerating dissolution of Spain's social and economic structure. Although Franco had never been a member of a political party, the growing anarchy impelled him to appeal to the government to declare a state of emergency. His appeal was refused, and he was removed from the general staff and sent to an obscure command in the Canary Islands. For some time he refused to commit himself to a military conspiracy against the government, but, as the political system disintegrated, he finally decided to join the rebels.

FRANCO'S MILITARY REBELLION

At dawn on July 18, 1936, Franco's manifesto acclaiming the military rebellion was broadcast from the Canary Islands, and the same morning the rising began on the mainland. The following day he flew to Morocco and within 24 hours was firmly in control of the protectorate and the Spanish army garrisoning it. After landing in Spain, Franco and his army marched toward Madrid, which was held by the government. When the Nationalist advance came to a halt on the outskirts of the city, the military leaders—in preparation of what they believed was the final assault that would deliver Madrid and the country into their hands—decided to choose a commander in chief, or generalissimo, who would also head the rebel Nationalist government in opposition to the republic. In part because he was not a typical Spanish "political general," Franco was chosen as the head of state of the new Nationalist regime on Oct. 1, 1936. The rebel government did not, however, gain complete control of the country for more than three years.

Franco presided over a government that was basically a military dictatorship, but he realized that it needed a regular civil structure to broaden its support. On April 19, 1937, he fused the Falange (the Spanish Fascist party) with the Carlists and created the rebel regime's official political movement. He became its head and assumed the title El Caudillo ("The Leader")

As commander in chief during the Civil War, Franco was a careful and systematic leader. Because of the relatively superior military quality of his army and the continuation of heavy German and Italian assistance, Franco won a complete and unconditional victory on April 1, 1939.

The Civil War had been largely a ruthless struggle of attrition, marked by atrocities on both sides. The tens of thousands of executions carried out by the Nationalist regime, which continued during the first years after the war ended, earned Franco more reproach than any other single aspect of his rule.

FRANCO'S DICTATORSHIP

Although Franco had visions of restoring Spanish grandeur after the Civil War, in reality he was the leader of an exhausted country still divided internally and impoverished by a long and costly war. The stability of his government was made more precarious by the outbreak of World War II only five months later. Franco declared Spanish neutrality in the conflict. After a failed attempt to negotiate with Hitler, his government thenceforth remained relatively sympathetic to the Axis powers while carefully avoiding any direct diplomatic and military commitment to them.

The most difficult period of Franco's regime began in the aftermath of World War II, when his government was ostracized by the newly formed United Nations. He was labeled by hostile foreign opinion as the "last surviving fascist dictator." For a time, Franco appeared to be the most hated of Western heads of state, but within his country, as many people supported him as opposed him. Relations with other nations regularized with the onset of the Cold War, as Franco became a leading anticommunist statesman.

Franco's domestic policies became somewhat more liberal during the 1950s and 1960s, and the continuity of his regime, with its capacity for creative evolution, won him a limited degree of respect from some of his critics. The Falange state party, downgraded in the early 1940s, in later years became known merely as the "Movement" and lost much of its original quasi-Fascist identity.

Unlike most rulers of rightist authoritarian regimes, Franco provided for the continuity of his government after his death through an official referendum in 1947. It made the Spanish state a monarchy and ratified Franco's powers as a sort of regent for life. In 1967 he opened direct elections for a small minority of deputies to the parliament. In 1969, Franco officially designated the then 32-year-old prince Juan Carlos—the eldest son of the nominal pretender to the Spanish throne—as his official successor upon his death. Franco resigned his position of premier in 1973 but retained his functions as head of state, commander in chief of the armed forces, and head of the Movement. Franco died in 1975 following a long illness.

MAO ZEDONG

(b. Dec. 26, 1893, Shaoshan, Hunan Province, China—d. Sept. 9, 1976, Beijing)

Mao Zedong was a Chinese Marxist theorist, soldier, and statesman who led his nation's Communist revolution. Leader of the Chinese Communist Party from 1935, he was chairman of the People's Republic of China from 1949 to 1959 and chairman of the party until his death.

EARLY YEARS

Born in the village of Shaoshan in Hunan Province, Mao was the son of a former peasant who had become affluent as a farmer and grain dealer. Mao's schooling was intermittent. During the Revolution of 1911–12 (to overthrow the Qing dynasty), he served in the army for six months. After that he drifted for a while without goals, but he managed to graduate from the First Provincial Normal

Mao Zedong. Encyclopædia Britannica, Inc.

School in Changsha in 1918. He then went to Peking (later Beijing) University, where he became embroiled in the revolutionary May Fourth Movement in 1919. This movement marked the decisive turn in Chinese revolutionary thought in favor of Marxist Communism as a solution to China's problems.

In 1921 Mao helped found the Chinese Communist Party. Two years later, when the Communists forged an alliance with Sun Yat-sen's Nationalist party, the Kuomintang, he left work to become a full-time revolutionary. It was at this time that Mao discovered the great potential of the peasant class for making revolution. This realization led him to the brilliant strategy he used to win control of China: gain control of the countryside and encircle the cities.

The Communists and the Nationalists coexisted in an uneasy relationship until the end of World War II. The Nationalist leader after 1925 was Chiang Kai-shek, who was determined to rule China. He never trusted the Communists, and at times he persecuted them. In October 1927 Mao led a few hundred peasants to a base in the Jinggang Mountains, on the Jiangxi-Hunan border, and embarked on a new type of revolutionary warfare in the countryside in which the Red Army would play the central role.

ROAD TO THE PEOPLE'S REPUBLIC OF CHINA

Mao Zedong's 22 years in the wilderness can be divided into four phases. The first of these is the initial three years when Mao and Zhu De, the commander in chief of the army, successfully developed the tactics of guerrilla warfare from base areas in the countryside.

The second phase (the Ziangxi period) centres on the founding in November 1931 of the Chinese Soviet Republic in a portion of Jiangxi Province, with Mao as chairman. The Red Army, grown to a strength of some 200,000

Jiang Qing and Mao Zedong, 1945. Library of Congress, Washington, D.C. (neg. no. LC-USZ62-126856)

soldiers, easily defeated large forces of inferior troops sent against it by Chiang Kai-shek. But it was unable to stand up against Chiang's own elite units, and in October of 1934, the major part of the Red Army and Mao abandoned the base in Jiangxi and set out for the northwest of China. This event became known as the Long March.

When some 8,000 troops who had survived the perils of the Long March arrived in Shaanxi Province in northwestern China in the autumn of 1935, events were already moving toward the third phase in Mao's rural odyssey. The third phase was to be characterized by a renewed united front with the Nationalists against Japan and by the rise of Mao to unchallenged supremacy in the party. This phase is often called the Yan'an period (for the town in Shaanxi where the Communists were based). By the time the Japanese began their attempt to subjugate all of China in July 1937, the terms of a new united front between the Communists and the Nationalists had been virtually settled, and the formal agreement was announced in September 1937.

In March of 1943, Mao became chairman of the Secretariat and of the Political Bureau. Shortly thereafter the Rectification Campaign took, for a time, the form of a harsh purge of elements not sufficiently loyal to Mao.

Mao's campaign in the countryside then moved into its fourth and last phase—that of civil war with the Nationalists. The People's Liberation Army took Nanjing in April of 1949. Mao's agrarian Marxism differed from the Soviet model, but, when the Communists succeeded in taking power in China in 1949, the Soviet Union agreed to provide the new state with technical assistance.

GREAT LEAP FORWARD

Mao's Great Leap Forward, an industrialization campaign, was formally launched in May 1958. The peasants were to be reorganized into "people's communes." However, neither the resources nor the administrative experience necessary to operate such enormous new social units of several thousand households were in fact available, and, not surprisingly, the consequences of these changes were chaos and economic disaster.

Mao's Great Leap Forward and his criticism of "new bourgeois elements" in the Soviet Union and China alienated the Soviet Union irrevocably; Soviet aid was withdrawn in 1960. The disorganization and waste created by the Great Leap, compounded by natural disasters and by the termination of Soviet economic aid, led to widespread famine in which, according to much later official Chinese accounts, millions of people died.

CULTURAL REVOLUTION

The movement that became known as the Great Proletarian Cultural Revolution represented an attempt by Mao to devise a new and more radical method for dealing with what he saw as the bureaucratic degeneration of the party. But it also represented, beyond any doubt, a deliberate effort to eliminate those in the leadership who, over the years, had dared to cross him. The victims, from throughout the party hierarchy, suffered more than mere political disgrace. All were publicly humiliated and detained for varying periods, sometimes under very harsh conditions. Many were beaten and tortured, and not a few were killed or driven to suicide.

This vast upheaval wrecked the Communist Party bureaucracy, paralyzed education and research, and left the economy almost a shambles. Only slowly did China begin to recover. By then Mao was old and ill. Other, more moderate hands guided policy. Zhou Enlai seemed to emerge as the nation's real leader when relations were reestablished with the United States. Nonetheless, Mao's personality cult remained strong until his death in 1976.

JUAN, EVA, AND ISABEL PERÓN

Respectively (b. Oct. 8, 1895, Lobos, Buenos Aires *provincia*, Argentina—d. July 1, 1974, Buenos Aires); (b. May 7, 1919, Los Toldos, Arg.—d. July 26, 1952, Buenos Aires); (b. Feb. 4, 1931, La Rioja, Arg.)

Juan Perón, his second wife Eva, and third wife Isabel were important figures in 20th-century Argentinian politics. Juan was an army colonel who became president of Argentina during the years 1946–52, 1952–55, and 1973–74 and was founder and leader of the Peronist movement. During Juan's first term as president, Eva (Evita) became a powerful, though unofficial, political leader, revered by the lower economic classes. His third wife, Isabel, although not as popular as Eva, served as president of Argentina from 1974 to 1976 after his death.

JUAN PERÓN

Juan Domingo Perón entered military school at 16 and made somewhat better than average progress through the officer ranks. He served in Chile as a military attaché and travelled to Italy to observe the rise of the Fascists and Nazis during 1938–40. Perón returned to Argentina in 1941, and in 1943 he helped overthrow Argentina's ineffective civilian government. He held several government posts but was ousted and briefly imprisoned in October 1945.

After a campaign marked by repression of the liberal opposition by the federal police and by strong-arm squads, Perón was elected president in February 1946 with 56 percent of the popular vote. Perón set Argentina on a course of industrialization and state intervention in the economy, calculated to provide greater economic and social benefits for the working class. During his first term his second wife, Eva, became a powerful, but unofficial, influence revered by the lower classes as Evita. She organized woman workers, obtained for women the right to vote, promoted welfare programs, and introduced compulsory religious education. Perón nationalized the railroads and other utilities and financed public works. He used the armed forces to stifle dissent.

Reelected leader of the Justicialist Party (Partido Justicialista) by a somewhat larger margin in 1951, Perón modified some of his policies. But he was overthrown and fled to Paraguay on September 19, 1955, after an army-navy revolt led by democratically inspired officers who reflected growing popular discontent with inflation, corruption, demagoguery, and oppression. Perón finally settled in Madrid. Evita had died of cancer in 1952, and he married for the third time in 1961. Perón's new wife was the former María Estela (called Isabel) Martínez, an Argentine dancer.

The military regime of General Alejandro Lanusse, which took power in Argentina in March 1971, proclaimed its intention to restore constitutional democracy by the end of 1973 and allowed the reestablishment of political parties, including the Peronist Party. Upon invitation from the military government, Perón returned to Argentina for a short time in November of 1972. In the elections of March 1973, Peronist candidates captured the presidency and majorities in the legislature, and, in June, Perón was welcomed back to Argentina with wild excitement. In October, in a special election, he was elected president and, at his insistence, his wife—whom the Argentines disliked and resented—became vice president. She failed to win the type of support Evita had received and was eventually ousted by the armed forces.

Eva Perón

María Eva Duarte married Juan Perón in 1945 after an undistinguished career as a stage and radio actress. She participated in her husband's 1945–46 presidential campaign, winning the adulation of the masses, whom she addressed as *los descamisados* (or "the shirtless ones").

Although she never held any government post, Evita, as she was affectionately called, acted as de facto minister of health and labour, awarding generous wage increases to the unions, who responded with political support for Perón. After cutting off government subsidies to the traditional Sociedad de Beneficencia ("Aid Society"), thereby making more enemies among the traditional elite, she replaced it with her own Eva Perón Foundation, which was supported by "voluntary" union and business contributions plus a substantial cut of the national lottery and other funds. These resources were used to establish thousands of hospitals, schools, orphanages, homes for the aged, and other charitable institutions. Evita was largely responsible for the passage of the woman suffrage law and formed the Peronista Feminist Party in 1949. She also introduced compulsory religious education into all Argentine schools. In 1951, although dying of cancer, she obtained the nomination for vice president, but the army forced her to withdraw her candidacy.

After her death, Evita remained a formidable influence in Argentine politics. Her working-class followers tried unsuccessfully to have her canonized, and her enemies— in an effort to exorcise her as a national symbol of Peronism—stole her embalmed body in 1955 after Juan Perón was overthrown and hid it in Italy for 16 years. In 1971 the military government, bowing to Peronist demands, turned over her remains to her exiled widower in Madrid. After Juan Perón died in office in 1974, his third wife, Isabel Perón, hoping to gain favour among the populace, repatriated the remains and installed them next to the deceased leader in a crypt in the presidential palace. Two years later a new military junta hostile to Peronism removed the bodies; Evita's remains were finally interred in the Duarte family crypt in Recoleta cemetery.

ISABEL PERÓN

María Estela Martínez Cartas was born to a lower-middle-class family, acquired the name Isabel (her saint's name) on her Roman Catholic confirmation, and adopted the name when she became a dancer. She met Juan Perón in either 1955 or 1956 and, giving up her career in show business, became his personal secretary. She accompanied him in exile to Madrid, where they were married in 1961. She visited Argentina several times in the 1960s and early 1970s, building support for Perón. When Perón finally returned to Argentina to run for president in 1973, Isabel was chosen as his running mate on the suggestion of Perón's close adviser José López Rega. Perón's illness elevated her several times to the position of acting president, and when he died on July 1, 1974, she succeeded him in office, becoming the world's first woman president.

Her regime inherited problems of inflation, labour unrest, and political violence. She attempted to solve the problems by appointing new cabinet ministers, printing money to pay foreign debts, and imposing a state of siege in November 1974 as the country was on the brink of anarchy. The controversy surrounding her social-welfare minister López Rega, who was forced into exile for graft and terrorist activities, did not help her situation. Moderate military officers urged her to resign, but she stubbornly refused. The economic and political situation continued to worsen, and on March 24, 1976, she was seized by air force officers and held under house arrest for five years. In 1981 she was convicted of corrupt practices, but she was paroled in the summer of that year and went into exile in Spain. Pardoned in late 1983, she submitted her resignation as head of the Partido Justicialista, the Peronist party, from her home in Madrid in 1985. In 2007 an Argentine judge issued a warrant for her arrest on charges of allowing the armed forces to commit human rights abuses during her presidency.

RUHOLLAH KHOMEINI

(b. Sept. 24, 1902?, Khomeyn, Iran—d. June 3, 1989, Tehrān)

Ruhollah Khomeini was one of the most influential figures in Iranian history, the Iranian Shī'ite cleric who led the revolution that overthrew Mohammad Reza Shah Pahlavi in 1979, and Iran's ultimate political and religious authority for the next 10 years.

Little is known of Khomeini's early life. There are various dates given for his birth, the most common being May 17, 1900, and Sept. 24, 1902. Originally named Ruhollah Musawi, he was the grandson and son of mullahs, or Shī'ite religious leaders. When he was five months old, his father was killed on the orders of a local landlord. The young Khomeini was raised by his mother and aunt and then by his older brother. He was educated in various Islamic schools, and he settled in the city of Qom about 1922. About 1930 he adopted the name of his home town, Khomayn (also spelled Khomeyn or Khomen), as his surname. As a Shī'ite scholar and teacher, Khomeini produced numerous writings on Islamic philosophy, law, and ethics. But it was his outspoken opposition to Iran's ruler, Mohammad Reza Shah Pahlavi, his denunciations of Western influences, and his uncompromising advocacy of Islamic purity that won him his initial following in Iran. In the 1950s he was acclaimed as an ayatollah, or major religious leader, and by the early 1960s he had received the title of grand ayatollah, thereby making him one of the supreme religious leaders of the Shī'ite community in Iran.

In 1962–63 Khomeini spoke out against the shah's reduction of religious estates in a land-reform program and against the emancipation of women. His ensuing arrest sparked antigovernment riots, and, after a year's imprisonment, Khomeini was forcibly exiled from Iran on Nov. 4, 1964. He eventually settled in the Shī'ite holy city of Al-Najaf, Iraq, from where he continued to call for the shah's overthrow and the establishment of an Islamic republic in Iran.

From the mid-1970s, Khomeini's influence inside Iran grew dramatically owing to mounting public dissatisfaction with the shah's regime. Iraq's ruler, Ṣaddām Ḥussein, forced Khomeini to leave Iraq on Oct. 6, 1978. Khomeini then settled in Neauphle-le-Château, a suburb of Paris. From there his supporters relayed his tape-recorded messages to an increasingly aroused Iranian populace, and massive demonstrations, strikes, and civil unrest in late 1978 forced the departure of the shah from the country on Jan. 16, 1979. Khomeini arrived in Tehrān in triumph on Feb. 1, 1979, and was acclaimed as the religious leader of Iran's revolution. He appointed a government four days later and on March 1 again took up residence in Qom. In December a referendum on a new constitution created an Islamic republic in Iran, with Khomeini named Iran's political and religious leader for life.

Khomeini himself proved unwavering in his determination to transform Iran into a theocratically ruled

Islamic state. Iran's Shī'ite clerics largely took over the formulation of governmental policy, while Khomeini arbitrated between the various revolutionary factions and made final decisions on important matters requiring his personal authority. First his regime took political vengeance, with hundreds of people who had worked for the shah's regime reportedly executed. The remaining domestic opposition was then suppressed, its members being systematically imprisoned or killed. Iranian women were required to wear the veil, Western music and alcohol were banned, and the punishments prescribed by Islamic law were reinstated.

The main thrust of Khomeini's foreign policy was the complete abandonment of the shah's pro-Western orientation and the adoption of an attitude of unrelenting hostility toward both superpowers. In addition, Iran tried to export its brand of Islamic revivalism to neighbouring Muslim countries. Khomeini sanctioned Iranian militants' seizure of the U.S. embassy in Tehrān on Nov. 4, 1979, and their holding of American diplomatic personnel as hostages for more than a year. He also refused to countenance a peaceful solution to the Iran-Iraq War, which had begun in 1980 and which he insisted on prolonging in the hope of overthrowing Ṣaddām. Khomeini finally approved a cease-fire in 1988 that effectively ended the war.

Iran's course of economic development foundered under Khomeini's rule, and his pursuit of victory in the Iran-Iraq War ultimately proved futile. Khomeini, however, was able to retain his charismatic hold over Iran's Shī'ite masses, and he remained the supreme political and religious arbiter in the country until his death in 1989. His gold-domed tomb in Tehrān's Behesht-e Zahrā' cemetery has since become a shrine for his supporters. Ideologically, he is best remembered for having developed the concept of *vilāyat-e faqīh* ("guardianship of the jurist") in a series of lectures and tracts first shared during his exile in Iraq in the late 1960s and 1970s. Khomeini argued therein for the establishment of a theocratic government administered by Islamic jurists in place of corrupt secular regimes. The Iranian constitution of 1979 embodies articles upholding this concept of juristic authority.

HIROHITO

(b. April 29, 1901, Tokyo, Japan—d. Jan. 7, 1989, Tokyo)

Hirohito was the longest-reigning monarch in Japan's history, serving as emperor of Japan from 1926 until his death in 1989.

Michinomiya Hirohito was born at the Aoyama Palace in Tokyo and was educated at the Peers' School and at the Crown Prince's Institute. Early in life he developed an interest in marine biology, on which he later wrote several books. In 1921 he visited Europe, becoming the first Japanese crown prince to travel abroad. Upon his return he was named prince regent when his father, the emperor Taishō, retired because of mental illness. In 1924 he married the princess Nagako Kuni.

Hirohito became emperor of Japan on Dec. 25, 1926, following the death of his father. His reign was designated Shōwa, or "Enlightened Peace." The Japanese constitution invested him with supreme authority, but in practice he merely ratified the policies that were formulated by his ministers and advisers. Many historians have asserted that Hirohito had grave misgivings about war with the United States and was opposed to Japan's alliance with Germany and Italy, but that he was powerless to resist the militarists who dominated the armed forces and the government. Other historians assert that Hirohito might have been involved in the planning of Japan's expansionist policies from 1931 to World War II. Whatever the truth may be, in

1945, Japan was close to defeat and opinion among the country's leaders was divided between those favouring surrender and those insisting on a desperate defense of the home islands against an anticipated invasion by the Allies. Hirohito settled the dispute in favour of those urging peace. He broke the precedent of imperial silence on Aug. 15, 1945, when he made a national radio broadcast to announce Japan's acceptance of the Allies' terms of surrender. In a second historic broadcast, made on Jan. 1, 1946, Hirohito rejected the traditional quasi-divine status of Japan's emperors.

Under the nation's new constitution, drafted by U.S. occupation authorities, Japan became a constitutional monarchy. Sovereignty resided in the people, not in the emperor, whose powers were severely curtailed. In an effort to bring the imperial family closer to the people, Hirohito began to make numerous public appearances and permitted publication of pictures and stories of his personal and family life. In 1959 his oldest son, Crown Prince Akihito, married a commoner, Shōda Michiko, breaking a 1,500-year tradition. In 1971 Hirohito broke another tradition when he toured Europe and became the first reigning Japanese monarch to visit abroad. In 1975 he made a state visit to the United States. Upon his death in 1989, Hirohito was succeeded as emperor by Akihito.

SUKARNO

(b. June 6, 1901, Surabaja, Java, Dutch East Indies—d. June 21, 1970, Jakarta, Indonesia)

Sukarno was the leader of the Indonesian independence movement and Indonesia's first president, serving from 1949 to 1966.

Born on the Indonesian island of Java in 1901, Sukarno was the only son of a poor Javanese schoolteacher. He attended the Bandung Technical Institute, graduating in 1925. As a student he excelled in languages, mastering Javanese, Sundanese, Balinese, and modern Indonesian, which he did much to create, and others. He had a degree in civil engineering but soon found politics far more appealing. His eloquent speaking ability soon made him Java's foremost proponent of independence. He was jailed (1929–31) and exiled (1933–42) for his views.

When the Japanese invaded the Indies in March of 1942, he welcomed them as personal and national liberators. During World War II, the Japanese made Sukarno their chief adviser. Immediately following Japan's defeat, he declared Indonesia's independence on Aug. 17, 1945. As president of the shaky new republic, he fueled a successful defiance of the Dutch, who, after two abortive police actions to regain control, formally transferred sovereignty on Dec. 27, 1949.

From his revolutionary capital in Jogjakarta, Sukarno returned in triumph to Jakarta on Dec. 28, 1949. There he established himself in the splendid palace of the Dutch governors-general. His increasingly numerous and outspoken critics maintained that Sukarno inspired no coherent programs of national organization and administration, rehabilitation, and development, such as were quite clearly necessary. He seemed instead to conduct a continuous series of formal and informal audiences and a nightly soiree of receptions, banquets, music, dancing, and entertainment. The Indonesian economy foundered while Sukarno encouraged the wildest of extravagances.

To be sure, the nation scored impressive gains in health, education, and cultural self-awareness and self-expression. It achieved, in fact, what Sukarno himself most joyously sought and acclaimed as national identity, an exhilarating sense of pride in being Indonesian. But this achievement came at a ruinous cost.

After "dreaming" in late 1956 of "burying" the feuding political parties in Indonesia and thus achieving national consensus and prosperity, Sukarno dismantled parliamentary democracy and destroyed free enterprise. He ordained "Guided Democracy" and "Guided Economy" for the achievement of Manipol-Usdek and Resopim-Nasakom—arcane acronyms symbolizing policies but signifying dictatorship. Sukarno narrowly escaped recurrent attempts at assassination, the first in 1957. Regional insurrections broke out in Sumatra and Sulawesi in 1958.

In 1965, still popular with the people, Sukarno was implicated in the murder of six army officers by Communist conspirators. The commander of the Jakarta garrison, General Suharto, put down a Communist insurrection. The public now demanded an end to Sukarno's rule. On March 11, 1966, he was forced to delegate wide powers to Suharto, who subsequently became acting president (March 1967) and then president (March 1968), as Sukarno sank into disgrace, dying at the age of 69 of a chronic kidney ailment and numerous complications.

DENG XIAOPING

(b. Aug. 22, 1904, Guang'an, Sichuan Province, China—d. Feb. 19, 1997, Beijing)

The Chinese Communist leader Deng Xiaoping was the most powerful figure in the People's Republic of China from the late 1970s until his death in 1997. He abandoned many orthodox Communist doctrines and attempted to incorporate elements of the free-enterprise system into the Chinese economy.

Deng was the son of a landowner and studied in France from 1920 to 1924—where he became active in the Communist movement—and in the Soviet Union in

1925–26. He then returned to China and later became a leading political and military organizer in the Jiangxi Soviet, an autonomous Communist enclave in southwestern China that had been established by Mao Zedong. Deng participated in the Long March (1934–35) of the Chinese Communists to a new base in northwestern China. After serving as the commissar (or political officer) of a division of the Communists' Eighth Route Army (1937–45), he was appointed a secretary of the Central Committee of the Chinese Communist Party (CCP) in 1945 and served as chief commissar of the Communists' Second Field Army during the Chinese Civil War (1947–49). After the Communist takeover of China in 1949, Deng became the regional party leader of southwestern China. In 1952 he was summoned to Beijing and became a vice premier. Rising rapidly, he became general secretary of the CCP in 1954 and a member of the ruling Political Bureau in 1955.

From the mid-1950s, Deng was a major policy maker in both foreign and domestic affairs. He became closely allied with such pragmatist leaders as Liu Shaoqi, who stressed the use of material incentives and the formation of skilled technical and managerial elites in China's quest for economic development. Deng thus came into increasing conflict with Mao, who stressed egalitarian policies and revolutionary enthusiasm as the key to economic growth, in opposition to Deng's emphasis on individual self-interest.

Deng was attacked during the Cultural Revolution (1966–76) by radical supporters of Mao—later dubbed the Gang of Four—and he was stripped of his high party and government posts sometime in the years 1967–69, after which he disappeared from public view. In 1973, however, Deng was reinstated under the sponsorship of Premier Zhou Enlai and was made deputy premier. In 1975 he became vice chairman of the party's Central Committee, a member of its Political Bureau, and chief of the general staff. As effective head of the government during the months preceding the death of Zhou, he was widely considered the likely successor to Zhou. However, upon Zhou's death in January 1976, the Gang of Four managed to purge Deng from the leadership once again. It was not until Mao's death in September 1976 and the consequent fall from power of the Gang of Four that Deng was rehabilitated, this time with the assent of Mao's chosen successor to the leadership of China, Hua Guofeng.

By July 1977 Deng had returned to his high posts. He soon embarked upon a struggle with Hua for control of the party and government. Deng's superior political skills and broad base of support soon led Hua to surrender the premiership and the chairmanship to protégés of Deng in 1980–81. Zhao Ziyang became premier of the government, and Hu Yaobang became general secretary of the CCP; both men looked to Deng for guidance.

From this point on, Deng proceeded to carry out his own policies for the economic development of China. Operating through consensus, compromise, and persuasion, Deng engineered important reforms in virtually all aspects of China's political, economic, and social life. His most important social reform was the institution of the world's most rigorous family-planning program in order to control China's burgeoning population. He instituted decentralized economic management and rational and flexible long-term planning to achieve efficient and controlled economic growth. China's peasant farmers were given individual control over and responsibility for their production and profits, a policy that resulted in greatly increased agricultural production within a few years of its initiation in 1981. Deng stressed individual responsibility in the making of economic decisions, material incentives as the reward for industry and initiative, and the formation of groups of skilled, well-educated technicians and managers to spearhead China's development. He freed many industrial enterprises from the control and supervision of the central government and gave factory managers the authority to determine production levels and to pursue profits for their enterprises. In foreign affairs, Deng strengthened China's trade and cultural ties with the West and opened up Chinese enterprises to foreign investment.

Deng eschewed the most conspicuous leadership posts in the party and government. But he was a member of the powerful Standing Committee of the Political Bureau, and he retained control of the armed forces by virtue of his being chairman of the CCP's Central Military Commission. He was also a vice-chairman of the CCP. Owing both to his posts and to the weight and authority of his voice within the party, he remained China's chief policy maker throughout the 1980s. In 1987 Deng stepped down from the CCP's Central Committee, thereby relinquishing his seat on the Political Bureau and its dominant Standing Committee. By doing so he compelled similar retirements by many aged party leaders who had remained opposed or resistant to his reforms.

Deng faced a critical test of his leadership in April–June 1989. Zhao had replaced the too-liberal Hu as general secretary of the CCP in 1987. Hu's death in April 1989 sparked a series of student demonstrations in Tiananmen Square in Beijing demanding greater political freedom and a more democratic government. After some hesitation, Deng supported those in the CCP leadership who favoured the use of force to suppress the protesters, and in June the army crushed the demonstrations with considerable loss of life. Zhao was replaced as party leader by the more authoritarian Jiang Zemin, to whom Deng yielded his chairmanship of the Military Commission in 1989. Though now lacking any formal post in the Communist leadership, Deng retained ultimate authority in the party. Although his direct involvement in government declined in the 1990s, he retained his influence until his death in 1997.

Deng restored China to domestic stability and economic growth after the disastrous excesses of the Cultural Revolution. Under his leadership, China acquired a rapidly growing economy, rising standards of living, considerably expanded personal and cultural freedoms, and growing ties to the world economy. Deng also left in place a mildly authoritarian government that remained committed to the CCP's one-party rule, even while it relied on free-market mechanisms to transform China into a developed nation.

DAG HAMMARSKJÖLD

(b. July 29, 1905, Jönköping, Sweden—d. Sept. 18, 1961, near Ndola, Northern Rhodesia [now Zambia])

Dag Hammarskjöld was a Swedish economist and statesman who served as second secretary-general of the United Nations from 1953 to 1961 and enhanced its prestige and effectiveness. He was posthumously awarded the Nobel Peace Prize in 1961.

The son of Hjalmar Hammarskjöld, prime minister of Sweden (1914–17) and chairman of the Nobel Prize Foundation (1929–47), Dag Hjalmar Agne Carl Hammarskjöld studied law and economics at the universities of Uppsala and Stockholm and taught political economy at Stockholm (1933–36). He then joined the Swedish civil service as permanent undersecretary in the Ministry of Finance and subsequently became president of the board of the Bank of Sweden. From 1947 he served in the Ministry of Foreign Affairs. In 1951 Hammarskjöld was chosen vice chairman of Sweden's delegation to the UN General Assembly, of which he became chairman in 1952. On April 10, 1953, five months after the resignation of Trygve Lie of Norway as secretary-general, Hammarskjöld was elected to the office for a term of five years. In September of 1957, he was reelected to another five-year term.

For several years Hammarskjöld was most concerned with combat and threats of fighting in the Middle East between Israel and the Arab states. He and the Canadian statesman Lester Pearson participated in the resolution of the Suez Canal crisis that arose in 1956. Hammarskjöld also played a prominent role in the 1958 crisis in Lebanon and Jordan.

The Belgian Congo became the independent Republic of the Congo (now Democratic Republic of the Congo) on June 30, 1960, and Hammarskjöld sent a UN force to suppress the civil strife that began there soon afterward. In September 1960, his action was denounced by the Soviet Union, which demanded that he resign and that the office of secretary-general be replaced by a three-man board (*troika*) comprising representatives of the Western, Communist, and neutral nations. Soon after, while on a peace mission to President Moise Tshombe of the Congolese province of Katanga, Hammarskjöld was killed in an airplane crash.

As secretary-general, Hammarskjöld is generally thought to have combined great moral force with subtlety in meeting international challenges. He insisted on the freedom of the secretary-general to take emergency action without prior approval by the Security Council or the General Assembly. He also allayed widespread fears that the UN would be completely dominated by its chief source of financial sustenance, the United States. The absence of a major international crisis during the first three years of his secretaryship enabled him to concentrate on quietly building public confidence in himself and his office.

KWAME NKRUMAH

(b. Sept. 21, 1909, Nkroful, Gold Coast [now Ghana]—d. April 27, 1972, Bucharest, Rom.)

Kwame Nkrumah was one of the most prominent leaders in the African struggles against colonialism in the 1950s. A Ghanaian nationalist leader, he led the Gold Coast's drive for independence from Britain and presided over its emergence as the new nation of Ghana. He headed the country from its independence in 1957 until he was overthrown by a coup in 1966.

EARLY YEARS

Kwame Nkrumah's father was a goldsmith, and his mother was a retail trader. Baptized a Roman Catholic, Nkrumah spent nine years at the Roman Catholic elementary school in nearby Half Assini. After graduation from Achimota College in 1930, he started his career as a teacher at Roman Catholic junior schools in Elmina and Axim and at a seminary.

Increasingly drawn to politics, Nkrumah decided to pursue further studies in the United States. He entered Lincoln University in Pennsylvania in 1935 and, after graduating in 1939, obtained master's degrees from Lincoln and from the University of Pennsylvania. He studied the literature of socialism, notably Karl Marx and Vladimir I. Lenin, and of nationalism—especially Marcus Garvey, the black American leader of the 1920s. Eventually, Nkrumah came to describe himself as a "nondenominational Christian and a Marxist socialist." He also immersed himself in political work, reorganizing and becoming president of the African Students' Organization of the United States and Canada. He left the United States in May 1945 and went to England, where he organized the fifth Pan-African Congress in Manchester.

Meanwhile, in the Gold Coast, J.B. Danquah had formed the United Gold Coast Convention (UGCC) to work for self-government by constitutional means. Invited to serve as the UGCC's general secretary, Nkrumah returned home in late 1947. As general secretary, he addressed meetings throughout the Gold Coast and began to create a mass base for the new movement. When extensive riots occurred in February of 1948, the British briefly arrested Nkrumah and other leaders of the UGCC.

When a split developed between the middle-class leaders of the UGCC and Nkrumah's more radical supporters, Nkrumah formed the new Convention Peoples' Party (CPP) in June 1949. This mass-based party was committed to a program of immediate self-government. In January 1950, Nkrumah initiated a campaign of "positive action," involving nonviolent protests, strikes, and noncooperation with the British colonial authorities.

FROM PRISON TO PRIME MINISTRY

In the ensuing crisis, services throughout the country were disrupted, and Nkrumah was again arrested and sentenced to one year's imprisonment. But the Gold Coast's first general election on February 8, 1951, demonstrated the support the CPP had already won. Elected to parliament, Nkrumah was released from prison to become leader of government business and, in 1952, prime minister of the Gold Coast.

When the Gold Coast and the British Togoland trust territory became an independent state within the British Commonwealth—as Ghana—in March 1957, Nkrumah became the new nation's first prime minister. In 1958 Nkrumah's government legalized the imprisonment without trial of those it regarded as security risks. It soon became apparent that Nkrumah's style of government was to be authoritarian. Nkrumah's popularity in the country rose, however, as new roads, schools, and health facilities were built, and as the policy of Africanization created better career opportunities for Ghanaians.

Determined by a plebiscite in 1960, Ghana became a republic and Nkrumah became its president, with wide legislative and executive powers under a new constitution. Nkrumah then concentrated his attention on campaigning for the political unity of black Africa, and he began to lose touch with realities in Ghana. His administration became involved in magnificent but often ruinous development projects, so that a once-prosperous country became crippled with foreign debt. His government's Second Development Plan, announced in 1959, had to be abandoned in 1961 when the deficit in the balance of payments rose to more than $125 million. Contraction of the economy led to widespread labour unrest and to a general strike in September 1961. From that time Nkrumah began to evolve a much more rigorous apparatus of political control and to turn increasingly to the Communist countries for support.

President of Ghana and Afterward

The attempted assassination of Nkrumah at Kulugungu in August 1962—the first of several—led to his increasing seclusion from public life and to the growth of a personality cult, as well as to a massive buildup of the country's internal security forces. Early in 1964 Ghana was officially designated a one-party state, with Nkrumah as life president of both nation and party. While the administration of the country passed increasingly into the hands of self-serving and corrupt party officials, Nkrumah busied himself with the ideological education of a new generation of black African political activists. Meanwhile, the economic crisis in Ghana worsened, and shortages of foodstuffs and other goods became chronic. On Feb. 24, 1966, while Nkrumah was visiting Beijing, the army and police in Ghana seized power. Returning to West Africa, Nkrumah found asylum in Guinea, where he spent the remainder of his life. He died of cancer in Bucharest in 1972.

RONALD W. REAGAN

(b. Feb. 6, 1911, Tampico, Ill., U.S.—d. June 5, 2004, Los Angeles, Calif.)

Conservative Republican Ronald Reagan, the 40th president of the United States, who served from 1981 to 1989, was noted for his appealing personal style, characterized by a jaunty affability and folksy charm. His remarkable skill as an orator earned him the title "the Great Communicator." His policies have been credited with contributing to the demise of Soviet Communism.

EARLY LIFE AND ACTING CAREER

Ronald Wilson Reagan was the second child of John Edward "Jack" Reagan, a struggling shoe salesman, and Nelle Wilson Reagan. Reagan's nickname, "Dutch," derived from his father's habit of referring to his infant

*Ronald Reagan (second from right)
with his parents, Jack and Nelle,
and his brother, Neil, c. 1915.*
Courtesy Ronald Reagan Library

son as his "fat little Dutchman." After several years of moving from town to town, the family settled in Dixon, Illinois, in 1920. At Eureka College in Eureka, Illinois, Reagan played gridiron football and was active in the drama society. After graduating, he landed a job as a sportscaster.

In 1937 Reagan took a screen test for the Warner Brothers studio and was signed to a contract. During the following 27 years, he made more than 50 full-length motion pictures as well as several short subject films. In 1938 Reagan became engaged to his costar Jane Wyman, and the couple married in Hollywood two years later. Their marriage ended in divorce in 1948. Commissioned a cavalry officer at the outbreak of World War II, Reagan was assigned to an army film unit based in Los Angeles, where he spent the rest of the war making training films. From 1947 to 1952 and again from 1959 to 1960, Reagan served as president of the Screen Actors Guild. Reagan met Nancy Davis in 1949, and the two were married in 1952.

Ronald Reagan visiting Nancy Reagan on the movie set of Donovan's Brain, *1953.* Courtesy Ronald Reagan Library

GOVERNORSHIP OF CALIFORNIA

Reagan announced his candidacy for governor of California in 1966. The incumbent, Democrat Edmund G. Brown ridiculed Reagan's lack of experience, but Reagan turned this apparent liability into an asset by portraying himself as an ordinary citizen who was fed up with a state government that had become inefficient and unaccountable and defeated Brown. During his two terms as governor (1966–74), Reagan erased a substantial budget deficit inherited from the Brown administration—through the largest tax increase in the history of any state to that time—and instituted reforms in the state's welfare programs.

Ronald Reagan as governor of California, c. 1967–71. Courtesy Ronald Reagan Library

ELECTION OF 1980

Reagan dominated the Republican presidential primary in 1980. He chose George Bush as his running mate, and the two men campaigned against Democratic incumbents Jimmy Carter and Walter Mondale on a platform promising steep tax cuts, increased defense spending, a balanced budget, and a constitutional amendment to ban abortion. On election day Reagan defeated Carter with slightly more than half the popular vote. The vote in the electoral college was 489 to Carter's 49.

PRESIDENCY

FIRST DAYS

Reagan's presidency began on a dramatic note when, after the inaugural ceremony, he announced that Iran, which had been holding American hostages since 1979, had

Ronald and Nancy Reagan waving to crowds on the day of his first inauguration, January 20, 1981. Courtesy Ronald Reagan Library

agreed to release them. Then, on March 30, 1981, Reagan was shot by John W. Hinckley, Jr. After his release from the hospital 12 days later, Reagan made a series of carefully staged public appearances designed to give the impression that he was recovering quickly, while in fact he remained seriously weakened for months and his workload was sharply curtailed.

DOMESTIC POLICIES

Domestically, the first Reagan term set a new tone, indicated in such themes as "getting the government off the backs of the people" and not letting it spend more than it

Presidents (left to right) Ronald Reagan, Gerald Ford, Jimmy Carter, and Richard Nixon, 1982. U.S. Department of Defense

takes in. He pushed through Congress a program of increased defense spending and budget and tax cuts. A severe recession in 1982–83 lessened the appeal of so-called Reaganomics, but a strong economic recovery aided his landslide reelection in 1984.

FOREIGN AFFAIRS

When he entered office in 1980, Reagan believed that the United States had grown weak militarily and had lost the respect it once commanded in world affairs. Aiming to restore the country to a position of moral, as well as military, preeminence in the world, he called for massive increases in the defense budget to expand and modernize the military and urged a more aggressive approach to combating Communism and related forms of leftist totalitarianism.

Reagan took an early stand against the Soviet Union. In March of 1983, he announced his Strategic Defense Initiative, popularly called Star Wars. It was perceived by the Soviets as a threat, but early in Reagan's second term they agreed to resume disarmament talks. Summits with Soviet secretary Mikhail Gorbachev in 1985, 1986, and 1987 resulted in a treaty reducing intermediate-range nuclear forces. In 1988 the two leaders met in Moscow for initial discussions on the control of long-range arsenals.

In 1983 there were crises in Lebanon, where 241 U.S. Marines were killed in a terrorist bombing, and Grenada, where U.S. forces were sent to depose a Marxist regime. In keeping with Reagan's belief that the United States should do more to prevent the spread of Communism, his administration expanded military and economic assistance to friendly Third World governments battling leftist insurgencies. He also actively supported guerrilla movements and other opposition forces in countries with leftist governments. This policy, which became known as the Reagan Doctrine, was applied with particular zeal in Latin America.

REELECTION AND THE IRAN-CONTRA AFFAIR

At the time of the presidential election of 1984, Reagan was at the height of his popularity, and Reagan and Bush easily defeated their Democratic opponents, Walter Mondale and Geraldine Ferraro, by 59 percent of the popular vote. In the electoral college, Reagan received 525 votes to Mondale's 13, the largest number of electoral votes of any candidate in history. Only two years later, however, he would become embroiled in the worst scandal of his political career, one that would cost him much popularity and party support and significantly impair his ability to lead the country. The clandestine sale of arms to Iran by some government officials, a vain attempt to bribe the Iranians into assisting with freeing U.S. hostages held in Lebanon, contradicted the administration's policy of refusing to negotiate with terrorists or aid countries that supported national terrorism. Profits from

U.S. president Ronald Reagan riding El Alamein at Rancho del Cielo, Santa Barbara, California, April 8, 1985. Courtesy Ronald Reagan Library

the sale had been illegally diverted to guerrillas (known as Contras) trying to topple the Nicaraguan government. Senate hearings on what became known as the Iran-Contra Affair began in 1987. Among those indicted were the National Security Council's John M. Poindexter and Lieut. Col. Oliver North. By 1990 six former Reagan officials had been convicted in the affair.

RETIREMENT AND DECLINING HEALTH

In the presidential election of 1988, Reagan campaigned actively for the Republican nominee, Vice President Bush. In large part because of Reagan's continued popularity,

Presidents (left to right) George Bush, Ronald Reagan, Jimmy Carter, Gerald Ford, and Richard Nixon attend the opening of the Ronald Reagan Presidential Library, Simi Valley, Calif., 1991. Marcy Nighswander— Associated Press/U.S. Department of Defense

Bush defeated Democratic candidate Michael Dukakis. Reagan retired to his home in Los Angeles, where he wrote his autobiography, *An American Life*, which was published in 1990. In 1994, in a letter to the American people, Reagan disclosed that he had been diagnosed with Alzheimer's disease, a degenerative brain disorder. He died in 2004.

KIM IL-SUNG AND KIM JONG IL

Respectively (b. April 15, 1912, Man'gyŏndae, near P'yŏngyang, Korea [now in North Korea]—d. July 8, 1994, P'yŏngyang); (b. Feb. 16, 1941, Siberia, Russia, U.S.S.R.)

Since 1948, North Korea has been ruled by the Communist leaders Kim Il-sung and his son Kim Jong Il. Kim Il-sung was the nation's premier from 1948 to 1972, chairman of its dominant Korean Workers' (Communist) Party (KWP) from 1949, and president and head of state from 1972 until his death in 1994. He was posthumously granted the title "eternal president of the republic." Kim Jong Il succeeded his father as ruler of North Korea.

KIM IL-SUNG

Kim Il-sung (original name Kim Song Ju) was the son of parents who fled to Manchuria in 1925 to escape the Japanese rule of Korea. He joined the Korean guerrilla resistance against the Japanese occupation in the 1930s and adopted the name of an earlier legendary Korean guerrilla fighter against the Japanese. Kim was noticed by the Soviet military authorities, who sent him to the Soviet Union for military and political training. There he joined the local Communist Party.

During World War II, Kim led a Korean contingent as a major in the Soviet army. After the Japanese surrender in 1945, Korea was effectively divided between a

Soviet-occupied northern half and a U.S.-supported southern half. At this time Kim returned with other Soviet-trained Koreans to establish a Communist provisional government under Soviet authority in what would become North Korea. He became the first premier of the newly formed Democratic People's Republic of Korea in 1948, and in 1949 he became chairman of the Korean Workers' (Communist) Party. Hoping to reunify Korea by force, Kim launched an invasion of South Korea in 1950, thereby igniting the Korean War. His attempt to extend his rule there was repelled by U.S. troops and other UN forces, however, and it was only through massive Chinese support that he was able to repel a subsequent invasion of North Korea by UN forces.

The Korean War ended in a stalemate in 1953. As head of state, Kim crushed the remaining domestic opposition and eliminated his last rivals for power within the Korean Workers' Party. He became his country's absolute ruler and set about transforming North Korea into an austere, militaristic, and highly regimented society devoted to the twin goals of industrialization and the reunification of the Korean Peninsula under North Korean rule. Kim introduced a philosophy of *juche*, or "self-reliance," under which North Korea tried to develop its economy with little or no help from foreign countries. North Korea's state-run economy grew rapidly in the 1950s and 1960s but eventually stagnated, with shortages of food occurring by the early 1990s. The omnipresent personality cult sponsored by Kim was part of a highly effective propaganda system that enabled him to rule unchallenged for 46 years over one of the world's most isolated and repressive societies. In his foreign policy, he cultivated close ties with both the Soviet Union and China and remained consistently hostile to South Korea and the United States. While retaining control of the Korean Workers' Party, Kim relinquished the office of premier and was elected president of North Korea in December 1972. In 1980 he raised his eldest son, Kim Jong Il, to high posts in the party and the military, in effect designating the younger Kim as his heir.

The dissolution of the Soviet Union in the early 1990s left China as North Korea's sole major ally, and even China cultivated more cordial relations with South Korea than with North Korea. Meanwhile, North Korean policy toward the South alternated between provocation and overtures of peace throughout the 1980s and early 1990s. Relations improved somewhat with Seoul's hosting of the Olympic Games in 1988, to which the North sent a team of athletes. In 1991 the two countries were simultaneously admitted to the United Nations, and a series of prime-ministerial talks produced two agreements between North and South Korea. One agreement pledged nonaggression, reconciliation, exchanges, and cooperation. The other was a joint declaration on the denuclearization of the Korean Peninsula. The agreements went into effect in February 1992, although little of substance came of them, especially after the North became embroiled in controversy over its nuclear program and suspended all contacts with the South in early 1993.

South Korean president Kim Young Sam was scheduled to travel to P'yŏngyang in July 1994 for an unprecedented summit between the two Korean leaders, but Kim Il-sung died before the meeting could take place. Kim Jong Il ascended to power after his father's death, and in the revised constitution that was announced in 1998, the office of president was written out and the elder Kim was written in as "eternal president of the republic."

KIM JONG IL

The official North Korean version of Kim Jong Il's life, different from the biography documented elsewhere, says that he was born at a guerrilla base camp on Mount Paektu, the highest point on the Korean Peninsula. It attributes many precocious abilities to him and claims his birth was accompanied by such auspicious signs as the appearance of a double rainbow in the sky. During the Korean War (1950–53), he was placed in safety in northeastern China (Manchuria) by his father, although the official biography does not mention the episode. After attending a pilot's training college in East Germany for two years, he graduated in 1963 from Kim Il-sung University. He served in numerous routine posts in the KWP before becoming his father's secretary. He worked closely with his father in the 1967 party purge and then was assigned several important jobs. Kim was appointed in September 1973 to the powerful position of party secretary in charge of organization, propaganda, and agitation.

Kim was officially designated his father's successor in October 1980, was given command of the armed forces in 1990–91, and held high-ranking posts on the Central Committee, in the Politburo, and in the Party Secretariat. When Kim Il-sung died of a heart attack in 1994, Kim Jong Il became North Korea's de facto leader. He was named chairman of the KWP in October 1997, and in September 1998 he formally assumed the country's highest post. Since the position of president had been eliminated by the Supreme People's Assembly, which reserved for Kim Il-sung the posthumous title of "eternal president," the younger Kim was reelected chairman of the National Defense Commission, an office whose powers were expanded.

During his leadership of the country, Kim built on the mystique already surrounding his father and himself. Conflicting information circulated regarding his personal life, most of it unreliable and—perhaps deliberately— serving to add to the mystery. It was known that Kim took an interest in the arts and encouraged greater creativity in literature and film, although the products remained primarily propaganda tools. A well-known film buff, Kim headed a movie studio before ascending to the country's leadership. It produced works celebrating socialist values, Kim Il-sung and his national policy of self-reliance (*juche*), and, later, Kim Jong Il himself and his "military first" (*sŏngun chŏngch'i*) policy. As part of his desire to create better films, in the late 1970s the younger Kim had a South Korean film director, Shin Sang-ok, and his wife, actress Choi Eun-hee, abducted to the North, where they were pressed into service until their 1986 escape.

After becoming North Korea's leader, and with his country facing a struggling economy and a famine, Kim made moves toward amending North Korea's long-standing policy of isolationism. Throughout the late 1990s and the early 21st century, Kim sought to improve ties with a number of countries. In addition, he appeared to be abiding by the terms of a 1994 agreement—called the Agreed Framework—with the United States, in which North Korea would dismantle its own nuclear program in return for arranging for the construction by an outside party of two nuclear reactors capable of producing electric power. South Korea was the primary contractor on the project.

Kim halted testing of a long-range missile in 1999 after the United States agreed to ease its economic sanctions against North Korea, and in June 2000 Kim met with South Korean leader Kim Dae Jung. In what was the first summit between leaders of the two countries, an agreement was reached to take steps toward reunification. Ties were also established with Australia and Italy.

At the same time, however, the Agreed Framework began falling apart in the face of North Korea's demonstrated reluctance to adhere to its terms. Relations with the United States deteriorated greatly in 2002, after Pres. George W. Bush characterized Kim's regime as part of an "axis of evil" (along with Iran and Iraq). It was suspected that North Korea was enriching uranium at one of the nuclear facilities whose activities were supposedly frozen by the terms of the Agreed Framework, and in December 2002 Kim expelled International Atomic Energy Agency inspectors from the site. The following year Kim announced that North Korea was pulling out of the Nuclear Non-proliferation Treaty and planning on developing nuclear weapons. The move was widely seen as a negotiating tactic to secure economic aid and a nonaggression pact from the United States. In 2005 North Korea claimed it was capable of building a nuclear weapon, and in October 2006 the country announced that it had conducted an underground test of such a weapon. Talks were suspended for several years, but another deal was struck in late 2007. The ability to verify North Korea's compliance remained an international issue.

The December 2007 election of Lee Myung-bak as South Korean president began another deterioration in inter-Korean relations as Lee took a harder line with his North Korean counterpart. In 2008 North Korea announced that it planned to close the land border and all nonmilitary telephone links with South Korea.

RICHARD M. NIXON

(b. Jan. 9, 1913, Yorba Linda, Calif., U.S.—d. April 22, 1994, New York, N.Y.)

Richard M. Nixon was the 37th president of the United States, serving from 1969 to 1974. Faced with almost certain impeachment and removal from office, he is the only president to have resigned from office.

Early Life and Congressional Career

Richard Milhous Nixon was the second of five children born to Frank Nixon, a service station owner and grocer, and Hannah Milhous Nixon, whose devout Quakerism would exert a strong influence on her son. Nixon graduated from Whittier College in Whittier, California, in 1934 and from Duke University Law School in Durham, North Carolina, in 1937. Returning to Whittier to practice law, he met Thelma Catherine "Pat" Ryan, a teacher and amateur actress, after the two were cast in the same play at a local community theatre. The couple married in 1940.

In August 1942, after a brief stint in the Office of Price Administration in Washington, D.C., Nixon served in the navy. Following his return to civilian life in 1946, he was elected to the U.S. House of Representatives. Running for reelection in 1948, Nixon entered and won both the Democratic and Republican primaries, which eliminated the need to participate in the general election. As a member of the House Un-American Activities Committee (HUAAC) in 1948–50, he took a leading role in the investigation of Alger Hiss, a former State Department official accused of spying for the Soviet Union.

In 1950 Nixon successfully ran for the United States Senate against Democratic representative Helen Gahagan Douglas. A small Southern California newspaper nicknamed him "Tricky Dick" because of some of his campaign tactics. The epithet later became a favourite among Nixon's opponents.

Vice Presidency

At the Republican convention in 1952, Nixon won nomination as vice president on a ticket with Dwight D. Eisenhower,

Vice Pres. Richard M. Nixon and his wife, Pat, receiving flowers from a young girl during a visit to South Korea in 1953. U.S. Department of Defense

largely because of his anticommunist credentials, but also because Republicans thought he could draw valuable support in the West. During the campaign he delivered a nationally televised address, the "Checkers" speech— named for the dog he admitted receiving as a political gift—to rebut charges of financial misconduct. He and Eisenhower were reelected easily in 1956.

Nixon's vice presidency was also noteworthy for his many well-publicized trips abroad, including a 1959 visit to the Soviet Union, highlighted by an impromptu profanity-filled "kitchen debate" in Moscow with Soviet premier Nikita Khrushchev.

Dwight D. Eisenhower (left) and Richard M. Nixon after being renominated at the 1956 Republican National Convention in San Francisco. Courtesy of the Dwight D. Eisenhower Library/U.S. Army

ELECTION OF 1960

Nixon received his party's presidential nomination in 1960 and was opposed in the general election by Democrat John F. Kennedy. The campaign was memorable for an unprecedented series of four televised debates between the two candidates. Although Nixon performed well rhetorically, Kennedy managed to convey an appealing image of youthfulness, energy, and physical poise, which convinced many that he had won the debates. In a close contest, Nixon lost to Kennedy by fewer than 120,000 popular votes. Citing irregularities in Illinois and Texas, many observers questioned whether Kennedy had legally won those states, and some prominent Republicans— including Eisenhower—even urged Nixon to contest the results. He chose not to, however. Nixon's supporters and critics alike, both then and later, praised him for the dignity and unselfishness with which he handled defeat and the suspicion that vote fraud had cost him the presidency.

Nixon then retired to private life in California, where he wrote a best-selling book, *Six Crises*. After failing to win the 1962 California gubernatorial race, he announced his retirement from politics and criticized the press, declaring that it would not "have Dick Nixon to kick around anymore." He moved to New York to practice law and, over the next few years, built a reputation as a strong leader in the Republican Party.

PRESIDENCY

Returning to politics, Nixon won the Republican nomination for president in 1968. With Maryland governor Spiro Agnew as his running mate, Nixon campaigned against Democrat Hubert H. Humphrey and third-party candidate George Wallace on a vague platform promising an honourable peace in Vietnam. Nixon won the election by a narrow margin, 31.7 million popular votes to Humphrey's nearly 30.9 million; the electoral vote was 301 to 191.

DOMESTIC POLICIES

Despite expectations from some observers that Nixon would be a "do-nothing" president, his administration increased funding for many federal civil rights agencies and proposed legislation that created the Occupational Safety and Health Administration (OSHA) and the Environmental Protection Agency (EPA). He responded to persistent inflation and increasing unemployment by

devaluing the dollar and imposing unprecedented peace-
time controls on wages and prices.

FOREIGN AFFAIRS

As president, Nixon began to withdraw U.S. military forces
from South Vietnam while resuming the bombing of North
Vietnam. His expansion of the Vietnam War to Cambodia
and Laos in 1970 provoked widespread protests in the
United States. One of these demonstrations—at Kent
State University on May 4, 1970—ended tragically when
soldiers of the Ohio National Guard fired into a crowd of
about 2,000 protesters, killing four and wounding nine.

Nixon's most significant achievement in foreign affairs
may have been the establishment of direct relations with
the People's Republic of China after a 21-year estrangement.
Nixon's visit to China in February and March of 1972, the
first by an American president while in office, concluded
with the Shanghai Communiqué, in which the United States
formally recognized the "one-China" principle—that there
is only one China, and that Taiwan is a part of China.

The rapprochement with China, undertaken in part to
take advantage of the growing Sino-Soviet rift in the late
1960s, gave Nixon more leverage in his dealings with the
Soviet Union. On a visit to the Soviet Union later that year,
he signed agreements resulting from the Strategic Arms
Limitation Talks between the United States and the Soviet
Union held between 1969 and 1972, known as SALT I.

Fearing Communist revolution in Latin America, the
Nixon administration helped to undermine the coalition
government of Chile's Marxist president Salvador Allende.

REELECTION AND WATERGATE

Renominated with Agnew in 1972, Nixon defeated his
Democratic challenger, Senator George S. McGovern, in

Richard M. Nixon, 1969. Department of Defense

one of the largest landslide victories in the history of American presidential elections: 46.7 million to 28.9 million in the popular vote and 520 to 17 in the electoral vote. Despite his resounding victory, Nixon would soon be forced to resign in disgrace in the worst political scandal in United States history.

Nixon's second term was overshadowed by the Watergate scandal, which stemmed from illegal activities by Nixon and his aides related to the burglary and wiretapping of the national headquarters of the Democratic Party at the Watergate office complex in Washington, D.C. Eventually it came to encompass allegations of other loosely related crimes committed both before and after the break-in. Faced with the near-certain prospect of impeachment by the House and conviction in the Senate, Nixon announced his resignation on the evening of Aug. 8, 1974, effective at noon the next day.

RETIREMENT AND DEATH

Nixon retired with his wife to the seclusion of his estate in San Clemente, California. He wrote *RN: The Memoirs of Richard Nixon* (1978) and several books on international affairs and American foreign policy, modestly rehabilitating his public reputation and earning a role as an elder statesman and foreign-policy expert. He died of a massive stroke in 1994.

MENACHEM BEGIN

(b. Aug. 16, 1913, Brest-Litovsk, Russia [now in Belarus] — d. March 9, 1992, Tel Aviv-Yafo, Israel)

Menachem Begin, Israel's sixth prime minister (1977–1983), along with Egyptian president Anwar el-Sādāt, was the corecipient of the 1978 Nobel Peace Prize for their achievement of a peace treaty between Israel and Egypt that was formally signed in 1979.

Menachem Wolfovitch Begin received a law degree from the University of Warsaw in 1935. Active in the Zionist movement throughout the 1930s, he became (1938) the leader of the Polish branch of the Betar youth movement, dedicated to the establishment of a Jewish state on both sides of the Jordan River. When the Germans invaded Warsaw in 1939, he escaped to Vilnius; his parents and a brother died in concentration camps. The Soviet authorities deported Begin to Siberia in 1940, but in 1941 he was released and joined the Polish army in exile. He went with them to Palestine in 1942.

Begin joined the militant Irgun Zvai Leumi and was its commander from 1943 to 1948. After Israel's independence in 1948, the Irgun formed the Ḥerut ("Freedom") Party with Begin as its head and leader of the opposition in the Knesset (Parliament) until 1967. Begin joined the National Unity government (1967–70) as a minister without portfolio and in 1970 became joint chairman of the Likud ("Unity") coalition.

On May 17, 1977, the Likud Party won a national electoral victory, and on June 21, Begin formed a government. He was perhaps best known for his uncompromising stand on the question of retaining the West Bank and the Gaza Strip, which had been occupied by Israel during the Arab-Israeli War of 1967. Prodded by U.S. president Jimmy Carter, however, Begin negotiated with President Anwar el-Sādāt of Egypt for peace in the Middle East, and the agreements they reached on September 17, 1978—known as the Camp David Accords—led directly to a peace treaty between Israel and Egypt that was signed on March 26, 1979. Under the terms of the treaty, Israel returned the Sinai Peninsula, which it had occupied since the 1967 war, to Egypt in exchange for full diplomatic recognition.

Begin formed another coalition government after the general election of 1980. Despite his willingness to return the Sinai Peninsula to Egypt under the terms of the peace agreement, he remained resolutely opposed to the establishment of a Palestinian state in the West Bank and Gaza Strip. In June 1982 his government mounted an invasion of Lebanon in an effort to oust the Palestine Liberation Organization (PLO) from its bases there. The PLO was driven from Lebanon, but the deaths of numerous Palestinian civilians there turned world opinion against Israel. Israel's continuing involvement in Lebanon and the death of Begin's wife in November 1982 were probably among the factors that prompted him to resign from office in October of 1983.

WILLY BRANDT

(b. Dec. 18, 1913, Lübeck, Ger.—d. Oct. 8/9, 1992, Unkel, near Bonn)

Willy Brandt was a German statesman who served as leader of the Social Democratic Party of Germany (Sozialdemokratische Partei Deutschlands, or SPD) from 1964 to 1987 and chancellor of the Federal Republic of Germany from 1969 to 1974. He was awarded the Nobel Peace Prize for in 1971 for his efforts to achieve reconciliation between West Germany and the countries of the Soviet bloc.

Born Herbert Ernst Karl Frahm, Brandt passed his university entrance examination in 1932. A year later, however, when the Nazis came to power, his activities as a young Social Democrat brought him into conflict with the Gestapo, and he was forced to flee the country to escape arrest. It was at this time, while living in Norway and earning a living as a journalist, that he assumed the name Willy Brandt. When the Germans occupied Norway, he escaped to Sweden, where he remained for the duration of World War II. After the war he returned to Germany as a Norwegian citizen and for a time was press attaché at the Norwegian mission in Berlin.

Pressed to return to politics, Brandt became a German citizen again and, after a period as Berlin representative of the Social Democratic Party Executive Committee, was elected a member of the federal parliament in 1949. Eight years later he became the mayor of West Berlin (1957–66), a post that brought him world fame. He showed great moral courage when in 1958 the Soviet Union demanded that West Berlin be given the title of a demilitarized free city and especially when the Berlin Wall was built in 1961. He succeeded Erich Ollenhauer as chairman of the SPD in 1964 and campaigned for the office of chancellor of West Germany three times—in 1961, 1965, and 1969.

When the grand coalition government of the Christian Democratic Union (CDU) and the SPD was formed in 1966, Brandt became foreign minister and vice chancellor. His party improved its performance at the federal election in 1969 and formed a coalition government with the small Free Democratic Party, pushing the CDU into the role of opposition party for the first time. His government's first major decisions included the revaluing of the West German mark and the signing of the Nuclear Nonproliferation Treaty.

The year following his election as chancellor, Brandt concentrated on foreign affairs, and he particularly sought to improve relations with East Germany, other Communist countries in eastern Europe, and the Soviet Union, formulating a policy known as *Ostpolitik* ("eastern policy"). His efforts led to a treaty with the Soviet Union in August 1970 calling for mutual renunciation of force and the acceptance of current European borders. They also led to a nonaggression treaty with Poland in December 1970, recognizing the Oder-Neisse Line as Poland's western boundary. Brandt's efforts also led to the Big Four agreement in September 1971 on the status of Berlin. His treaty with Poland was controversial. Detractors claimed that it signaled West Germany's acceptance of the permanent loss of those eastern lands stripped from Germany after World War II, while supporters praised it for opening the possibility of reuniting West and East Germany and stabilizing relations with eastern Europe. A firm supporter of a united Europe, Brandt exerted his influence to break down French objections to enlarging the European Economic Community (EEC). More than any other statesman he helped promote the entry of Britain and other countries to the EEC.

Brandt resigned in May 1974 after his close aide Gunther Guillaume was unmasked as an East German spy. He remained the chairman of the SPD until 1987 and was also head of the Socialist International (the Social Democrats' umbrella organization) from 1976 to 1992. From 1979 he also headed the Independent Commission on International Development Issues, known as the Brandt Commission—a prestigious independent panel that studied world economic policies.

Brandt wrote several books, including *Willy Brandt in Exile: Essays, Reflections and Letters, 1933–1947*, translated from the German by R.W. Last (1971), and *People and Politics: The Years 1960–1975*, translated by J.M. Brownjohn (1978). The latter comprises Brandt's political memoirs.

AUGUSTO PINOCHET

(b. Nov. 25, 1915, Valparaiso, Chile—d. Dec. 10, 2006, Santiago)

Augusto Pinochet was the leader of the military junta that overthrew the socialist government of Pres.

Salvador Allende of Chile on Sept. 11, 1973, and head of Chile's military government from 1974 to 1990.

Augusto Pinochet Ugarte, a 1936 graduate of the military academy in Santiago, was a career military officer who was appointed army commander in chief by President Allende 18 days before the coup, which he planned and led. Pinochet was named head of the victorious junta's governing council, and he moved to crush Chile's liberal opposition. In its first three years, the regime arrested approximately 130,000, many of whom were tortured. In June 1974 Pinochet assumed sole power as president, relegating the rest of the junta to an advisory role.

Pinochet was determined to exterminate leftism in Chile and to reassert free-market policies in the country's economy. His junta was widely condemned for its harsh suppression of dissent, even though its reversal of the Allende government's socialist policies resulted in a lower rate of inflation and an economic boom in the period from 1976 to 1979. A modest political liberalization began in 1978 after the regime announced that, in a plebiscite, 75 percent of the electorate had endorsed Pinochet's rule.

Under a new constitution adopted in March 1981, Pinochet remained president for an eight-year term until 1989, when a national referendum would determine whether he could serve an additional eight-year term. During the 1980s, Pinochet's free-market policies were credited with maintaining a low rate of inflation and an acceptable rate of economic growth despite a severe recession in 1980–83. Pinochet permitted no meaningful political opposition, but he fulfilled his constitutional obligation to hold the plebiscite scheduled, which took place earlier than mandated in October 1988. The result was a "no" vote of 55 percent and a "yes" vote of 43 percent. Although rejected by the electorate, Pinochet remained in office until free elections installed a new president, the Christian Democrat Patricio Aylwin, on March 11, 1990.

As commander of the armed forces until 1998, Pinochet frequently thwarted human-rights prosecutions against members of the security forces. After stepping down, he became a senator-for-life, a post granted to former presidents under the 1981 constitution. Later in 1998, while visiting London, he was detained by British authorities after the Spanish government requested his extradition in connection with the torture of Spanish citizens in Chile during his rule. The unprecedented case stirred worldwide controversy and galvanized human-rights organizations in Chile. The United States and other countries were prompted to release formerly classified documents concerning Chileans who had "disappeared"—were kidnapped and presumably killed by the Pinochet regime. The disclosures brought to light details of Operation Colombo, in which more than 100 Chilean leftists had disappeared in 1975, and Operation Condor, in which several South American military governments coordinated their efforts to systematically eliminate opponents in the 1970s and 1980s. In January 2000 Pinochet was allowed to return home after a British court ruled that he was physically unfit to stand trial. Nevertheless, he continued to face investigations by Chilean authorities.

Later in 2000 Pinochet was stripped of his immunity from prosecution—which he had enjoyed as a former president—and ordered to stand trial on charges of human-rights abuses (in Chile immunity is lifted on a case-by-case basis). The charges were dropped in 2002, however, after Chile's Supreme Court upheld a ruling that he was mentally incapable of defending himself in court. Soon afterward Pinochet resigned his post as a senator-for-life. In 2005 he was again stripped of immunity and ordered to stand trial on charges stemming from Operation Colombo and on separate charges relating to tax evasion.

INDIRA GANDHI

(b. Nov. 19, 1917, Allahabad, India—d. Oct. 31, 1984, New Delhi)

I ndira Gandhi served as prime minister of India for three consecutive terms from 1966 to 1977 and a fourth term from 1980 to 1984 before she was assassinated by Sikh extremists.

Indira Priyadarshini Gandhi was the only child of Jawaharlal Nehru, the first prime minister of independent India. She attended Visva-Bharati University, West Bengal, and the University of Oxford, and in 1942, she married Feroze Gandhi (d. 1960), a fellow member of the Indian National Congress (Congress Party). She was a member of the working committee of the ruling Congress Party from 1955, and in 1959 she was elected to the largely honorary post of party president. Lal Bahadur Shastri, who succeeded Nehru as prime minister in 1964, named her minister of information and broadcasting in his government.

Upon Shastri's sudden death in January 1966, Gandhi became leader of the Congress Party—and thus also prime minister—in a compromise between the right and left wings of the party. Her leadership, however, came under continual challenge from the right wing of the party, led by a former minister of finance, Morarji Desai. In the election of 1967, she won a slim majority and had to accept Desai as deputy prime minister. In 1971, however, she won a sweeping electoral victory over a coalition of conservative parties. Gandhi strongly supported East Bengal (now Bangladesh) in its secessionist conflict with Pakistan in late 1971, and India's armed forces achieved a swift and decisive victory over Pakistan that led to the creation of Bangladesh.

In March 1972, buoyed by the country's success against Pakistan, Gandhi again led her new Congress Party to a landslide victory in national elections. Shortly afterward her defeated Socialist Party opponent charged that she had violated the election laws. In June 1975 the High Court of Allahabad ruled against her, which meant that she would be deprived of her seat in Parliament and would have to stay out of politics for six years. In response, she declared a state of emergency throughout India, imprisoned her political opponents, and assumed emergency powers, passing many laws limiting personal freedoms. During this period she implemented several unpopular policies, including large-scale sterilization as a form of birth control. When long-postponed national elections were held in 1977, Gandhi and her party were soundly defeated, and she left office. The Janata Party took over the reins of government.

Early in 1978 Gandhi's supporters split from the Congress Party and formed the Congress (I) Party—the "I" signifying Indira. She was briefly imprisoned in October 1977 and December 1978 on charges of official corruption. Despite these setbacks, she won a new seat in Parliament in November 1978, and her Congress (I) Party began to gather strength. Dissension within the ruling Janata Party led to the fall of its government in August 1979. When new elections for the Lok Sabha (lower house of Parliament) were held in January 1980, Gandhi and her Congress (I) Party were swept back into power in a landslide victory. Her son Sanjay Gandhi, who had become her chief political adviser, also won a seat in the Lok Sabha. All legal cases against Indira, as well as against her son, were withdrawn.

Sanjay Gandhi's death in an airplane crash in June 1980 eliminated Indira's chosen successor from the political leadership of India. After Sanjay's death, Indira groomed her other son, Rajiv, for the leadership of her party. Gandhi adhered to the quasi-socialist policies of industrial development that had been begun by her father. She established closer relations with the Soviet Union, depending on that nation for support in India's long-standing conflict with Pakistan.

During the early 1980s, Indira Gandhi was faced with threats to the political integrity of India. Several states sought a larger measure of independence from the central government, and Sikh extremists in Punjab State used violence to assert their demands for an autonomous state. In response, Gandhi ordered an army attack in June 1984 on the Harimandir (Golden Temple) at Amritsar, the Sikhs' holiest shrine. This attack led to the deaths of more than 450 Sikhs. Five months later Gandhi was killed in her garden by a fusillade of bullets fired by two of her own Sikh bodyguards in revenge for the attack on the Golden Temple.

NELSON MANDELA

(b. July 18, 1918, Umtata, Cape of Good Hope, S.Af.)

One of the most influential South Africans of the 20th century, Nelson Mandela was a black nationalist and statesman whose long imprisonment (1962–90) and subsequent ascension to the presidency in 1994 symbolized the aspirations of South Africa's black majority. He led the country until 1999.

The son of Chief Henry Mandela of the Xhosa-speaking Tembu people, Nelson Rolihlahla Mandela renounced his claim to the chieftainship to become a lawyer. He attended the University College of Fort Hare and studied law at the University of Witwatersrand. He later passed the qualification exam to become a lawyer and in 1952 opened a firm with Oliver Tambo. In 1944 he joined the African National Congress (ANC), a black-liberation group, and in 1949 became one of its leaders, helping to revitalize the organization and opposing the apartheid policies of the ruling National Party. Mandela went on trial for treason in 1956–61 but was acquitted. During the extended court proceedings, he divorced his first wife and married Nomzamo Winifred Madikizela. They divorced in 1996. After the massacre of unarmed Africans by police forces at Sharpeville in 1960 and the subsequent banning of the ANC, Mandela abandoned his nonviolent stance and began advocating acts of sabotage against the South African regime. In 1962 he was jailed and sentenced to five years in prison.

In 1963 the imprisoned Mandela and several other men were tried for sabotage, treason, and violent conspiracy. The celebrated Rivonia Trial was named after a fashionable suburb of Johannesburg where raiding police had discovered quantities of arms and equipment at the headquarters of the underground Umkhonto We Sizwe ("Spear of the Nation," the ANC's military wing). Mandela had been a founder of the organization and admitted the truth of some of the charges that were made against him. On June 12, 1964, he was sentenced to life imprisonment.

From 1964 to 1982, Mandela was incarcerated at Robben Island Prison, off Cape Town. He was subsequently kept at the maximum-security Pollsmoor Prison until 1988, at which time he was hospitalized for tuberculosis. Mandela retained wide support among South Africa's black population, and his imprisonment became a cause célèbre among the international community that condemned apartheid. The South African government under President F.W. de Klerk released Mandela from prison on Feb. 11, 1990. On March 2 Mandela was chosen deputy president of the ANC, the president, Tambo, being ill, and he replaced Tambo as president in July 1991. Mandela and de Klerk worked to end apartheid and bring about a peaceful transition to nonracial democracy in South Africa. In 1993 they were awarded the Nobel Peace Prize for their efforts.

In April 1994 South Africa held its first all-race elections, which were won by Mandela and the ANC. As president, he established the Truth and Reconciliation Commission (TRC), which investigated human rights violations under apartheid, and introduced housing, education, and economic development initiatives designed to improve the living standards of the country's black population. In 1996 he oversaw the enactment of a new democratic constitution. The following year Mandela resigned his post with the ANC and in 1999 did not seek a second term as South African president. After leaving office in June, he retired from active politics.

ANWAR EL-SĀDĀT

(b. Dec. 25, 1918, Mit Abū al-Kawm, Al-Minūfiyyah governorate, Egypt—d. Oct. 6, 1981, Cairo)

Egyptian army officer and politician Anwar el-Sādāt was president of Egypt from 1970 until his assassination in 1981. He initiated serious peace negotiations with Israel, an achievement for which he shared the 1978 Nobel Peace Prize with Israeli prime minister Menachem Begin. Under their leadership, Egypt and Israel made peace with each other in 1979.

Muḥammad Anwar el-Sādāt graduated from the Cairo Military Academy in 1938. During World War II he plotted to expel the British from Egypt with the help of the Germans. The British arrested and imprisoned him in 1942, but he escaped two years later. In 1946 Sādāt was arrested after being implicated in the assassination of pro-British minister Amīn 'Uthmān. He was imprisoned until his acquittal in 1948. In 1950 he joined Gamal Abdel Nasser's Free Officers organization. He participated in its armed coup against the Egyptian monarchy in 1952 and supported Nasser's election to the presidency in 1956. Sādāt held various high offices that led to his serving in the vice presidency during the years 1964–66 and 1969–70. He became acting president upon Nasser's death, on Sept. 28, 1970, and was elected president in a plebiscite on October 15.

Sādāt's domestic and foreign policies were partly a reaction against those of Nasser and reflected Sādāt's efforts to emerge from his predecessor's shadow. One of Sādāt's most important domestic initiatives was the open-door policy known as *infitāḥ* ("opening"). This program of dramatic economic change included decentralization and diversification of the economy as well as efforts to attract trade and foreign investment. Sādāt's efforts to liberalize the economy came at significant cost, including high inflation and an uneven distribution of wealth, deepening inequality and leading to discontent that would later contribute to food riots in January 1977.

It was in foreign affairs that Sādāt made his most dramatic efforts. Feeling that the Soviet Union gave him inadequate support in Egypt's continuing confrontation with Israel, he expelled thousands of Soviet technicians and advisers from the country in 1972. In addition, Egyptian peace overtures toward Israel were initiated early in Sādāt's presidency, when he made known his willingness to reach a peaceful settlement if Israel returned the Sinai Peninsula, which had been captured by that country in the June (Six-Day) War of 1967. Following the failure of this initiative, Sādāt launched a military attack in coordination with Syria to retake the territory, sparking the October (Yom Kippur) War of 1973. The Egyptian army achieved a tactical surprise in its attack on the Israeli-held territory, and, though Israel successfully counterattacked, Sādāt emerged from the war with greatly enhanced prestige as the first Arab leader to have actually retaken some territory from Israel.

After the war, Sādāt began to work toward peace in the Middle East. He made a historic visit to Israel on Nov. 19–20, 1977, during which he traveled to Jerusalem to place his plan for a peace settlement before the Israeli Knesset (parliament). This initiated a series of diplomatic efforts that Sādāt continued despite strong opposition from most of the Arab world and the Soviet Union. U.S. president Jimmy Carter mediated the negotiations between Sādāt and Begin that resulted in the Camp David Accords on Sept. 17, 1978, a preliminary peace agreement between Egypt and Israel. Sādāt and Begin were awarded the Nobel in 1978, and their continued political negotiations resulted in the signing on March 26, 1979, of a treaty of peace between Egypt and Israel—the first between the latter and any Arab country.

While Sādāt's popularity rose in the West, it fell dramatically in Egypt because of internal opposition to the treaty, a worsening economic crisis, and Sādāt's suppression of the resulting public dissent. In September 1981 he ordered a massive police strike against his opponents, jailing more than 1,500 people from across the political spectrum. The following month Sādāt was assassinated by Muslim extremists during the Armed Forces Day military parade commemorating the Yom Kippur War.

PIERRE ELLIOTT TRUDEAU

(b. Oct. 18, 1919, Montreal, Quebec, Can.—d. Sept. 28, 2000, Montreal)

Pierre Elliott Trudeau was a Liberal politician and prime minister of Canada from 1968–79 and 1980–84. His terms in office were marked by the establishment of diplomatic relations with China (1970) and improved relations with France, the defeat of the French separatist movement, constitutional independence from the British Parliament, and the formation of a new Canadian constitution with the principal additions of a bill of rights and an amending formula.

Trudeau grew up in a family of French and Scots-French descent, in the affluent Montreal suburb of Outremont. He studied at Jean-de-Brébeuf, an elite Jesuit preparatory school, and at the University of Montreal, from which he received a law degree in 1943. He served on the Privy Council for three years as a desk officer, and in 1950 he helped found the *Cité Libre* ("Free City"), a monthly critical review. He practiced law from 1951 to 1961, specializing in labour and civil liberties cases.

Trudeau was assistant professor of law at the University of Montreal from 1961 to 1965, when he was elected as a "new wave" Liberal to the House of Commons. In 1967 he toured the French-speaking African nations on behalf of the prime minister, Lester B. Pearson, who had appointed him parliamentary secretary (1966) and minister of justice and attorney general. As minister of justice, Trudeau won passage of three unpopular social welfare measures—stricter gun-control legislation and reform of the laws regarding abortion and homosexuality.

On Pearson's announcement of his plan to retire, Trudeau campaigned for the leadership of the Liberal Party.

His colourful personality and disregard of unnecessary formality, combined with his progressive ideas, made him the most popular of the 20 candidates. He became party leader on April 6, 1968, and prime minister two weeks later. As a determined antiseparatist, Trudeau in 1970 took a strong stand against terrorists from the Front de Libération du Québec during the October Crisis.

The elections of October 1972 left Trudeau and the Liberals much weakened, with a minority government dependent on the coalition support of the New Democratic Party (NDP). During the next year and a half, the prime minister faced a series of no-confidence votes in Parliament, but in the national elections on July 8 the Liberal Party won a clear majority and an increased number of seats in Parliament.

Throughout the 1970s, Trudeau struggled against increasing economic and domestic problems. In the national general elections of May 22, 1979, his Liberal Party failed to win a majority (although Trudeau maintained his seat in Parliament), and the Progressive Conservative Party won power as a minority government.

The Liberal Party was returned to power in the general election of Feb. 18, 1980, and Trudeau began his fourth term as prime minister on March 3. The proposal of French separatism in Quebec was defeated in a provincial referendum on May 20, 1980, and Trudeau then began work on his plans to reform Canada's constitution. Proposed reforms included "patriation" (that the British Parliament transfer the authority to amend Canada's constitution to Canada), a charter of human rights, broadened federal economic powers, and institutional changes in federal structures such as the Supreme Court.

On Dec. 2, 1981, the Canadian House of Commons approved Trudeau's constitutional reform resolution with a vote of 246 to 24 — only the representatives from Quebec dissented. On April 17, 1982, Queen Elizabeth II declared Canada's independence from the British Parliament. With these major political aims realized, Trudeau spent his final years in office seeking greater economic independence for Canada, forming better trade relations between industrialized democracies and Third World nations, and urging further international disarmament talks. On Feb. 29, 1984, Trudeau resigned from the leadership of the Liberal Party, but he remained in office until John Turner was chosen to succeed him at the party leadership convention in June of that same year.

JOHN PAUL II

(b. May 18, 1920, Wadowice, Pol. — d. April 2, 2005, Vatican City)

Born Karol Józef Wojtyła, John Paul II was the first non-Italian pope in 455 years and the first ever from a Slavic country. He served as the bishop of Rome and head of the Roman Catholic Church from 1978 to 2005.

The first two decades of Wojtyła's life coincided with the only period of independence that Poland would know between 1772 and 1989. He thus grew up experiencing national freedom but also understanding its vulnerability. After one year at the Jagiellonian University in Kraków, Wojtyła's formal studies were interrupted when German forces invaded Poland in September 1939. He continued his studies in the university's clandestine classes, and, to avoid Nazi arrest, worked for chemical manufacturer Solvay — making him the only pope in modern times to have been a laborer.

Wojtyła was ordained into the Catholic priesthood in November 1946. He immediately left Poland for two years of study in Rome, earning his first doctorate in philosophy

(Angelicum University, 1948). Returning to Poland, Wojtyła became an assistant pastor in the village of Niegowić in 1948. Within a year he was moved to Kraków's St. Florian's parish. Over the next decade, Wojtyła taught at the Jagiellonian University, where he also completed a master's degree in theology and a doctorate in sacred theology (both in 1948). He was appointed chair of ethics at the Catholic University of Lublin in 1954.

In 1958 Pope Pius XII appointed him auxiliary bishop of Kraków. Wojtyła was a prominent participant in the Second Vatican Council (1962–65). Pope Paul VI designated him archbishop of Kraków in 1963 and added the rank of cardinal in 1967.

He was elected pope on Oct. 16, 1978, and was installed on October 22 as John Paul II. From the moment of his inauguration, John Paul presented an activist image that was amplified by his travels. Parading his message through many cultures and speaking in many languages, the energetic and handsome 58-year-old pope became a media icon. His potent mix of religion and politics — and its deep roots in Poland — was dramatized in his trips abroad, which, in effect, surrounded the Soviet Union with messages of religious freedom, national independence, and human rights. In the first 10 years of his papacy, John Paul supported Poland's dissident Solidarity trade union, advising Poles to advance slowly so that the Communist regime would have little excuse to impose martial law. This strategy was thrown into crisis when John Paul was shot and nearly killed by a Turkish gunman, Mehmet Ali Ağca, on May 13, 1981. The assassination attempt was almost certainly a conspiracy, but investigators have never proved who sponsored it. Throughout the 1980s, however, it was widely believed that the Soviets had been behind the attempt in the hope of demoralizing Solidarity. In 1989 the Communists asked for negotiations with the trade union. This was followed within months by the dissolution of the Soviet bloc and, eventually, the collapse of the U.S.S.R. Visits from John Paul also weakened several dictatorships and juntas in such countries as Brazil, the Philippines, Haiti, Paraguay, and Chile. He was awarded the U.S. Congressional Gold Medal in January 2001.

John Paul made constant efforts to reach out to people of other religions, most notably Jews and Muslims. He declared anti-Semitism a sin and held numerous meetings with Islam's top religious authorities.

Hoping to strengthen the Catholic faith in many cultures, John Paul canonized many more Catholic saints—drawn from a broader geographic and occupational spectrum—than had any of his predecessors. With the February 2001 installation of 44 cardinals representing five continents, John Paul had named more than 150 new cardinals during his long pontificate. He directed the rewriting of several major church texts and spoke out on an array of highly contentious issues, denouncing abortion, premarital sex, and homosexual practices (though not homosexual inclination). He continually rebuffed new pleas for priests to be allowed to marry and, although he blocked women from entering the priesthood, he nonetheless advocated full equality for women in other realms of life.

JULIUS NYERERE

(b. March 1922, Butiama, Tanganyika—d. Oct. 14, 1999, London, Eng.)

Julius Nyerere was the first prime minister of independent Tanganyika in 1961 and later the first president of the new state of Tanzania in 1964. He was also the major force behind the Organization of African Unity (OAU; now the African Union).

Julius Kambarage Nyerere was a son of the chief of the small Zanaki ethnic group. He was educated at Tabora Secondary School and Makerere College in Kampala, Uganda. A convert to Roman Catholicism, he taught in several Roman Catholic schools before going to Edinburgh University. He graduated with an M.A. in history and economics in 1952 and returned to Tanganyika to teach.

By the time Nyerere entered politics, the old League of Nations mandate that Britain had exercised in Tanganyika had been converted into a United Nations trusteeship, with independence the ultimate goal. Seeking to hasten the process of emancipation, Nyerere joined the Tanganyika African Association, quickly becoming its president in 1953. In 1954 he converted the organization into the politically oriented Tanganyika African National Union (TANU). Under Nyerere's leadership the organization espoused peaceful change, social equality, and racial harmony and rejected tribalism and all forms of racial and ethnic discrimination.

In 1955 and 1956, he journeyed to the United Nations in New York City as a petitioner to the Trusteeship Council and the Fourth Committee on trusts and non-self-governing territories. After a debate that ended in his being granted a hearing, he asked for a target date for the independence of Tanganyika. The British administration rejected the demand, but a dialogue was begun that established Nyerere as the preeminent nationalist spokesman for his country.

The British administration nominated him a member of the Tanganyikan Legislative Council, but he resigned in 1957 in protest against the slowness of progress toward independence. In elections held in 1958–59, Nyerere and

TANU won a large number of seats on the Legislative Council. In a subsequent election in August 1960, his organization managed to win 70 of 71 seats in Tanganyika's new Legislative Assembly. Progress toward independence owed much to the understanding and mutual trust that developed during the course of negotiations between Nyerere and the British governor, Sir Richard Turnbull. Tanganyika finally gained responsible self-government in September 1960, and Nyerere became chief minister at this time. Tanganyika became independent on Dec. 9, 1961, with Nyerere as its first prime minister. The next month, however, he resigned from this position to devote his time to writing and synthesizing his views of government and of African unity. One of Nyerere's more important works was a paper called *Ujamaa—The Basis for African Socialism*, which later served as the philosophical basis for the Arusha Declaration in 1967. When Tanganyika became a republic in 1962, he was elected president, and in 1964 he became president of the United Republic of Tanzania, which included Tanganyika and Zanzibar.

Nyerere was reelected president of Tanzania in 1965 and returned to serve three more successive five-year terms before he resigned as president in 1985. From independence on, Nyerere also headed Tanzania's only political party, Chama Cha Mapinduzi (CCM).

As outlined in his political program, the Arusha Declaration, Nyerere was committed to the creation of an egalitarian socialist society based on cooperative agriculture in Tanzania. He collectivized village farmlands, carried out mass literacy campaigns, and instituted free and universal education. He also emphasized Tanzania's need to become economically self-sufficient rather than remain dependent on foreign aid and foreign investment. Nyerere termed his socialist experimentation *ujamaa* ("familyhood" in Swahili), a name that emphasized the blend of economic cooperation, racial and tribal harmony, and moralistic self-sacrifice that he sought to achieve. Tanzania became a one-party state, though certain democratic opportunities were permitted within that framework.

As a major force behind the modern Pan-African movement and one of the founders in 1963 of the OAU, Nyerere was a key figure in African events in the 1970s. He was a strong advocate of economic and political measures in dealing with the apartheid policies of South Africa. Nyerere was chairman of a group of five frontline African presidents who advocated the overthrow of white supremacy in Rhodesia (now Zimbabwe), South Africa, and South West Africa/Namibia (now Namibia).

Nyerere's concerns on the domestic front were dominated by economic hardships and by difficulties between Nyerere and Idi Amin of Uganda. When Ugandan troops occupied a small border area of Tanzania in 1978, Nyerere pledged to bring about the downfall of Amin, and in 1979 the Tanzanian army invaded Uganda in support of a local movement to overthrow him.

After Nyerere stepped down from the presidency in 1985, he continued as chairman of the CCM until 1990. Thereafter he assumed the role of elder statesman and was regularly called upon to act as arbiter in international crises.

JIMMY CARTER

(b. Oct. 1, 1924, Plains, Ga., U.S.)

Jimmy Carter was the 39th president of the United States, serving from 1977 to 1981. He served as the nation's chief executive during a time of serious problems at home and abroad. After losing his bid for a second term as president, he left office and embarked on a career of diplomacy and advocacy, for which he was awarded the Nobel Peace Prize in 2002.

James Earl Carter, Jr., was the son of Earl Carter, a peanut warehouser who had served in the Georgia state legislature, and Lillian Gordy Carter, a registered nurse who went to India as a Peace Corps volunteer at age 68. Carter attended Georgia Southwestern College and the Georgia Institute of Technology before graduating from the U.S. Naval Academy at Annapolis, Md., in 1946. After marrying Rosalynn Smith—who came from Carter's small hometown, Plains, Ga.—he served in the U.S. Navy until 1953, when he left to manage the family peanut business. He served in the state senate from 1962 to 1966. He ran unsuccessfully for governor in 1966. Depressed by this experience, he found solace in evangelical Christianity, becoming a born-again Baptist. In 1970 he ran again and won. As governor (1971–75), he opened Georgia's government offices to African Americans and women and introduced stricter budgeting procedures for state agencies.

Although lacking a national political base or major backing, Carter managed to win the Democratic nomination in July 1976. He chose the liberal Sen. Walter F. Mondale of Minnesota as his running mate. Carter's opponent was the unelected incumbent Republican president, Gerald R. Ford, who had come into office in 1974 when Richard Nixon resigned in the wake of Watergate. In November 1976 the Carter-Mondale ticket won the election, capturing 51 percent of the popular vote and garnering 297 electoral votes to Ford's 240.

Carter tried to reinforce his image as a man of the people. He adopted an informal style of dress and speech in public appearances, held frequent press conferences, and reduced the pomp of the presidency. Early on in his administration, Carter introduced a dizzying array of

Jimmy Carter. Courtesy of Jimmy Carter Library

ambitious programs for social, administrative, and economic reform. Most of those programs, however, met with opposition in Congress despite the Democratic majorities in both the House of Representatives and the Senate. Carter's difficulties with Congress undermined the success of his administration, and by 1978 his initial popularity had dissipated in the face of his inability to convert his ideas into legislative realities.

Two scandals also damaged Carter's credibility. In summer 1977 Bert Lance, the director of the Office of Management and Budget and one of Carter's closest friends, was accused of financial improprieties as a Georgia banker. When Carter stood by Lance—whom he eventually asked to resign and who later was acquitted of all charges—many questioned the president's vaunted scruples. Carter's image suffered again—though less—in the summer of 1980 when his younger brother, Billy (widely perceived as a buffoon), was accused of acting as an influence peddler for the Libyan government of Muammar al-Qaddafi. Senate investigators concluded that, while Billy had acted improperly, he had no real influence on the president.

In foreign affairs, Carter received accolades for championing international human rights, though his critics charged that his vision of the world was naive. In 1977 he obtained two treaties between the United States and Panama that gave the latter control over the Panama Canal at the end of 1999 and guaranteed the neutrality of that waterway thereafter. In 1978 Carter brought together Egyptian president Anwar el-Sādāt and Israeli prime minister Menachem Begin at the presidential retreat in Camp David, Maryland, and secured their agreement to the Camp David Accords, which ended the state of war that had existed between the two countries since Israel's founding in 1948. On Jan. 1, 1979, Carter established full diplomatic relations between the United States and China and simultaneously broke official ties with Taiwan. Also in 1979, in Vienna, Carter and Soviet leader Leonid Brezhnev signed a new bilateral strategic arms limitation treaty (SALT II) intended to establish parity in strategic nuclear weapons delivery systems between the two superpowers on terms that could be adequately verified. Carter removed the treaty from consideration by the Senate in January 1980, however, after the Soviet Union invaded Afghanistan. He also placed an embargo on the shipment of American grain to the Soviet Union and pressed for a U.S. boycott of the 1980 Summer Olympics due to be held in Moscow.

Carter's substantial foreign policy successes were overshadowed by a serious crisis in foreign affairs and by a groundswell of popular discontent over his economic policies. On Nov. 4, 1979, a mob of Iranian students stormed the U.S. embassy in Tehrān and took the diplomatic staff there hostage. A standoff developed between the United States and Iran over the issue of the captive diplomats. Carter's inability to obtain the release of the hostages became a major political liability. The failure of a secret U.S. military mission to rescue the hostages—which ended almost before it began with a crash in the desert of a plane and helicopter—in April 1980 seemed to typify the inefficacy and misfortune of the Carter administration.

On the home front, Carter's management of the economy aroused widespread concern, as inflation increased and unemployment remained high. The faltering economy was due in part to the energy crisis that had originated in the early 1970s as a result of the country's overdependence on foreign oil.

Carter was able to fend off the challenge of Massachusetts senator Edward Kennedy to win the Democratic presidential nomination in 1980. However, the public's confidence in Carter's executive abilities had fallen to an irretrievable low. In the elections held that November, Carter was overwhelmingly defeated by the Republican nominee, a former actor and governor of California, Ronald W. Reagan.

In his final months in office, Carter was able to push through important legislation that created the Superfund to clean up abandoned toxic waste dumps and that set aside some 100 million acres (40 million hectares) of land in Alaska to protect it from development.

After leaving office, Carter served as a sort of diplomat without portfolio in various conflicts in a number of countries. His efforts on behalf of international peace and his highly visible participation in building homes for the poor through Habitat for Humanity established in the public mind a much more favourable image of Carter than had been the case during his presidency. Carter also became a prolific author, writing on a variety of topics. Two books on the Middle East were *Palestine: Peace Not Apartheid* (2006) and *We Can Have Peace in the Holy Land: A Plan That Will Work* (2009).

POL POT

(b. May 19, 1925, Kompong Thom Province, Camb.—d. April 15, 1998, near Anlong Veng, along the Cambodia-Thailand border)

Pol Pot was a Khmer political leader whose totalitarian regime, which lasted from 1975 to 1979, imposed severe hardships on the Cambodian people. His radical Communist government forced the mass evacuations of cities, killed or displaced millions of people, and left a legacy of brutality and impoverishment.

The son of a landowning farmer, Saloth Sar, as he was originally named, was sent at age five or six to live with an older brother in Phnom Penh, where he was educated. A mediocre student, he failed the entrance examinations for high school and so instead studied carpentry for a year at a technical school in Phnom Penh. In 1949 he went to Paris on a scholarship to study radio electronics. There he became involved with the French Communist Party and joined a group of young left-wing Cambodian nationalists who later became his fellow leaders in the Khmer Rouge. In France he spent more time on revolutionary activities than on his studies. His scholarship was cut short after he failed examinations, and he returned to Phnom Penh in 1953.

Pol Pot taught at a private school in Phnom Penh from 1956 to 1963, when he left the capital because his Communist ties were suspected by the police. By 1963 he had adopted his revolutionary pseudonym, Pol Pot. He spent the next 12 years building up the Communist Party that had been organized in Cambodia in 1960, and he served as the party's secretary. An opponent of the Norodom Sihanouk government and of the military government of General Lon Nol, he led the Khmer Rouge guerrilla forces in their overthrow of Lon Nol's regime in 1975. Pol Pot was prime minister of the new Khmer Rouge government from 1976 until he was overthrown by invading Vietnamese in January 1979. It is estimated that from 1975 to 1979, under the leadership of Pol Pot, the government caused the deaths of more than one million people from forced labour, starvation, disease, torture, or execution while carrying out a program of radical social and agricultural reforms.

Following the Vietnamese invasion of his country, Pol Pot withdrew to bases in Thailand to lead the Khmer Rouge forces against the new Hanoi-supported government in Phnom Penh, which refused to consider peace negotiations as long as he remained at the head of the party. Although ostensibly removed from the military and political leadership of the Khmer Rouge in 1985, he remained a guiding force in the organization, which continued its guerrilla campaign into the 1990s, though with diminishing intensity. By 1997 the Khmer Rouge were in deep decline, their ranks riddled by desertions and factionalism. In June of that year, Pol Pot was forcibly ousted from the organization's leadership and placed under house arrest by his colleagues, and in July he was convicted of treason. Pol Pot died of natural causes in 1998.

MARGARET THATCHER

(b. Oct. 13, 1925, Grantham, Lincolnshire, Eng.)

In 1979 Margaret Thatcher became Europe's first woman prime minister, serving as prime minister of the United Kingdom until 1990. The "Iron Lady," as she was commonly known, gave her name to an era (Thatcherism) and was the only British prime minister in the 20th century to win three consecutive terms.

EARLY YEARS

The daughter of Alfred Roberts, a grocer and local alderman (and later mayor of Grantham), and Beatrice Ethel Stephenson, Margaret Thatcher (born Margaret Hilda Roberts) formed an early desire to be a politician. Her intellectual ability led her to the University of Oxford, where she studied chemistry and was immediately active in politics, becoming one of the first woman presidents of the Oxford University Conservative Association. After graduating in 1946, she worked as a research chemist. After her marriage to Denis Thatcher in 1951, she read for the bar and specialized in tax law.

Thatcher was elected to Parliament in 1959 and served as secretary of state for education and science from 1970 to 1974. As a member of the Conservative Party's newly energetic right wing, she succeeded Edward Heath as party leader in 1975.

PRIME MINISTER

Thatcher led the Conservatives to a decisive electoral victory in 1979. As a prime minister representing the Conservative Party, Thatcher advocated greater independence of the

Ronald Reagan and Margaret Thatcher at the White House, Washington, D.C., July 17, 1987. Courtesy Ronald Reagan Library

individual from the state. This included an end to allegedly excessive government interference in the economy,
including privatization of state-owned enterprises and the
sale of public housing to tenants; reductions in expenditures on social services such as health care, education, and
housing; limitations on the printing of money in accord
with the economic doctrine of monetarism; and legal
restrictions on trade unions. The term *Thatcherism* came
to refer not just to these policies but also to certain aspects
of her ethical outlook and personal style, including moral
absolutism, fierce nationalism, a zealous regard for the
interests of the individual, and a combative, uncompromising approach to achieving political goals.

Rising unemployment and social tensions during her
first term made her deeply unpopular. Her unpopularity
would have ensured her defeat in the general election of
1983 were it not for two factors: her decisive leadership in
the Falkland Islands War (1982) between Britain and
Argentina and Britain's victory, and the deep divisions
within the Labour Party. Thatcher won election to a second term in a landslide.

By the end of Thatcher's second term, few aspects of
British life had escaped the most sweeping transformation
of Britain since the postwar reforms of the Labour Party.

Thatcher's most significant international relationship
was with Ronald Reagan, president of the United States
from 1981 to 1989. Thatcher and Reagan's partnership
ensured that the Cold War continued in all its frigidity
until the rise to power of the reform-minded Soviet leader
Mikhail Gorbachev in 1985. In keeping with her strong
anticommunism—a 1976 speech condemning Communism
earned her the nickname "Iron Lady" in the Soviet press—
Thatcher strongly supported the North Atlantic Treaty
Organization (NATO) and Britain's independent nuclear
deterrent. This stance proved popular with the electorate,

given the Labour Party's repudiation of Britain's traditional nuclear and defense policies. In Africa, Thatcher
presided over the orderly establishment of an independent Zimbabwe (formerly Rhodesia) in 1980, after 15 years
of illegal separation from British colonial rule under a
white minority. However, she encountered considerable
criticism both at home and abroad for her opposition to
international sanctions against the apartheid regime of
South Africa. The second half of Thatcher's tenure was
marked by an inextinguishable controversy over Britain's
relationship with the European Community (EC).

Spurred by public disapproval of the poll tax implemented in 1989—which produced outbreaks of street
violence—and Thatcher's increasingly strident tone,
Conservative members of Parliament moved against her
in November 1990. Although she defeated her most senior
opponent, former defense minister Michael Heseltine, by
204 votes to Heseltine's 152, her total fell four votes short
of the necessary majority plus 15 percent, and she decided
not to contest the election in a second ballot. On November
22 she announced her resignation as Conservative Party
leader and prime minister, paving the way for her replacement by John Major six days later.

LATER YEARS

In retirement, Margaret Thatcher remained a political
force. She continued to influence internal Conservative
Party politics (often to the dismay of Major), and
Thatcherism shaped the priorities of the Labour Party,
which she had kept out of office for more than a decade.
She remained a member of Parliament until the 1992 election and was subsequently elevated, as a peeress for life, to
the House of Lords. She continued to speak and lecture,
notably in the United States and Asia, and established the

Thatcher Foundation to support free enterprise and democracy—particularly in the newly liberated countries of central and eastern Europe. In 1995 she became a member of the Order of the Garter. Following a series of minor strokes, Thatcher retired from public speaking in 2002.

FIDEL CASTRO

(b. Aug. 13, 1926, near Birán, Cuba)

A symbol of Communist revolution in Latin America, Fidel Castro Ruz transformed Cuba into the first Communist state in the Western Hemisphere.

Castro was born on his family's sugar plantation at Mayarí in Oriente Province in southeastern Cuba. As a boy he worked in the sugar fields. He attended Jesuit schools and Belén College in Havana.In 1945 he entered the School of Law of the University of Havana. In 1947 he played a minor role in an attempt to overthrow the dictator in the Dominican Republic. He escaped capture and returned to the university to study law, receiving his degree in 1950. Castro began to practice law and worked on behalf of the poor in Havana. He was a candidate for Cuba's legislature when General Fulgencio Batista overthrew the government in 1952. He organized a rebellion against Batista in 1953, but it failed, and Castro was captured and served time in prison. He and his brother Raúl were released in a political amnesty in 1955, and they went to Mexico to continue their campaign against the Batista regime. There Fidel Castro organized Cuban exiles into a revolutionary group called the 26th of July Movement.

On Dec. 2, 1956, Castro and an armed expedition of 81 men landed on the eastern coast of Cuba, from the yacht *Granma*. All of them were killed or captured except Fidel and Raúl Castro, Ernesto "Che" Guevara, and nine others, who retreated into the Sierra Maestra to wage guerrilla warfare against the Batista forces. In 1959 Batista was forced to flee the country.

As the undisputed revolutionary leader, Castro became commander in chief of the armed forces in Cuba's new provisional government, which had Manuel Urrutia, a moderate liberal, as its president. In February 1959 Castro became premier and thus head of the government. By the time Urrutia was forced to resign in July 1959, Castro had taken effective political power into his own hands.

Castro had come to power with the support of most Cuban city dwellers on the basis of his promises to restore the 1940 constitution, create an honest administration, reinstate full civil and political liberties, and undertake moderate reforms. But once established as Cuba's leader, he began to pursue more radical policies. Cuba's private commerce and industry were nationalized, sweeping land reforms were instituted, and American businesses and agricultural estates were expropriated. The United States was alienated by these policies and offended by Castro's fiery new anti-American rhetoric. His trade agreement with the Soviet Union in February 1960 further deepened American distrust. In 1960 most economic ties between Cuba and the United States were severed, and the United States broke diplomatic relations with the island country in January 1961. In April of that year, the U.S. government secretly equipped thousands of Cuban exiles to overthrow Castro's government. Their landing at the Bay of Pigs in April 1961, however, was crushed by Castro's armed forces.

Cuba also began acquiring weapons from the Soviet Union, which soon became the country's chief supporter and trade partner. In 1962 the Soviet Union secretly stationed ballistic missiles in Cuba that could deliver nuclear warheads to American cities, and in the ensuing confrontation with the United States, the world came close to a nuclear war. The Cuban Missile Crisis ended when the Soviet Union agreed to withdraw its nuclear weapons from Cuba in exchange for a pledge that the United States would withdraw the nuclear-armed missiles it had stationed in Turkey and no longer seek to overthrow Castro's regime.

In the meantime Castro created a one-party government to exercise dictatorial control over all aspects of Cuba's political, economic, and cultural life. All political dissent and opposition were ruthlessly suppressed. Many members of the Cuban upper and middle classes felt betrayed by these measures and chose to immigrate to the United States. At the same time, Castro vastly expanded the country's social services, extending them to all classes of society on an equal basis. Educational and health services were made available to Cubans free of charge, and every citizen was guaranteed employment. The Cuban economy, however, failed to achieve significant growth or to reduce its dependence on the country's chief export, cane sugar. With inefficient industries and a stagnant agriculture, Cuba became increasingly dependent on favourable Soviet trade policies to maintain its modest standard of living in the face of the United States' continuing trade embargo.

Castro remained premier until 1976, when a new constitution created a National Assembly and Castro became president of that body's Council of State and the Council of Ministers. He retained the posts of commander in chief of the armed forces and secretary-general of the Communist Party of Cuba—the only legal political party—and he continued to exercise unquestioned and total control over the government. Castro's brother Raúl, minister of the armed forces, ranked second to him in all government and party posts.

The collapse of the Soviet Union in 1991 took Castro by surprise and meant the end of generous Soviet subsidies to Cuba. Castro countered the resulting economic decline and shortages of consumer goods by allowing some economic liberalization and free-market activities while retaining tight controls over the country's political life.

In 2003 the National Assembly confirmed Castro as president for another five-year term. On July 31, 2006, while recovering from surgery, Fidel Castro passed power on a provisional basis to his brother Raúl. It was the first time since the 1959 revolution that he had ceded control. In February 2008, just days before the National Assembly was to vote for the country's leader, Fidel Castro officially declared that he would not accept another term as president.

CHE GUEVARA

(b. June 14, 1928, Rosario, Argentina—d. October 1967, Bolivia)

Ernesto "Che" Guevara, a noted theoretician and tactician of guerrilla warfare, played a major military role in the Cuban Revolution of the late 1950s. After his execution by the Bolivian army, he was regarded as a martyred hero by generations of leftists worldwide, and his image became an icon of leftist radicalism and anti-imperialism.

Ernesto Guevara de la Serna was the eldest of five children in a middle-class family of Spanish-Irish descent and leftist leanings. Although suffering from asthma, he excelled as an athlete and a scholar, completing his medical studies in 1953. He spent many of his holidays traveling in Latin America, and his observations of the great poverty of the masses convinced him that the only solution lay in violent revolution. He came to look upon Latin America not as a collection of separate nations but as a cultural and economic entity, the liberation of which would require an intercontinental strategy.

In 1953 Guevara went to Guatemala, where Jacobo Arbenz headed a progressive regime that was attempting to bring about a social revolution. (Around this time Guevara acquired his nickname, from a verbal mannerism of Argentines who punctuate their speech with the interjection *che*.) The overthrow of the Arbenz regime in 1954 in a coup supported by the U.S. Central Intelligence Agency persuaded Guevara that the United States would always oppose progressive leftist governments. This conviction became the cornerstone of his plans to bring about socialism by means of a worldwide revolution.

He left Guatemala for Mexico, where he met the Cuban brothers Fidel and Raúl Castro, political exiles who were preparing an attempt to overthrow the dictatorship of Fulgencio Batista in Cuba. Guevara joined Fidel Castro's force, which landed in the Cuban province of Oriente late in November 1956. Immediately detected by Batista's army, they were almost wiped out. The few survivors, including the wounded Guevara and Raúl and Fidel Castro, reached the Sierra Maestra, where they became the nucleus of a guerrilla army. The rebels slowly gained in strength, seizing weapons from Batista's forces and winning support and new recruits, and Guevara became one of Castro's most-trusted aides. Guevara later recorded the two years spent overthrowing Batista's government in *Pasajes de la guerra revolucionaria* (1963; *Reminiscences of the Cuban Revolutionary War*, 1968).

After Castro's victorious troops entered Havana on January 2, 1959, and established a Marxist government, Guevara became a Cuban citizen, as prominent in the new government as he had been in the revolutionary army, representing Cuba on many commercial missions. He also became well known in the West for his opposition to all forms of imperialism and neocolonialism and for his attacks on U.S. foreign policy. He served as chief of the Industrial Department of the National Institute of Agrarian Reform, president of the National Bank of Cuba, and minister of industry.

During the early 1960s, he defined Cuba's policies and his own views in many speeches and writings, notably *El socialismo y el hombre en Cuba* (1965; *Man and Socialism in Cuba*, 1967)—an examination of Cuba's new brand of Communism—and a highly influential manual, *La guerra de guerrillas* (1960; *Guerrilla Warfare*, 1961). After April of 1965 Guevara dropped out of public life. His movements and whereabouts for the next two years remained secret. It was later learned that he had spent some time in what is now the Democratic Republic of the Congo with other Cuban guerrilla fighters, helping to organize the Patrice Lumumba Battalion, which fought in the civil war there.

In the autumn of 1966 Guevara went to Bolivia, incognito, to create and lead a guerrilla group in the region of Santa Cruz. On Oct. 8, 1967, the group was almost annihilated by a special detachment of the Bolivian army. Guevara, who was wounded in the attack, was captured and shot.

MARTIN LUTHER KING, JR.

(b. Jan. 15, 1929, Atlanta, Ga., U.S.—d. April 4, 1968, Memphis, Tenn.)

Baptist minister Martin Luther King, Jr., was one of the most influential social activists of the 20th century. He led the civil rights movement in the United States from the mid-1950s until his death by assassination in 1968. His leadership was fundamental to that movement's success in ending the legal segregation of African Americans in the

President Lyndon B. Johnson talking with Martin Luther King, Jr., in the Oval Office at the White House, Washington, D.C., 1963. Yoichi Okamoto/ Lyndon B. Johnson Library Photo

South and other parts of the United States. He was awarded the Nobel Peace Prize in 1964.

EARLY YEARS

King came from a comfortable middle-class family steeped in the tradition of the Southern black ministry. Both his father and maternal grandfather were Baptist preachers. His parents were college-educated, and King's father had succeeded his father-in-law as pastor of the prestigious

Ebenezer Baptist Church in Atlanta. This secure upbring-
ing, however, did not prevent King from experiencing the
prejudices then common in the South.

A bright student, he was admitted to Morehouse
College at 15, without completing high school. He decided
to become a minister and at 18 was ordained in his father's
church. After graduating from Morehouse in 1948, he
entered Crozer Theological Seminary in Chester, Pa. He
was the valedictorian of his class in 1951 and won a graduate fellowship. At Boston University he received a Ph.D. in
theology in 1955.

The Montgomery Bus Boycott

While in Boston, King met Coretta Scott. They were married in 1953 and had four children. King had been pastor of
the Dexter Avenue Baptist Church in Montgomery,
Alabama, slightly more than a year when the city's small
group of civil rights advocates decided to contest racial segregation on that city's public bus system. On Dec. 1, 1955,
Rosa Parks, an African American woman, refused to surrender her bus seat to a white passenger and was consequently
arrested for violating the city's segregation law. Activists
formed the Montgomery Improvement Association to boycott the transit system and chose King as their leader.
Although King's home was dynamited and his family's safety
threatened, he continued to lead the boycott until, one year
and a few weeks later, the city's buses were desegregated.

The Southern Christian
Leadership Conference

Recognizing the need for a mass movement to capitalize
on the successful Montgomery action, King set about

organizing the Southern Christian Leadership Conference (SCLC), which gave him a base of operation throughout the South, as well as a national platform from which to speak. King became increasingly convinced that nonviolent resistance was the most potent weapon available to oppressed people in their struggle for freedom.

In 1960 King moved to his native city of Atlanta, where he became co-pastor with his father of the Ebenezer Baptist Church. In late October he was arrested with 33 young people while protesting segregation at the lunch counter in an Atlanta department store. Charges were dropped, but King was sentenced to Reidsville State Prison Farm on the pretext that he had violated his probation on a minor traffic offense committed several months earlier. The case assumed national proportions, with outrage at Georgia's flouting of legal forms and the failure of President Dwight Eisenhower to intervene. King was released only upon the intercession of Democratic presidential candidate John F. Kennedy.

THE LETTER FROM THE BIRMINGHAM JAIL

In Birmingham, Alabama, in the spring of 1963, King's campaign to end segregation at lunch counters and in hiring practices drew nationwide attention when police turned dogs and fire hoses on the demonstrators. King was jailed along with large numbers of his supporters, including hundreds of schoolchildren. From the Birmingham jail, King wrote a letter of great eloquence in which he spelled out his philosophy of nonviolence. On Aug. 28, 1963, an interracial assembly of more than 200,000 people gathered peaceably in the shadow of the Lincoln Memorial to demand equal justice for all citizens under the law. Here the crowds were uplifted by the emotional strength and prophetic quality of King's famous "I Have a Dream" speech, in which he emphasized his faith that all men, someday, would be brothers.

The rising tide of civil rights agitation produced, as King had hoped, a strong effect on national opinion and resulted in the passage of the Civil Rights Act of 1964. This act authorized the federal government to enforce desegregation of public accommodations and outlawed discrimination in publicly owned facilities, as well as in employment. That eventful year was climaxed by the award to King of the Nobel Peace Prize in Oslo, Norway, in December.

Martin Luther King, Jr. (centre), and Malcolm X (right), 1964. Library of Congress, Washington, D.C. (digital file no. 3d01847u)

CHALLENGES OF THE FINAL YEARS

In March 1965 King was criticized for yielding to state troopers at a Selma, Ala., march that was aimed at the need for a federal voting-rights law that would provide legal support for the enfranchisement of African Americans in the South. He was also criticized for failing in the effort to change Chicago's housing segregation policies. King was now being challenged and even publicly derided by young black-power enthusiasts. While King stood for patience, middle-class respectability, and a measured approach to social change, more revolutionary leaders like Malcolm X stood for confrontation and immediate change.

The strain and changing dynamics of the civil rights movement had taken a toll on King, especially in the final months of his life. In the opinion of many of his followers and biographers, King seemed to sense his end was near. As King prophetically told a crowd at the Mason Temple Church in Memphis on April 3, the night before he died, "I've seen the promised land. I may not get there with you. But I want you to know tonight that we, as a people, will get to the promised land." The next day, while standing on the second-story balcony of the Lorraine Motel in Memphis, King was killed by a sniper's bullet. The killing sparked riots and disturbances in over 100 cities across the country.

On March 10, 1969, the accused white assassin, James Earl Ray, pleaded guilty to the murder and was sentenced to 99 years in prison. Ray later recanted his confession. In a surprising turn of events, members of the King family eventually came to Ray's defense, believing his pleas of innocence. Although the U.S. government conducted several investigations into the murder of King and each

Building in Washington, D.C., destroyed during the riots that followed the assassination of Martin Luther King, Jr., April 1968. Library of Congress, Washington, D.C. (digital file no. 03132u)

time concluded that Ray was the sole assassin, the killing remains a matter of controversy.

YĀSIR 'ARAFĀT

(b. Aug. 24?, 1929, Cairo?, Egypt—d. Nov. 11, 2004, Paris, France)

In his efforts to lead the Palestinian people in their attempts for statehood, Yāsir 'Arafāt served as president (1996–2004) of the Palestinian Authority, chairman (1969–2004) of the Palestine Liberation Organization (PLO), and leader of Fatah, the largest of the constituent

PLO groups. In 1993 he led the PLO to a peace agreement with the Israeli government. Arafāt, Yitzhak Rabin, and Shimon Peres of Israel were jointly awarded the Nobel Peace Prize in 1994.

Born Muḥammad 'Abd al-Ra'ūf al-Qudwah al-Ḥusaynī, Arafāt was one of seven children of a well-to-do merchant whose wife was related to the anti-Zionist grand mufti of Jerusalem, Amīn al-Ḥusaynī (d. 1974). The date and place of 'Arafāt's birth are disputed. A birth certificate registered in Cairo, Egypt, gives Aug. 24, 1929. Some sources, however, have supported 'Arafāt's claim to have been born in Jerusalem on Aug. 4, 1929, and still others have given Gaza, Palestine, as his birthplace. 'Arafāt attended the University of Cairo, graduating as a civil engineer. He joined the Muslim Brotherhood and the Union of Palestinian Students, of which he was president from 1952 to 1956, and was commissioned into the Egyptian army. In 1956 he served in the Suez campaign.

After Suez, 'Arafāt went to Kuwait, where he worked as an engineer and set up his own contracting firm. In Kuwait he helped found Fatah, which was to become the leading military component of the PLO. After being named chairman of the PLO in 1969, he became commander in chief of the Palestinian Revolutionary Forces in 1971 and, two years later, head of the PLO's political department. Subsequently, he directed his efforts increasingly toward political persuasion rather than confrontation and terrorism against Israel. In November 1974 'Arafāt became the first representative of a nongovernmental organization—the PLO—to address a plenary session of the United Nations General Assembly.

In 1982 'Arafāt became the target of criticism from Syria and from various Syrian-supported factions within the PLO. The criticisms escalated after the Israeli invasion of Lebanon forced ʿArafāt to abandon his Beirut headquarters at the end of August 1982 and set up a base in Tunisia and later in Baghdad, Iraq. ʿArafāt was subsequently able to reaffirm his leadership as the split in the PLO's ranks healed.

On April 2, 1989, ʿArafāt was elected by the Central Council of the Palestine National Council (the governing body of the PLO) to be the president of a hypothetical Palestinian state. In 1993 he took a further step toward peace when, as head of the PLO, he formally recognized Israel's right to exist and helped negotiate the Israel-PLO accord, which envisaged the gradual implementation of Palestinian self-rule in the West Bank and Gaza Strip over a five-year period. ʿArafāt began directing Palestinian self-rule in 1994, and in 1996 he was elected president of the Palestinian Authority, which governed Palestinian-controlled areas of the West Bank and the Gaza Strip.

In mid-1996 Israeli-Palestinian relations became acrimonious with the election of Israeli prime minister Benjamin Netanyahu, who favoured a slower transition to self-rule. Growing distrust between ʿArafāt and Netanyahu resulted in a 19-month-long deadlock. In 1998 U.S. president Bill Clinton intervened, arranging a summit meeting with the two leaders at Wye Mills, Maryland. The resulting Wye Memorandum detailed the steps to be taken by Israel and Palestine to complete the peace process. ʿArafāt pledged to continue the process with Netanyahu's successor, Ehud Barak.

In 2000, in talks mediated by Clinton at Camp David, where the historic Camp David Accords between Israel and Egypt were negotiated in 1978, ʿArafāt rejected an offer by Barak that would have created an independent Palestinian state because it did not grant the Palestinians full control over East Jerusalem or adequately guarantee, in his view, the right of Palestinian refugees to return. 'Arafāt's decision was widely hailed by Palestinians, and Barak was ousted from office in 2001 by Ariel Sharon, whose visit to the Temple Mount in Jerusalem in September 2000 had sparked a wave of Palestinian violence. In 2001, following suicide attacks in Israel that Sharon blamed 'Arafāt for instigating, 'Arafāt was confined by Israel to his headquarters in Ramallah. In October 2004, 'Arafāt fell ill and was transported for medical treatment to Paris, where he died the following month.

HELMUT KOHL

(b. April 3, 1930, Ludwigshafen am Rhein, Ger.)

Helmut Kohl was chancellor of West Germany from 1982 to 1990 and of the reunified German nation from 1990 to 1998. He presided over the integration of East Germany into West Germany in 1990 and thus became the first chancellor of a unified Germany since 1945.

Kohl grew up in a conservative Roman Catholic family. As a teenager in wartime Germany, he was drafted and sent to basic training, but the war ended before he had to fight. His interest in politics manifested itself early. In 1947 he began working in a Christian Democratic Union (CDU) youth organization in his native town. Kohl earned a doctorate in political science at the University of Heidelberg in 1958. He was elected in 1959 to the Rhineland-Palatinate state legislature and in 1969 to the state's post of minister president (prime minister). He soon developed a reputation as a capable administrator. He also became the CDU's national deputy chairman in 1969, and he was elected chairman of the party in 1973.

Kohl entered the 1976 federal elections as the chancellor candidate of the CDU and its Bavarian sister party, the Christian Social Union (CSU), but lost to the Social Democratic Party (SDP) led by Helmut Schmidt. In 1982 many members of Schmidt's coalition partners, the Free Democratic Party (FDP), deserted their alliance with him. The combined forces of the CDU, the CSU, and the FDP defectors passed a vote of no confidence against Schmidt in the Bundestag (West German parliament) on Oct. 1, 1982, and immediately forced him from office by giving Kohl the required absolute majority in the ensuing vote for a new chancellor.

The CDU-CSU-FDP coalition won a 58-seat majority in federal elections held on March 6, 1983. Kohl's government went on to follow centrist policies that included modest cuts in government spending and strong support for West German commitments to NATO. These policies were confirmed by victory in the federal elections of Jan. 25, 1987, although the CDU-CSU-FDP coalition held a reduced majority of 45 seats.

As the Soviet Union abandoned its control over eastern Europe in 1989–90, Kohl led the drive for the speedy reunification of West with East Germany. The opposition SDP, by contrast, approached this momentous issue much more warily. When East Germany held its first democratic parliamentary elections in March 1990, Kohl campaigned vigorously for the CDU's sister parties in East Germany, which were able to form a government committed to reunification. In May 1990 Kohl's government concluded a treaty with East Germany that unified the two countries' economic and social-welfare systems and granted East Germany an equal exchange of their now-worthless East German currency for the powerful deutsche mark. Kohl worked strenuously to obtain the assent of both his NATO allies and the Soviet Union to German reunification, and on Oct. 3, 1990, East Germany was dissolved and its constituent states joined West Germany in a reunified Germany. On Dec. 2, 1990, in the first free, all-German parliamentary elections since 1932, Kohl and his governing CDU-CSU-FDP coalition won a 134-seat majority in the Bundestag.

Absorption of the moribund eastern German economy proved more expensive and difficult than predicted, and Kohl's government had to commit itself to tax increases and cuts in government spending in order to finance unification. Voter discontent over these harsh realities, compounded by resentment over a severe recession in 1992–93, were reflected in the parliamentary elections of Oct. 16, 1994, which reduced Kohl's parliamentary majority to 10 seats.

Continuing high unemployment in Germany and voter weariness with Kohl after 16 years in office enabled the SDP, led by Gerhardt Schröder, to defeat the CDU-CSU in parliamentary elections held on Sept. 27, 1998. In 1999 Kohl was involved in a scandal arising from the collection of illegal campaign contributions. In January 2000 he resigned his party offices and faced serious charges of misusing funds. He was assessed a stiff fine in February 2001.

MIKHAIL GORBACHEV

(b. March 2, 1931, Privolye, Stavropol *kray*, Russia, U.S.S.R.)

Mikhail Gorbachev served as the general secretary of the Communist Party of the Soviet Union (CPSU) from 1985 to 1991 and president of the Soviet Union in 1990–91. His efforts to democratize his country's political system and decentralize its economy led to the downfall of Communism and the breakup of the Soviet Union in 1991.

Mikhail Sergeyevich Gorbachev was the son of Russian peasants in Stavropol territory in southwestern Russia. He joined the Komsomol (Young Communist League) in 1946 and drove a combine harvester at a state farm in Stavropol for the next four years. He proved a promising Komsomol member, and in 1952 he entered the law school of Moscow State University and became a member of the Communist Party. He graduated with a degree in law in 1955 and went on to hold a number of posts in the Komsomol and regular party organizations in Stavropol, rising to become first secretary of the regional party committee in 1970.

Gorbachev was named a member of the Central Committee of the Communist Party of the Soviet Union in 1971, and he was appointed a party secretary of agriculture in 1978. He became a candidate member of the Politburo in 1979 and a full member in 1980. Following the death of Konstantin Chernenko in March 1985, Gorbachev succeeded him as general secretary of the CPSU.

Gorbachev quickly set about consolidating his personal power in the Soviet leadership. His primary domestic goal was to resuscitate the stagnant Soviet economy. To this end, he called for rapid technological modernization and increased worker productivity, and he tried to make the cumbersome Soviet bureaucracy more efficient and responsive.

When these superficial changes failed to yield tangible results, Gorbachev in 1987–88 proceeded to initiate deeper reforms of the Soviet economic and political system. Under his new policy of *glasnost* ("openness"), a major cultural thaw took place, as freedoms of expression and of information were significantly expanded. Under Gorbachev's policy of *perestroika* ("restructuring"), the first modest attempts to democratize the Soviet political system were undertaken. Multicandidate contests and the secret ballot were introduced in some elections to party and government posts. Under *perestroika*, some limited free-market mechanisms also began to be introduced into the Soviet economy, but encountered serious resistance from party and government bureaucrats.

In foreign affairs, Gorbachev from the beginning cultivated warmer relations and trade with the developed nations of both West and East. In December 1987 he signed an agreement with U.S. president Ronald Reagan for their two countries to destroy all existing stocks of intermediate-range nuclear-tipped missiles. In 1988–89 he oversaw the withdrawal of Soviet troops from Afghanistan after their nine-year occupation of that country.

In October of 1988, Gorbachev was able to consolidate his power by his election to the chairmanship of the presidium of the Supreme Soviet (the national legislature). Under changes made to the constitution in December 1988, a new bicameral parliament called the U.S.S.R. Congress of People's Deputies was created, with some of its members directly elected by the people in multicandidate elections. In 1989 the newly elected Congress of People's Deputies elected from its ranks a new U.S.S.R. Supreme Soviet that, in contrast to its predecessor of that name, was a real standing parliament with substantial legislative powers. In May 1989 Gorbachev was elected chairman of this Supreme Soviet, retaining the national presidency.

Throughout 1989 Gorbachev had seized every opportunity to voice his support for reformist Communists in the Soviet-bloc countries of eastern Europe, and, when Communist regimes in those countries collapsed like dominoes late that year, Gorbachev tacitly accepted their fall. As democratically elected, noncommunist governments came to power in East Germany, Poland, Hungary, and Czechoslovakia in late 1989–90, Gorbachev agreed to the phased withdrawal of Soviet troops from those countries. By the summer of 1990, he had agreed to the reunification of East with West Germany and even assented to the prospect of that reunified nation's becoming a member of the Soviet Union's longtime enemy, the North Atlantic Treaty Organization. In 1990 Gorbachev received the Nobel Peace Prize for his striking achievements in international relations.

The new freedoms arising from Gorbachev's democratization and decentralization of his nation's political system led to civil unrest in several of the constituent republics—Azerbaijan, Georgia, and Uzbekistan—and to outright attempts to achieve independence in others, such as Lithuania. In response, Gorbachev used military force to suppress bloody interethnic strife in several of the Central Asian republics in 1989–90, while constitutional mechanisms were devised that could provide for the lawful secession of a republic from the U.S.S.R.

In 1990 Gorbachev further accelerated the transfer of power from the party to elected governmental institutions. In March of that year, the Congress of People's Deputies elected him to the newly created post of president of the U.S.S.R., with extensive executive powers. At the same time, the Congress, under his leadership, abolished the Communist Party's constitutionally guaranteed monopoly of political power in the Soviet Union, thus paving the way for the legalization of other political parties.

Gorbachev and his family were briefly held under house arrest from August 19 to 21, 1991, during a short-lived coup by the hard-liners. After the coup foundered in the face of staunch resistance by Russian president Boris Yeltsin and other reformers who had risen to power under the democratic reforms, Gorbachev resumed his duties as Soviet president, but his position had by now been irretrievably weakened. Entering into an unavoidable alliance with Yeltsin, Gorbachev quit the Communist Party, disbanded its Central Committee, and supported measures to strip the party of its control over the KGB and the armed forces. Gorbachev also moved quickly to shift fundamental political powers to the Soviet Union's constituent republics. Events outpaced him, however, and the Russian government under Yeltsin readily assumed the functions of the collapsing Soviet government as the various republics agreed to form a new commonwealth under Yeltsin's leadership. On Dec. 25, 1991, Gorbachev resigned the presidency of the Soviet Union, which ceased to exist that same day.

In 1996 Gorbachev ran for president of Russia but garnered less than 1 percent of the vote. He nevertheless remained active in public life, as a speaker and as a member of various global and Russian think tanks.

DALAI LAMA XIV

(b. July 6, 1935, Tibet)

Dalai Lama XIV is the title of the Tibetan Buddhist monk Bstan-'dzin-rgya-mtsho (Tenzin Gyatso). He is a global figure, largely known for his advocacy of Buddhism and of the rights of the people of Tibet.

To Tibetan Buddhists, a Dalai Lama is the incarnation of the lord of compassion who takes earthly forms in order to help humankind. The title is often translated as "Ocean Teacher." The Dalai Lama is the head of the religious order called Dge-lugs-pa (or Yellow Hat). Since the order achieved supremacy in Tibet in the mid-17th century, the Dalai Lama has been the spiritual leader of Tibetan Buddhism. Until the mid-20th century, when the 14th Dalai Lama was forced into exile, the Dalai Lama also ruled Tibet politically.

LIFE IN TIBET

The 13th Dalai Lama died in Lhasa, the capital of Tibet, on Dec. 17, 1933. According to custom, executive authority was given to a regent, whose chief task was to identify and educate the next Dalai Lama, who would typically assume control at about the age of 20. After consulting various oracles, the regent sent out search parties to locate the child. One party made its way to Amdo, in the far northeast region of the Tibetan cultural domain, where it encountered a young boy named Lha-mo-don-grub, the son of a farmer. After passing a number of tests (including the selection of personal items that had belonged to the 13th Dalai Lama), he was proclaimed the next Dalai Lama. But before he and his family could leave for Lhasa, they were held for ransom by a powerful Chinese warlord, Ma Bufeng. The ransom was paid by the Tibetan government, and the child and his family made the long trip, where he was enthroned on Feb. 22, 1940.

Ordained as a Buddhist monk, the young Dalai Lama moved (without his family) into the vast Potala Palace—the residence of the Dalai Lamas and the seat of Tibetan government—where he began a rigorous monastic education under the tutelage of distinguished scholars. Affairs of state remained, however, in the hands of the regent. The Dalai Lama assumed his full role as ruler of Tibet on Nov. 17, 1950, at age 15. A month later he fled the advance of the Chinese armies, which had invaded Tibet in 1949. He returned to Lhasa in 1951 and spent several unsuccessful years attempting to make a peaceful and workable arrangement with China.

As tensions continued to escalate, rumours that Chinese authorities planned to kidnap the Dalai Lama led to a popular uprising in Lhasa on March 10, 1959, with crowds surrounding the Dalai Lama's summer palace to protect him. During the ensuing chaos, the Dalai Lama (disguised as a Tibetan soldier) escaped under cover of darkness on March 17. Accompanied by a small party of his family and teachers and escorted by guerrilla fighters, the Dalai Lama made his way on foot and horseback across the Himalayas, pursued by Chinese troops. On March 31 he and his escorts arrived in India, where the Indian government offered them asylum.

LIFE IN EXILE

In the wake of the Lhasa uprising and the Chinese consolidation of power across Tibet, tens of thousands of Tibetans followed the Dalai Lama into exile. In 1960 he established his government-in-exile in Dharamsala, a former British hill station in the Indian state of Himachal Pradesh, where he continued to reside. The government of India, however, was reluctant to allow all the Tibetan refugees to concentrate in one region and thus created settlements across the subcontinent, where the Tibetans established farming communities and built monasteries. The welfare of the refugees and the preservation of Tibetan culture in exile, especially in light of reports of the systematic destruction of Tibetan institutions during China's Cultural Revolution (1966–76), were the primary concerns of the Dalai Lama during this period.

The Dalai Lama traveled little during the early part of his exile and published only two books, an introduction to Buddhism and an autobiography. In later years, however, he traveled quite extensively, delivering addresses at colleges and universities, meeting with political and religious leaders, and lecturing on Buddhism.

His activities focused on two main goals, one of which was to build and sustain international awareness of the plight of Tibet. He continued to advocate what he called a "middle way approach" between the complete independence of Tibet and its complete absorption into the People's Republic of China. He also sent numerous delegations to China to discuss such proposals, but they met with little success. In recognition of his efforts, he was awarded the Nobel Peace Prize in 1989. His other goal was to disseminate the central tenets of Buddhism to a wide audience.

After the Dalai Lama reached the age of 70, the question of his successor was repeatedly raised. In the 1980s his public speculation about whether there would be a need for another Dalai Lama was taken by some as a call to the Tibetan community to preserve its culture in exile. During the first decade of the 21st century, however, he declared that there will be a 15th Dalai Lama and that he will be discovered not in Chinese-controlled Tibet, but in exile.

VÁCLAV HAVEL

(b. Oct. 5, 1936, Prague, Czechoslovakia [now in Czech Republic])

Václav Havel is a Czech playwright, poet, and political dissident, who, after the fall of Communism, was president of Czechoslovakia from 1989 to 1992 and of the Czech Republic from 1993 to 2003.

Havel was the son of a wealthy restaurateur whose property was confiscated by the Communist government of Czechoslovakia in 1948. As the son of bourgeois parents, Havel was denied easy access to education but managed to finish high school and study on the university level. He found work as a stagehand in a Prague theatrical company in 1959 and soon began writing plays with Ivan Vyskowil. By 1968 Havel had progressed to the position of resident playwright of the Theatre of the Balustrade company. He was a prominent participant in the liberal reforms of 1968 (known as the Prague Spring), and, after the Soviet clampdown on Czechoslovakia that year, his plays were banned and his passport was confiscated. During the 1970s and 1980s, he was repeatedly arrested and served four years in prison (1979–83) for his activities on behalf of human rights in Czechoslovakia. After his release from prison, Havel remained in his homeland.

Havel's first solo play, *Zahradní slavnost* (1963; *The Garden Party*), typified his work in its absurdist, satirical examination of bureaucratic routines and their dehumanizing effects. In his best-known play, *Vyrozumění* (1965; *The Memorandum*), an incomprehensible artificial language is imposed on a large bureaucratic enterprise, causing the breakdown of human relationships and their replacement by unscrupulous struggles for power. In these and subsequent works, Havel explored the self-deluding rationalizations and moral compromises that characterize life under a totalitarian political system. Havel continued to write plays steadily until the late 1980s. These works include *Ztížená možnost soustředění* (1968; *The Increased Difficulty of Concentration*); the three one-act plays *Audience* (1975), *Vernisáž* (1975; *Private View*), and *Protest* (1978); *Largo Desolato* (1985); and *Zítra to Spustíme* (1988; *Tomorrow*).

When massive antigovernment demonstrations erupted in Prague in November 1989, Havel became the leading figure in the Civic Forum, a new coalition of noncommunist opposition groups pressing for democratic reforms. In early December, the Communist Party capitulated and formed a coalition government with the Civic Forum. As a result of an agreement between the partners in this bloodless "Velvet Revolution," Havel was elected to the post of interim president of Czechoslovakia on Dec. 29, 1989, and he was reelected to the presidency in July

1990, becoming the country's first noncommunist leader since 1948. As the Czechoslovak union faced dissolution in 1992, Havel, who opposed the division, resigned from office. The following year he was elected president of the new Czech Republic. His political role, however, was limited, as Prime Minister Václav Klaus (1993–97) commanded much of the power. In 1998 Havel was reelected by a narrow margin, and, under his presidency, the Czech Republic joined the North Atlantic Treaty Organization (NATO) in 1999. Barred constitutionally from seeking a third term, he stepped down as president in 2003.

Havel's first new play in more than 20 years, *Odcházení* (*Leaving*)—a tragicomedy that draws on his experiences as president and presents a chancellor leaving his post while grappling with a political enemy—premiered in 2008.

SADDĀM HUSSEIN

(b. April 28, 1937, Tikrīt, Iraq—d. Dec. 30, 2006, Baghdad)

As president of Iraq (1979–2003), Saddām Hussein's rule was marked by brutality as well as costly and unsuccessful wars against neighbouring countries.

Saddām Hussein al-Tikrītī was born into a peasant family in northern Iraq. He joined the Ba'th Party in 1957. In 1959 he participated in an unsuccessful attempt by Ba'thists to assassinate the Iraqi prime minister, 'Abd al-Karīm Qāsim. Wounded in the attempt, Saddām escaped, first to Syria and then to Egypt. He attended Cairo Law School (1962–63) and continued his studies at Baghdad Law College after the Ba'thists took power in Iraq in 1963. The Ba'thists were overthrown that same year, however, and Saddām spent several years in prison in Iraq. He escaped, becoming a leader of the Ba'th Party, and was instrumental in the coup that brought the party back to power in 1968.

Ṣaddām effectively held power in Iraq along with the head of state, President Aḥmad Ḥasan al-Bakr, and in 1972 he directed the nationalization of Iraq's oil industry.

Ṣaddām began to assert open control of the government in 1979 and became president upon Bakr's resignation. He then became chairman of the Revolutionary Command Council and prime minister, among other positions. He used an extensive secret-police establishment to suppress any internal opposition to his rule, and he made himself the object of an extensive personality cult among the Iraqi public.

Ṣaddām launched an invasion of Iran's oil fields in September 1980, but the campaign bogged down in a war of attrition. The cost of the war and the interruption of Iraq's oil exports caused Ṣaddām to scale down his ambitious programs for economic development. The Iran-Iraq War dragged on in a stalemate until 1988, when both countries accepted a cease-fire that ended the fighting. Despite the large foreign debt with which Iraq found itself saddled by war's end, Ṣaddām continued to build up his armed forces.

In August 1990 the Iraqi army overran neighbouring Kuwait. Ṣaddām apparently intended to use that nation's vast oil revenues to bolster Iraq's economy, but his occupation of Kuwait quickly triggered a worldwide trade embargo against Iraq. He ignored appeals to withdraw his forces from Kuwait, despite the buildup of a large U.S.-led military force in Saudi Arabia and the passage of United Nations (UN) resolutions condemning the occupation and authorizing the use of force to end it. The Persian Gulf War began on Jan. 16, 1991, and ended six weeks later when the allied military coalition drove Iraq's armies out of Kuwait. Iraq's crushing defeat triggered internal rebellions by both Shīʿites and Kurds, but Ṣaddām suppressed

Thirty-foot-tall bronze sculptures of former Iraqi dictator Ṣaddām Ḥussein, on the grounds of the Republican Palace, Baghdad, 2005. Jim Gordon, CIV/ U.S. Department of Defense

their uprisings, causing thousands to flee to refugee camps along the country's northern border. Untold thousands more were murdered, many simply disappearing into the regime's prisons.

As part of the cease-fire agreement with the UN, Iraq was prohibited from producing or possessing chemical, biological, and nuclear weapons. Numerous sanctions were leveled on the country pending compliance, and these caused severe disruption of the economy. Ṣaddām's continued refusal to cooperate with UN arms inspectors led to a four-day air strike by the United States and Great Britain in late 1998 (Operation Desert Fox).

In the wake of the September 11 attacks in the United States in 2001, the U.S. government, asserting that Ṣaddām might provide terrorist groups with chemical or biological weapons, sought to renew the disarmament process. While Ṣaddām allowed UN weapons inspectors to return to Iraq in November 2002, his failure to cooperate fully with the investigations frustrated the United States and Great Britain and led them to declare an end to diplomacy. On March 17, 2003, U.S. president George W. Bush ordered Ṣaddām to step down from office and leave Iraq within 48 hours or face war. When Ṣaddām refused to leave, U.S. and allied forces launched an attack on Iraq on March 20.

Ṣaddām Hussein, following his capture by U.S. forces in Tikrīt, Iraq, Dec. 14, 2003. U.S. Department of Defense

The Iraq War broke out with an assault by U.S. aircraft on a bunker complex in which Ṣaddām was thought to be meeting with subordinates. Although the attack failed to kill the Iraqi leader, subsequent attacks directed against Ṣaddām made it clear that eliminating him was a major goal of the invasion. On April 9, the day Baghdad fell to U.S. soldiers, Ṣaddām fled into hiding. He took with him the bulk of the national treasury and was initially able to evade capture by U.S.

troops. It was not until December 13, 2003, that Ṣaddām was finally captured from a small underground hiding place near a farmhouse in the vicinity of his native Tikrīt.

In October 2005 Ṣaddām went on trial before the Iraqi High Tribunal. He and several codefendants were charged with the killing of 148 townspeople in Dujail, a mainly Shī'ite town, in 1982. The tribunal finally adjourned in July 2006 and handed down its verdicts in November. Ṣaddām was convicted of crimes against humanity, including willful killing, illegal imprisonment, deportation, and torture, and was sentenced to death by hanging. Days after an Iraqi court upheld his sentence in December 2006, Ṣaddām was executed.

Ṣaddām Hussein sitting before an Iraqi judge at a courthouse in Baghdad, 2004. SSGT D. Myles Cullen, USAF/U.S. Department of Defense

KOFI ANNAN

(b. April 8, 1938, Kumasi, Gold Coast [now Ghana])

G hanaian Kofi Annan served as the secretary-general of the United Nations (UN) from 1997 to 2006. He was the corecipient, with the United Nations, of the Nobel Peace Prize in 2001.

Kofi Atta Annan, whose father was governor of Asante Province and a hereditary paramount chief of the Fante people, studied at the University of Science and Technology in Kumasi before enrolling at Macalester College in St. Paul, Minn., where he received a bachelor's degree in economics. He continued his studies at the Institute for Advanced International Studies in Geneva. He earned a master's degree while a Sloan fellow at the Massachusetts Institute of Technology in 1971–72.

Annan began his career with the UN as a budget officer for the World Health Organization in Geneva in 1962. With the exception of a brief stint as the director of tourism in Ghana (1974–76), he spent his entire career with the UN, serving in several administrative posts. On March 1, 1993, he was elevated to undersecretary-general for peacekeeping operations. In that position, he distinguished himself during the civil war in Bosnia and Herzegovina, particularly in his skillful handling of the transition of peacekeeping operations from UN forces to NATO forces.

Because Boutros Boutros-Ghali, Annan's predecessor as secretary-general, had alienated some member nations — most notably the United States — with his independent and aloof style, Annan entered office with the tasks of repairing relations with the United States and reforming the UN bureaucracy. Soon after becoming secretary-general, he introduced a reform plan that sought to reduce the organization's budget and streamline its operations, moves that were welcomed by the United States. Other priorities included restoring public confidence in the UN, combating the AIDS virus, especially in Africa, and ending human rights abuses.

In 2001 Annan was appointed to a second term. Later that year the September 11 attacks occurred in the United States, and global security and terrorism became major issues for Annan. In 2003 the United States launched a war against Iraq without receiving approval from the UN Security Council, and Annan's subsequent criticism of the war strained relations with the United States. Later in 2003 Annan appointed a panel to explore the UN's response to global threats, and he included many of its recommendations in a major reform package presented to the UN General Assembly in 2005. A number of measures were later adopted; the proposal to expand the Security Council from 15 to 24 members was among those rejected. In 2005 Annan was at the centre of controversy following an investigation into the oil-for-food program, which had allowed Iraq—under UN supervision—to sell a set amount of oil in order to purchase food, medicine, and other necessities. A report described major corruption within the program and revealed that Annan's son was part of a Swiss business that had won an oil-for-food contract. Although Annan was cleared of wrongdoing, he was criticized for his failure to properly oversee the program. In 2006 Annan's term ended, and he was succeeded by Ban Ki-moon.

In 2007 Annan was named chairperson of the Alliance for a Green Revolution in Africa (AGRA), an organization aiding small-scale farmers. AGRA was funded by the Bill & Melinda Gates Foundation and the Rockefeller Foundation. He later played a crucial role in resolving the Kenyan election crisis that began in late December 2007, eventually brokering a power-sharing agreement between the government and the opposition on Feb. 28, 2008. In the same year, he received the Peace of Westphalia Prize, awarded biannually for contributions to unity and peace in Europe, and became chancellor of the University of Ghana.

MUAMMAR AL-QADDAFI

(b. 1942, near Surt, Libya)

Since 1969 Muammar al-Qaddafi has been the de facto leader of Libya, known for his outspoken and controversial policies, particularly toward the West.

The son of an itinerant Bedouin farmer, Qaddafi was born in a tent in the Libyan desert. He proved a talented student and graduated from the University of Libya in 1963. A devout Muslim and ardent Arab nationalist, Qaddafi early began plotting to overthrow the Libyan monarchy of King Idrīs I. He graduated from the Libyan military academy in 1965 and thereafter rose steadily through the ranks, all the while continuing to plan a coup with the help of his fellow army officers. Captain Qaddafi seized control of the government in a military coup that deposed King Idrīs in September 1969. Qaddafi was named commander in chief of the armed forces and chairman of Libya's new governing body, the Revolutionary Command Council.

Qaddafi removed the U.S. and British military bases from Libya in 1970. He expelled most members of the native Italian and Jewish communities from Libya that same year, and in 1973 he nationalized all foreign-owned petroleum assets in the country. He also outlawed alcoholic beverages and gambling, in accordance with his own strict Islamic principles. Qaddafi also began a series of persistent but unsuccessful attempts to unify Libya with other Arab countries. He was adamantly opposed to negotiations with Israel and became a leader of the so-called rejectionist front of Arab nations in this regard. He also earned a reputation for military adventurism. His government was implicated in several abortive coup attempts in Egypt and Sudan, and Libyan forces persistently intervened in the long-running civil war in neighbouring Chad.

From 1974 onward Qaddafi espoused a form of Islamic socialism as expressed in his collection of political writings, *The Green Book*. This combined the nationalization of many economic sectors with a brand of populist government ostensibly operating through people's congresses, labour unions, and other mass organizations. Meanwhile, Qaddafi was becoming known for his erratic and unpredictable behaviour on the international scene. His government financed a broad spectrum of revolutionary or terrorist groups worldwide, including the Black Panthers, the Nation of Islam in the United States, and the Irish Republican Army in Northern Ireland. Squads of Libyan agents assassinated émigré opponents abroad, and his government was allegedly involved in several bloody terrorist incidents in Europe perpetrated by Palestinian or other Arab extremists. These activities brought him into growing conflict with the U.S. government, and in April 1986, a force of British-based U.S. warplanes bombed several sites in Libya, killing or wounding several of his children and narrowly missing Qaddafi himself.

Libya's purported involvement in the destruction of a civilian airliner over Lockerbie, Scotland, in 1988, led to UN and U.S. sanctions that further isolated Qaddafi from the international community. In the late 1990s, however, Qaddafi turned over the alleged perpetrators of the bombing to international authorities. UN sanctions against Libya were subsequently lifted in 2003, and following Qaddafi's announcement that Libya would cease its unconventional-weapons program, the United States dropped most of its sanctions as well. Although some observers remained critical, these measures provided an opportunity for the rehabilitation of Qaddafi's image abroad and facilitated his country's gradual return to the global community. In 2009 Qaddafi was elected chairman of the African Union.

LECH WAŁĘSA

(b. Sept. 29, 1943, Popowo, near Włocławek, Pol.)

Originally a labour activist who helped form and lead (1980–90) Communist Poland's first independent trade union, Solidarity, Lech Wałęsa went on to become the president of Poland from 1990 to 1995. He received the Nobel Peace Prize in 1983.

Wałęsa, the son of a carpenter, received only primary and vocational education and in 1967 began work as an electrician at the huge Lenin Shipyard in Gdańsk, Poland. He witnessed the 1970 food riots in Gdańsk in which police killed a number of demonstrators. When new protests against Poland's Communist government erupted in 1976, Wałęsa emerged as an antigovernment union activist and lost his job as a result. On Aug. 14, 1980, during protests at the Lenin shipyards caused by an increase in food prices, Wałęsa climbed over the shipyard fence and joined the workers inside, who elected him head of a strike committee to negotiate with management. Three days later the strikers' demands were conceded, but when strikers in other Gdańsk enterprises asked Wałęsa to continue his strike out of solidarity, he immediately agreed. Wałęsa took charge of an Interfactory Strike Committee that united the enterprises of the Gdańsk-Sopot-Gdynia area.

This committee issued a set of bold political demands, including the right to strike and form free trade unions, and it proclaimed a general strike. Fearing a national revolt, the Communist authorities yielded to the workers' principal demands, and on August 31, Wałęsa and Mieczysław Jagielski, Poland's first deputy premier, signed an agreement conceding to the workers the right to organize freely and independently.

When some 10 million Polish workers and farmers joined semiautonomous unions in response to this momentous agreement, the Interfactory Strike Committee was transformed into a national federation of unions under the name Solidarity (Solidarność), with Wałęsa as its chairman and chief spokesman. Solidarity was officially recognized by the Polish government in October, and Wałęsa steered the federation on a course of carefully limited confrontations with the government in order to avert the possibility of Soviet military intervention in Poland. The federation's gains proved ephemeral, however. On Dec. 13, 1981, the Polish government imposed martial law. Solidarity was outlawed, and most of the leaders of Solidarity were arrested, including Wałęsa, who was detained for nearly a year. The awarding of the Nobel Peace Prize to Wałęsa in 1983 was criticized by the Polish government. Fearing involuntary exile, he remained in Poland while his wife, Danuta, traveled to Oslo, Norway, to accept the prize on his behalf.

As the leader of the now-underground Solidarity movement, Wałęsa was subjected to constant harassment until collapsing economic conditions and a new wave of labour unrest in 1988 forced Poland's government to negotiate with him and other Solidarity leaders. These negotiations led to an agreement that restored Solidarity to legal status and sanctioned free elections for a limited number of seats in the newly restored upper house of the Sejm (Parliament).

Solidarity won an overwhelming majority of those seats in June 1989, and after Wałęsa refused to form a coalition government with the Communists, the Parliament was forced to accept a Solidarity-led government—though Wałęsa himself refused to serve as premier.

Wałęsa helped his Solidarity colleague Tadeusz Mazowiecki become premier of this government in 1989, but he ran against Mazowiecki for president in 1990 and won Poland's first direct presidential election by a landslide. As president, Wałęsa helped guide Poland through its first free parliamentary elections in 1991 and watched as successive ministries converted Poland's state-run economy into a free-market system. Wałęsa had displayed remarkable political skills as the leader of Solidarity, but his plain speech, confrontational style, and refusal to approve a relaxation of Poland's strict new prohibitions on abortion eroded his popularity late in his term as president. In 1995 he sought reelection but was narrowly defeated by the former Communist Aleksander Kwasniewski, head of the Democratic Left Alliance. Wałęsa ran for president once again in 2000 but carried only a tiny fraction of the vote.

AUNG SAN SUU KYI

(b. June 19, 1945, Rangoon, Burma [now Yangon, Myanmar])

Aung San Suu Kyi is a prodemocracy opposition leader in Myanmar who in 1991 was awarded the Nobel Peace Prize. For much of the period since 1989, she has been held under house detention by Myanmar authorities.

The daughter of Aung San (a martyred national hero of independent Burma) and Khin Kyi (a prominent Burmese diplomat), Aung San Suu Kyi was two years old when her father, Aung San—then the de facto prime minister of what would shortly become independent Burma—was assassinated. Aung San Suu Kyi attended schools in Burma until 1960, when her mother was appointed ambassador to India. After further study in India, she attended the University of Oxford, where she met her future husband. She had two children and lived a rather quiet life until 1988, when she returned to Burma to nurse her dying mother. There, the mass slaughter of protesters against the brutal and unresponsive rule of the military strongman U Ne Win led her to speak out against him and to begin a nonviolent struggle for democracy and human rights. In July 1989 the military government of the newly named Union of Myanmar placed Aung San Suu Kyi under house arrest and held her incommunicado. The military offered to free her if she agreed to leave Myanmar, but she refused to do so until the country was returned to civilian government and political prisoners were freed. The newly formed group with which she became affiliated, the National League for Democracy (NLD), won more than 80 percent of the parliamentary seats that were contested in 1990, but the results of that election were ignored by the military government.

Aung San Suu Kyi was freed from house arrest in July 1995. The following year she attended the NLD party congress, but the military government continued to harass both her and her party. In 1998 she announced the formation of a representative committee that she declared was the country's legitimate ruling parliament. The military junta once again placed her under house arrest from September 2000 to May 2002. Following clashes between the NLD and progovernment demonstrators in 2003, the government returned her to house arrest. In 2009 a United Nations body declared her detention illegal under Myanmar's own law. In 2008 the conditions of her house arrest were somewhat loosened, allowing her to receive some magazines as well as letters from her children. In May 2009, shortly before her most recent sentence was to be completed, Aung

San Suu Kyi was arrested and charged with breaching the terms of her house arrest. In August she was convicted and sentenced to three years in prison, though the sentence immediately was reduced to 18 months, and she was allowed to serve it while remaining under house arrest.

VLADIMIR PUTIN

(b. Oct. 7, 1952, Leningrad, U.S.S.R. [now St. Petersburg, Russia])

Vladimir Putin has been the leading figure in Russia since 1999, serving as the country's prime minister in 1999, as its president from New Year's Eve 1999 to 2008, and again as prime minister since 2008.

Vladimir Vladimirovich Putin studied law at Leningrad State University, where his tutor was Anatoly Sobchak, later one of the leading reform politicians of the *perestroika* period. Putin served 15 years as a foreign intelligence officer for the KGB (Committee for State Security), including six years in Dresden, East Germany (now Germany). In 1990 he retired from active KGB service with the rank of lieutenant colonel and returned to Russia to become prorector of Leningrad State University with responsibility for the institution's external relations. Soon afterward, Putin became an adviser to Sobchak, the first democratically elected mayor of St. Petersburg. He quickly won Sobchak's confidence and became known for his ability to get things done. By 1994 he had risen to the post of first deputy mayor.

In 1996 Putin moved to Moscow, where he joined the presidential staff as deputy to Pavel Borodin, the Kremlin's chief administrator. Putin grew close to fellow Leningrader Anatoly Chubais and moved up in administrative positions. In July 1998 President Boris Yeltsin made Putin director of the Federal Security Service (the KGB's domestic successor), and shortly thereafter he became secretary of the influential Security Council. Yeltsin, who was searching for an heir to assume his mantle, appointed Putin prime minister in 1999.

Although he was virtually unknown, Putin's public-approval ratings soared when he launched a well-organized military operation against secessionist rebels in Chechnya. Wearied by years of Yeltsin's erratic behaviour, the Russian public appreciated Putin's coolness and decisiveness under pressure. Putin's support for a new electoral bloc, Unity, ensured its success in the December parliamentary elections.

On Dec. 31, 1999, Yeltsin unexpectedly announced his resignation and named Putin acting president. Promising to rebuild a weakened Russia, the austere and reserved Putin easily won the March 2000 elections with about 53 percent of the vote. As president, he sought to end corruption and create a strongly regulated market economy.

Putin quickly reasserted control over Russia's 89 regions and republics, dividing them into seven new federal districts, each headed by a representative appointed by the president. He also removed the right of regional governors to sit in the Federation Council, the upper house of the Russian parliament. Putin moved to reduce the power of Russia's unpopular financiers and media tycoons—the so-called "oligarchs"—by closing several media outlets and launching criminal proceedings against numerous leading figures. He faced a difficult situation in Chechnya, particularly from rebels who staged terrorist attacks in Moscow and guerrilla attacks on Russian troops from the region's mountains. In 2002 Putin declared the military campaign over, but casualties remained high.

Putin strongly objected to U.S. president George W. Bush's decision in 2001 to abandon the 1972 Anti-Ballistic Missile Treaty. In response to the September 11 attacks on the United States in 2001, he pledged Russia's assistance and cooperation in the U.S.-led campaign against terrorists and their allies, offering the use of Russia's airspace for humanitarian deliveries and help in search-and-rescue operations. Nevertheless, Putin joined German chancellor Gerhard Schröder and French president Jacques Chirac in 2002–03 to oppose U.S. and British plans to use force to oust Ṣaddām Ḥussein's government in Iraq.

Overseeing an economy that enjoyed growth after a prolonged recession in the 1990s, Putin was easily reelected in March 2004. In parliamentary elections in December 2007, Putin's party, United Russia, won an overwhelming majority of seats. Although the fairness of the elections was questioned by international observers and by the Communist Party of the Russian Federation, the results nonetheless affirmed Putin's power. With a constitutional provision forcing Putin to step down in 2008, he chose Dmitry Medvedev as his successor. Soon after Medvedev won the March 2008 presidential election by a landslide, Putin announced that he had accepted the position of chairman of the United Russia Party. Confirming widespread expectations, Medvedev nominated Putin as the country's prime minister within hours of taking office on May 7, 2008. Russia's parliament confirmed the appointment the following day.

BENAZIR BHUTTO

(b. June 21, 1953, Karachi, Pak.—d. Dec. 27, 2007, Rawalpindi)

B enazir Bhutto was the first woman to attain political leadership of a Muslim country in modern times. She served two terms as prime minister of Pakistan, in 1988–90 and in 1993–96, and looked set to win a third term when she was assassinated in 2007.

Bhutto was the daughter of the politician Zulfikar Ali Bhutto, the leader of Pakistan from 1971 until 1977. She

was educated at Harvard University (B.A., 1973) and subsequently studied philosophy, political science, and
economics at the University of Oxford (B.A., 1977).

After her father's execution in 1979 during the rule of
the military dictator Mohammad Zia-ul-Haq, Bhutto
became the titular head of her father's party, the Pakistan
People's Party (PPP), and endured frequent house arrest
from 1979 to 1984. In exile from 1984 to 1986, she returned
to Pakistan after the lifting of martial law and soon became
the foremost figure in the political opposition to Zia.
President Zia died in August 1988 in a mysterious plane
crash, leaving a power vacuum at the centre of Pakistani
politics. In the ensuing elections, Bhutto's PPP won the
single largest bloc of seats in the National Assembly. She
became prime minister on Dec. 1, 1988, heading a coalition government.

Bhutto was unable to do much to combat Pakistan's
widespread poverty, governmental corruption, and
increasing crime. In August 1990, the president of
Pakistan, Ghulam Ishaq Khan, dismissed Bhutto's government on charges of corruption and other malfeasance
and called for new elections. Bhutto's PPP suffered a
defeat in the national elections of October 1990. She
then led the parliamentary opposition against her successor, Nawaz Sharif.

In elections held in October 1993, the PPP won a plu-
rality of votes, and Bhutto again became head of a coalition
government. Under renewed allegations of corruption,
economic mismanagement, and a decline of law and order,
her government was dismissed in November 1996 by Pres.
Farooq Leghari.

Voter turnout was low in the 1997 elections, in which
Bhutto's PPP suffered a decisive loss to Sharif's Pakistan
Muslim League party. With British and Swiss coopera-
tion, Sharif's administration continued to pursue the

corruption charges against Bhutto. In 1999 Bhutto and her husband, the controversial businessman and senator Asif Ali Zardari—jailed since 1996 on a variety of additional charges—were both convicted of corruption by a Lahore court. This decision was overturned by the Supreme Court in 2001 because of evidence of governmental interference. Bhutto did not achieve political accommodation with Gen. Pervez Musharraf's seizure of power in a 1999 coup d'état. Her demands that the charges against her and her husband be dropped were denied, undercutting negotiations with the Musharraf government regarding a return to the country from her self-imposed exile. Facing standing arrest warrants should she return to Pakistan, Bhutto remained in exile in London and Dubai from the late 1990s.

Because of Musharraf's 2002 decree banning prime ministers from serving a third term, Bhutto was not permitted to stand for elections that same year. In addition, legislation in 2000 that prohibited a court-convicted individual from holding party office hindered her party, as Bhutto's unanimously elected leadership would have excluded the PPP from participating in elections. In response to these obstacles, the PPP split, registering a new, legally distinct branch called the Pakistan People's Party Parliamentarians (PPPP). Legally separate and free from the restrictions brought upon the PPP by Bhutto's leadership, the PPPP participated in the 2002 elections and earned a strong vote. However, Bhutto's terms for cooperation with the military government—that all charges against her and against her husband be withdrawn—continued to be denied. In 2004 Bhutto's husband was released from prison on bail and joined Bhutto in exile. Just before the 2007 elections, talk began to circulate of Bhutto's return to Pakistan.

Shortly before Musharraf's reelection to the presidency, amid unresolved discussions of a power-sharing deal between Bhutto and Musharraf's military regime, he finally granted Bhutto a long-sought amnesty for the corruption charges brought against her by the Sharif administration. The Supreme Court challenged Musharraf's right to grant the amnesty, however, criticizing it as unconstitutional. Nevertheless, in October 2007 Bhutto returned to Karachi from Dubai after eight years of self-imposed exile. Celebrations marking her return were marred by a suicide attack on her motorcade, in which numerous supporters were killed. Bhutto was assassinated in December in a similar attack while campaigning for upcoming parliamentary elections.

Bhutto's autobiography, *Daughter of the East*, was published in 1988 (also published as *Daughter of Destiny*, 1989). She also wrote *Reconciliation: Islam, Democracy, and the West*, which was published posthumously in 2008.

HUGO CHÁVEZ

(b. July 28, 1954, Sabaneta, Venez.)

Hugo Chávez became president of Venezuela in 1999 and has been a leading leftist, both in Latin America and the world, forging alliances with Cuba and Iran.

After graduating from a Venezuelan military academy in 1975, Hugo Rafael Chávez Frías entered the army. He became increasingly critical of the government, which he viewed as corrupt, and in 1992 he helped stage an unsuccessful coup against Pres. Carlos Andrés Pérez. He was imprisoned and exiled from political life until 1994, when Pres. Rafael Caldera pardoned him. An admirer of Simón Bolívar ("the Liberator"), Chávez subsequently cofounded the left-wing Movement for the Fifth Republic. In 1998 he ran for president, promising to end political corruption, revive the stagnating economy, and make sweeping constitutional changes to bring "true democracy" to the country.

His platform proved popular with the poor, who accounted for some 80 percent of the population, and Chávez won a landslide victory.

After taking office in 1999, Chávez oversaw the passage of a new constitution that greatly expanded his powers, reorganized the judiciary, and replaced the existing legislature with the National Assembly. He also increased control of the oil industry, using its revenues to fund his "Bolivarian Revolution," which included free education, low-cost housing, and health care. The creation of a new legislature led to another round of national elections in 2000, and Chávez won a landslide victory amid charges of electoral fraud. Critics accused him of assuming dictatorial powers, and a series of antigovernment strikes culminated in a military coup on April 12, 2002, in which Chávez was ousted. Two days later, however, he was returned to power. Unrest with his government continued, and opponents forced a recall election in August 2004. Backed by the urban poor and rural peasants, Chávez easily won the election.

Much of Chávez's foreign policy centred on strengthening ties with other Latin American countries, especially Cuba. Following the 2002 coup, which he claimed was supported by the U.S. government, Chávez's relationship with the United States grew highly contentious. He adopted anti-American rhetoric, threatened to end oil sales to the United States, and purchased arms and other military equipment—acquisitions he claimed were necessary to defend Venezuela from the "imperialistic power."

In December 2006, Chávez was reelected to a third term, capturing 63 percent of the vote. He continued his efforts to turn Venezuela into a socialist state and promoted a program that included the takeover of the petroleum sector in 2007 and the nationalization of telecommunications, electricity, steel, and cement companies in 2008. At the end of 2007, Chávez lost a referendum on constitutional changes, including one that would have allowed him to run for reelection indefinitely. He took the narrow defeat (51 to 49 percent) in stride and continued to promote a socialist agenda in Venezuela that included modifying the country's name, its coat of arms, and its flag, as well as creating a new currency (the bolívar fuerte) and a new time zone for Venezuela. In February 2009, Chávez went to the electorate with another constitutional referendum. In a vote to eliminate term limits for all elected officials, Chavez won, as more than 54 percent of Venezuelans approved the elimination of all term limits. Chávez characterized the vote as a mandate for continued revolutionary change, while his critics saw in it the threat of perpetual rule.

OSAMA BIN LADEN

(b. 1957, Riyadh, Saudi Arabia)

Osama bin Laden is the mastermind of numerous acts of terrorism against the United States and other Western powers, including the 1993 bombing of New York City's World Trade Center, the 2000 suicide bombing of the U.S. warship *Cole* in the Yemeni port of Aden, and the Sept. 11, 2001, attacks on the World Trade Center in New York City and the Pentagon near Washington, D.C.

Bin Laden was one of more than 50 children of one of Saudi Arabia's wealthiest families. He attended King Abdul Aziz University, where he received a degree in civil engineering. Shortly after the Soviet Union invaded Afghanistan in 1979, bin Laden, like thousands of other Muslims from throughout the world, joined the Afghan resistance, viewing it as his Muslim duty to repel the occupation. After the Soviet withdrawal in 1989, bin Laden returned home as a hero, but he was quickly disappointed with what he perceived as the corruption of the Saudi government and of his own family. His objection to the presence of U.S. troops in Saudi Arabia during the Persian Gulf War led to a growing rift with his country's leaders. By 1993 he had purportedly formed a network known as al-Qaeda ("the Base"), which consisted largely of militant Muslims bin Laden had met in Afghanistan. The group funded and organized several attacks worldwide, including detonating truck bombs against American targets in Saudi Arabia in 1996, killing tourists in Egypt in 1997, and simultaneously bombing the U.S. embassies in Nairobi, Kenya, and Dar es Salaam, Tanzania, in 1998. These attacks altogether killed nearly 300 people. In 1994 the Saudi government confiscated bin Laden's passport after accusing him of subversion, and he fled to Sudan, where he organized camps that trained militants in terrorist methods, and from where he was eventually expelled in 1996. He later returned to Afghanistan, where he received protection from its ruling Taliban militia.

In 1996–98 bin Laden, a self-styled scholar, issued a series of *fatwās* ("religious opinions") declaring a holy war against the United States, which he accused, among other things, of looting the natural resources of the Muslim world and aiding and abetting the enemies of Islam. Bin Laden's apparent goal was to draw the United States into a large-scale war in the Muslim world that would overthrow moderate Muslim governments and reestablish the Caliphate (a single Islamic state). To this end, al-Qaeda, aided by bin Laden's considerable wealth, trained militants and funded terrorist attacks. It had thousands of followers worldwide, in places as diverse as Saudi Arabia, Yemen, Libya, Bosnia, Chechnya, and the Philippines. Following the September 11 attacks, the United States led a coalition in late 2001 that overthrew the Taliban and sent bin Laden into hiding. Nearly three years passed, during which time U.S. forces hunted bin Laden along the Afghanistan-Pakistan border. Bin Laden emerged in a videotaped message in October 2004, less than a week before that year's U.S. presidential election, in which he claimed responsibility for the September 11 attacks.

BARACK OBAMA

(b. Aug. 4, 1961, Honolulu, Hawaii, U.S.)

Barack Hussein Obama, II, 44th president of the United States (2009–), became the first African American to hold the country's highest office.

Obama's father, Barack Obama, Sr., was a teenage goatherd in rural Kenya. He won a scholarship to study in the United States and eventually became a senior economist in the Kenyan government. Obama's mother, S. Ann Dunham, grew up in Kansas, Texas, and Washington State before her family settled in Honolulu. In 1961 she and Barack Sr. met and married less than a year later.

When Obama was age two, Barack Sr. left to study at Harvard University. Shortly thereafter, in 1964, Ann and Barack Sr. divorced. Later Ann married Lolo Soetoro from Indonesia, with whom she had a second child, Maya. Obama lived for several years in Jakarta with his half sister, mother, and stepfather. While there, Obama attended both a government-run school where he received some instruction in Islam and a Catholic private school where he took part in Christian schooling. He returned to Hawaii in 1971, and in 1979 graduated from Punahou School, an elite college preparatory academy in Honolulu.

Obama attended Occidental College in suburban Los Angeles for two years and then transferred to Columbia University in New York City, where in 1983 he received a bachelor's degree in political science. In 1985 he took a position as a community organizer on Chicago's largely impoverished Far South Side. He returned to school three

Barack Obama. Courtesy of the Office of U.S. Senator Barack Obama

years later and graduated magna cum laude in 1991 from Harvard University's law school, where he was the first African American to serve as president of the *Harvard Law Review*. While a summer associate in 1989 at the Chicago law firm of Sidley Austin, Obama met Chicago native Michelle Robinson, a young lawyer at the firm. The two married in 1992.

After receiving his law degree, Obama moved to Chicago and became active in the Democratic Party. During this period, Obama wrote his first book, the memoir, *Dreams from My Father* (1995), and saw it published. Obama lectured on constitutional law at the University of Chicago and worked as an attorney on civil rights issues. In 1996 he was elected to the Illinois Senate.

In 2004 he was elected to the U.S. Senate, defeating Republican Alan Keyes in the first U.S. Senate race in which the two leading candidates were African Americans. While campaigning for the U.S. Senate, Obama gained national recognition by delivering the keynote address at the Democratic National Convention in July 2004. Obama quickly became a major figure in his party. His second book, *The Audacity of Hope* (2006), a mainstream polemic on his vision for the United States, was published weeks later, instantly becoming a major best seller. In February 2007 he announced that he would seek the Democratic Party's presidential nomination in 2008.

On Jan. 3, 2008, Obama won a surprise victory in the first major nomination, the Iowa caucus, over Sen. Hillary Clinton, who was the overwhelming favourite to win the nomination. Five days later, however, Obama finished second to Clinton in the New Hampshire primary, and a bruising—and sometimes bitter—primary race ensued. On June 3, following the final primaries in Montana and South Dakota, the number of delegates pledged to Obama surpassed the total necessary to claim the Democratic nomination.

On August 27 Obama became the first African American to be nominated for the presidency by either major party and went on to challenge Republican Sen. John McCain for the country's highest office. McCain criticized Obama, still a first-term senator, as being too inexperienced for the job. To counter, Obama selected Joe Biden, a veteran senator from Delaware who had a long resume of foreign policy expertise, to be his vice-presidential running mate. Obama and McCain waged a fierce and expensive contest. Obama, still bolstered by a fever of popular support, eschewed federal financing of his campaign and raised hundreds of millions of dollars, much of it coming in small donations and over the Internet from a record number of donors. Obama's fund-raising advantage helped him buy massive amounts of television advertising and organize deep grassroots organizations in key battleground states and in states that had voted Republican in previous presidential cycles.

The two candidates offered a stark ideological choice for voters. Obama called for a swift withdrawal of most

Memorabilia from Barack Obama's presidential campaign. Obama for America

Barack Obama—with his wife, Michelle—being sworn in as the 44th president of the United States, Jan. 20, 2009. MSgt Cecilio Ricardo, U.S. Air Force/U.S. Department of Defense

combat forces from Iraq and a restructuring of tax policy that would bring more relief to lower- and middle-class voters, while McCain said the United States must wait for full victory in Iraq and charged that Obama's rhetoric was long on eloquence but short on substance. Just weeks before election day, Obama's campaign seized on the economic meltdown that had resulted from the catastrophic failure of U.S. banks and financial institutions in September, calling it a result of the Republican free-market-driven policies of the eight-year administration of George W. Bush.

Obama won the election, capturing nearly 53 percent of the popular vote and 365 electoral votes. Not only did

Pres. Barack Obama delivers his inaugural address from the west steps of the U.S. Capitol, Washington, D.C., Jan. 20, 2009. SMSgt Thomas Meneguin, U.S. Air Force/U.S. Department of Defense

he hold all the states that John Kerry had won in the 2004 election, but he also captured a number of states (e.g., Colorado, Florida, Nevada, Ohio, and Virginia) that the Republicans had carried in the previous two presidential elections. On election night tens of thousands gathered in Chicago's Grant Park to see Obama claim victory. Shortly after his win, Obama resigned from the Senate. On Jan. 20, 2009, hundreds of thousands turned out in Washington, D.C., to witness Obama taking the oath of office as president. In 2009 he was awarded the Nobel Peace Prize "for his extraordinary efforts to strengthen international diplomacy and cooperation between peoples."

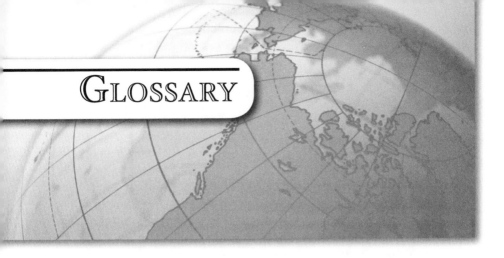

GLOSSARY

apocryphal Of doubtful authorship or authenticity.

appanage Source of revenue, such as land within the royal domain, for the maintenance of a member of a ruling family.

arteriosclerosis Degenerative disorder characterized by abnormal thickening and hardening of arterial walls and loss of elasticity, causing decreased blood flow and increasing the risk of heart attack.

ascetic A person who dedicates his or her life to the pursuit of spiritual contemplation and ideas.

bellicose Hostile; eager to fight.

caliph A leader who serves as the successor of Muhammad as temporal and spiritual head of Islam.

covenant In theology, an agreement that brings about a relationship of commitment between God and his people.

dichotomous Divided into two parts.

draconian Rigorous, unusually severe.

embryonic Rudimentary; underdeveloped.

envisage To visualize.

eschatological Concerning the end of the world or the ultimate destiny of humankind.

expropriate To dispossess a person's ownership of property.

extant In existence, not destroyed or lost.

fealty Loyalty or fidelity to a lord by a tenant or vassal.

incipient Beginning; in the initial stage.

incursion A hostile invasion of a territory.

indefatigable Untiring.

junta A small group ruling a country, usually following a governmental coup d'état.

kibbutz A community settlement, organized by a collective, especially in Israel.

malfeasance Wrongdoing or illegal act perpetrated by a public official.

moribund Near death; dying.

mullah An educated Muslim trained in traditional religious law and doctrine.

penurious Given to extreme frugality.

plebiscite A direct vote by the people of an entire country or district for or against a proposal, especially on a choice of government or ruler.

polemic An aggressive attack on the principles of another.

pontificate The office or term of a bishop or pope.

posthumous Following or occurring after one's death.

presidium In Communist countries, the committee that acts with full powers when its parent body is in recess.

sagacity Wisdom; soundness of judgment.

satrap A governor of a province in ancient Persia.

sentient Having the power of perception; conscious.

tactician A person adept at planning military maneuvers.

vanguard The forefront in any movement or field.

virtuosity Technical skill and fluency.

FOR FURTHER READING

Balaghi, Shiva. *Saddam Hussein: A Biography*. Westport, CT: Greenwood Publishing Group, 2006.

Bhutto, Benazir. *Reconciliation: Islam, Democracy, and the West*. New York, NY: HarperCollins Publishers, 2008.

Bin Laden, Osama. Bruce Lawrence, ed. *Messages to the World: The Statements of Osama bin Laden*. New York, NY: Verso, 2005.

Black, Conrad. *A Life in Full: Richard M. Nixon*. New York, NY: PublicAffairs, 2007.

Brocheux, Pierre. *Ho Chi Minh: A Biography*. Cambridge, UK: Cambridge University Press, 2003.

Cartledge, Paul. *Alexander the Great*. New York, NY: Overlook Hardcover, 2004.

Castro, Fidel, and Ignacio Ramonet. *Fidel Castro: My Life: A Spoken Autobiography*. New York, NY: Simon & Schuster, Inc., 2006.

Coomaraswamy, Ananda K., and I. B. Horner. *The Living Thoughts of Gotama the Buddha*. New York, NY: BiblioBazaar, 2008.

Cunningham, Kevin. *Joseph Stalin and the Soviet Union*. New York, NY: Morgan Reynolds Publishing, 2006.

Dalai Lama. Jeffrey Hopkins, trans. *How to See Yourself As You Really Are*. New York, NY: Simon & Schuster, 2006.

Gandhi, Mohandas Karamchand. *Gandhi, an Autobiography: The Story of Experiments with Truth*. Boston, MA: Beacon Press Books, 1957.

Goldsworthy, Adrian. *Caesar: Life of a Colossus*. New Haven, CT: Yale University Press, 2006.

Gorbachev, Mikhail, and George Shriver. *Gorbachev*. Columbia University Press, 2000.

Guevara, Ernesto Che. *Che Guevara Reader: Writings on Politics & Revolution*. New York, NY: Ocean Press, 2003.

Jackson, Julian. *De Gaulle* (Life & Times). London, UK: Haus Publishing Limited, 2003.

King, Martin Luther, Jr. *The Autobiography of Martin Luther King, Jr*. New York, NY: Warner Books, Inc.

Kirsch, Jonathan. *Moses: A Life*. New York, NY: Ballantine Publishing Group, 1998.

Lim, Jae-Cheon. *Kim Jong Il's Leadership of North Korea*. New York, NY: Routledge, 2008.

Lings, Martin. *Muhammad: His Life Based on the Earliest Sources*. London, UK: Inner Traditions, 2006.

Man, John. *Attila: The Barbarian King Who Challenged Rome*. New York, NY: St. Martin's Press, 2005.

Mandela, Nelson. *The Long Walk to Freedom: The Autobiography of Nelson Mandela*. New York, NY: Back Bay Books, 1995.

McKitterick, Rosamond. *Charlemagne: The Formation of a European Identity*. Cambridge, UK: Cambridge University Press, 2008.

Meisler, Stanley. *Kofi Annan: A Man of Peace in a World of War*. Hoboken, NJ: John Wiley & Sons, 2007.

Meisner, Maurice. *Mao Zedong: A Political and Intellectual Portrait*. Cambridge, UK: Polity Press, 2007.

Naden, Corinne J. *Heroes & Villains: Muammar al-Qaddafi*. New York, NY: Lucent, 2004.

Obama, Barack. *The Audacity of Hope: Thoughts on Reclaiming the American Dream*. New York, NY: Crown Publishing Group, 2006.

Pentecost, J. Dwight. *The Words and Works of Jesus Christ: A Study of the Life of Christ*. Grand Rapids, MI: The Zondervan Corporation, 2000.

Plaidy, Jean. *Victoria Victorious: The Story of Queen Victoria*. New York, NY: Three Rivers Press, 2005.

Putin, Vladimir. *First Person*. New York, NY: Perseus Books Group, 2000.

Rubin, Barry, and Judith Colp Rubin. *Yasir Arafat: A Political Biography*. Oxford, UK: Oxford University Press, 2003.

Tyldesley, Joyce. *Cleopatra: Last Queen of Egypt*. London, UK: Profile Books Ltd., 1996.

Waley, Arthur. *The Analects of Confucius*. New York, NY: First Vintage Books, 1989.

INDEX